JESUS REDEEMING IN MARY

The Role of the Blessed Virgin Mary in Redemption
According to St. Louis Marie Grignion de Montfort

St. Louis Marie Grignion de Montfort

JESUS REDEEMING IN MARY

The Role of the Blessed Virgin Mary in Redemption
According to St. Louis Marie Grignion de Montfort

THE REV. JUDITH MARIE GENTLE, PH.D.

MONTFORT
PUBLICATIONS

2003
Montfort Publications
26 South Saxon Ave.
Bay Shore, NY 11706

Designed and typeset by Joe Gannon, Mulberry Tree Press, Inc., Northport, NY

Cover design by Alan Colavecchio, Winsted, CT

Cover Statue: Our Lady of Wisdom, hand carved,
attributed to St. Louis de Montfort.

Library Of Congress Cataloging-in-Publications Data
is available from the publisher upon request.

First Edition:

Bay Shore, NY 240 pp. One Volume

ISBN: 0-910984-62-X

Printed in Canada

Preface

THIS BOOK IS A SHORTENED AND EDITED VERSION of the dissertation I defended to receive my Doctor of Philosophy degree in systematic and historical theology at Boston College on February 14, 2001. While writing my dissertation, I was constantly aware of how desperately the Church, in all its branches, needs to understand the role of the Blessed Virgin Mary in Redemption for its own health.

In readying this version, I became even more painfully aware of this critical need as the universal Church struggles to proclaim and embody the Gospel of Jesus Christ anew to both the world and the members of its own various households in this 3rd millennium, amidst much turmoil. More than ever, St. Louis-Marie de Montfort seems to be a prophet for our times in saying that only if the Blessed Virgin's place in the economy of salvation is fully known and embraced will Jesus Christ and His kingdom be completely known and able to enter the world.[1] Nothing could be more true, for both the entire Church and the world, in these perilous times. It is my great hope and humble prayer that all who read and ponder this meager offering might be aided by the Holy Spirit to come into a deeper awareness of the entire Blessed Trinity's Marian mystery in a way that leads not to mere esoteric knowledge but rather, more importantly, to saving knowledge.

---

[1] St. Louis Marie de Montfort, "True Devotion to Mary", *God Alone: The Collected Writings of St. Louis Marie de Montfort* , trans. team (Bay Shore, NY: Montfort Publications, 1987) 293–4.

As the culminating project of my doctoral work, this book represents the integration of many insights I have been blessed to ponder due to having received the incomparable gift of the Catholic Faith passed on to me by many teachers, throughout the years. Some have passed this gift on to me in classrooms, from pulpits, through personal conversations and example. Others have left an indelible impression upon me through their enduring writings. To all these, both named and unnamed, I owe a great debt for faithfully passing on the gifts they have received.

I specifically wish to express my indebtedness and thanks to the many members of the Society of Jesus and their colleagues who have served as my teachers, mentors, spiritual directors, and supporters for many years. I am especially grateful to Harvey D. Egan, S.J., who served as my dissertation director at Boston College. I am also grateful to Brian E. Daley, S.J., who passed onto me his faithful appropriation of the teachings of the Fathers of the Church.

I also wish to express my deep gratitude to all those at Montfort Publications who have encouraged and helped me see this project to completion, especially Roger M. Charest, S.M.M., J. Patrick Gaffney, S.M.M., Tom and Eileen Lloyd, and Richard J. Payne.

In closing, I most humbly offer thanks and praise to our divine Lord and Savior, Jesus Christ, Who both led me to undertake this work and enabled me to accomplish it by the Power of the Holy Spirit working only through, with, and in the most Blessed Virgin Mary. *Ad Jesum per Mariam.*

July 16, 2003
Rev. Judith Marie Gentle, Ph.D.
Feast of Our Lady of Mt. Carmel

Contents

Why Continue to Discuss Marian Mediation?

Setting the Scene

As you walk up the central aisle of the Great Upper Church in the Basilica of the National Shrine of the Immaculate Conception in Washington, D.C., your gaze cannot help but be lifted up toward an enormous mosaic in the arched ceiling of the apse of this great Marian shrine. Upon finally reaching the central altar that rests beneath the immense Marian blue dome of the shrine, we come face to face with this vivid and even somewhat terrifying mosaic. We find ourselves looking directly into the penetrating, fire-filled eyes of an image of the risen Lord Jesus Christ, reigning in power and great glory. This all-embracing mosaic of the risen and victorious Christ calls to mind the scriptural images of the apocalyptic Lord seated upon His throne, as depicted in the Book of Revelation.

This mosaic is called *Christ in Majesty*. Appropriately, it was the only artistic embellishment beneath the Marian blue dome of the shrine on the day of the Basilica's dedication, November 20, 1959.[2] The centrality of this image of the risen Christ reigning over all from the arched inner walls of this Marian shrine cannot help but confront the contemplative pilgrim with the central mystery of the Christian faith. Namely, the divine Son of God, Incarnate for our redemption, chose to come down to us through, with, and, as most graphically depicted by the womb-like positioning of this mosaic inside a Marian blue dome, in Mary.

For one who is immersed in the questions being raised by the renewed theological conversation about the role of the Blessed Virgin Mary in the acquisition and distribution of the grace of Redemption, the mosaic's depiction of the risen Lord, rather than the divine Infant, cannot help but cause one to wonder if indeed the divine Son of God is not still choosing to reign in the hearts of those He has redeemed through, with, and somehow, even in Mary. Is our risen Savior somehow recreating, redeeming, and giving birth to us anew by the power of the Holy Spirit-through, with, and even in the womb-like Immaculate Heart of the Blessed Virgin Mary?

In this third millennium since the birth of Jesus Christ, there are yet many unresolved questions among Christians about both the initial and the ongoing role of the Blessed Virgin Mary in salvation. These questions are long standing and have been debated since the Church's early Christological controversies. The Council of Ephesus in 431 remains a significant witness to this fact. This ecumenical council, which was concerned primarily with upholding orthodox Christology, ended up giving the universal Church its first dogmatic definition about Mary.

It is a matter of record that at the Council of Ephesus the Blessed Virgin was officially declared to be the "Mother of God" or *Theotókos*. The exact wording used by the Council to confer this title is quoted here because of its significance for understanding both who Mary is and Jesus Christ's relationship to her:

> It was not that an ordinary man was born first of the holy Virgin, on whom afterwards the Word descended; what we say is that, being united with the flesh from the womb, [the Word] has undergone birth in the flesh, making the birth in the flesh His own . . . . Thus [the holy Fathers] have unhesitatingly called the holy Virgin "Mother of

God" (*Theotókos*). This does not mean that the nature of the Word or His divinity received the beginning of its existence from the holy Virgin, but that, since the holy body, animated by a rational soul, which the Word united to Himself according to the hypostasis (*kath'hupostasin*), was born from her, the Word was born according to the flesh. If anyone does not confess that the Emmanuel is truly God and, therefore, that the holy Virgin is the Mother of God (*Theotókos*) (since she begot according to the flesh the Word of God made flesh), *anathema sit*.[3]

While this title is not found as such in any New Testament writings, the first known mention of this Marian title was made by St. Hippolytus of Rome (c.235).[4] In 428, Nestorius, a monk from Antioch, was appointed Patriarch of Constantinople. He disputed the title, "Mother of God," as a true title for Mary because of his Christological views. He believed that the Son of God was *one* thing and the son of Mary was *another* thing, in the sense that he saw in Christ two persons, one divine (the *Logos*) and the other human (Jesus). Nestorius said it was heresy to call the Blessed Virgin Mary the "Mother of God" because she was merely mother of the human person, Jesus. He preferred that she be called *Christókos* rather than *Theotókos*.[5]

In order to safeguard the union of the two natures, the human and the divine, in the one Person of the divine Word of God, the Council of Ephesus formally declared Mary to be the Mother of God, i.e., the Mother of the Second Person of the Blessed Trinity who had taken a human nature to Himself through, with, and in her, by the power of the Holy Spirit. In so doing, this council upheld a Christological principle called the *communicatio idiomatum*. This means that what the human Christ did and suffered may be attributed to the divine Person, precisely because of the union of the two natures in the one, divine Person.[6]

The Council of Ephesus' Christological and Mariological decrees set the stage for the key question about the Blessed Virgin Mary that we are still asking today. Namely, did her freely offered *fiat* in response to the archangel Gabriel's message that God had uniquely chosen her to become the virgin Mother of God the Son irrevocably involve her in God's very work of Redemption-yesterday, today, and forever? In other words, did Mary's *fiat* make her not only the Mother of God but also the Mother of the entire work of Redemption?

Not surprisingly, it is in some of the exuberant Marian preaching which occurred in the wake of the victory of the Council of Ephesus over Nestorius that we find many of the threads of sacred tradition which claim that Mary is indeed more than a mere disciple of her Son. One such example is a sermon attributed to St. Cyril of Alexandria, whose anathemas against Nestorius and other theological writings formed the core of the decrees made at Ephesus in 431. In this sermon which many have called "the most famous Marian sermon of antiquity,"[7] the Blessed Virgin is given a series of glowing titles which indicate that through her all the glories of salvation and sanctification have been wrought.

> Through thee, the Trinity is glorified;
> through thee, the Cross is venerated in the whole
>   world . . .
> through thee, angels and archangels rejoice,
> through thee, demons are chased . . .
> through thee, the fallen creature is raised to
>   heaven . . .
> through thee, churches are founded in the whole
>   world,
> through thee, peoples are led to conversion.[8]

If we return once again to the Basilica of the National Shrine of the Immaculate Conception in Washington, D.C., we do not have to look very far for evidence of how this central Marian question continues to be raised in the Church today. Only this time, let us allow our vision to be attracted to the impressive marble sculpture that fills the south wall of the nave immediately above the shrine's entry. As we leave through the cathedral doors of the Great Upper Church, we cannot help but look up and notice another significant piece of art dedicated on November 14, 1999. It is entitled *The Universal Call to Holiness*. This marble relief is massive, weighing more than 35 tons, and demands your attention as you end your pilgrimage. In the center of the sculpture is a large dove, depicting the Holy Spirit, with rays emanating from the dove to symbolize the gift of grace in the life of the believer. On either side of this symbol of the Holy Spirit, there are human figures, all facing upwards and towards the center where the dove is located. They are depicted as male and female, of various ages, ethnic origins and vocations. They are clearly intended to represent all humanity and serve as an effective reminder that the journey toward holiness is intended for everyone. The close proximity of these figures to one another, with some of them actually reaching out as if to touch each other, reminds us that the journey toward holiness is never a solitary one.

Mary is also depicted in this sculpture. As we gaze at this sculpture, we notice that her image is on the left side of the symbol of the Holy Spirit, as the first in a long line of those glancing toward the symbol of the Holy Spirit from that side of the sculpture. While her representation in this sculpture is slightly larger than that of the other persons depicted, we cannot help but notice that she has not been placed in the center of the sculpture, directly under the Holy Spirit, with the rays of grace proceeding from the Holy Spirit through her to the others. In fact, there is nothing in the content of this sculpture to indicate clearly that she is an instrument of the mediation of grace itself to the other persons depicted on the marble relief. She is seen merely as someone who is offering a guiding hand by way of personal example. In the words of the rector of the shrine, Mary is meant to be seen in this representation as "a constant reminder of the perfect response to God's invitation."[9]

In sharp contrast to our encounter with *Christ in Majesty*, the contemplative pilgrim comes away from this artistic representation of *The Universal Call to Holiness* thinking that while the Blessed Virgin may indeed be the first and most prominent in a long line of those having been sanctified by the fruits of her Son's redeeming work, she is not necessarily the Mother of Redemption itself.

A Deeper Look at the Dilemma and its Ramifications

In his encyclical, *Ut unum sint,* Pope John Paul II echoes the necessity of working toward Christian unity sounded by the Second Vatican Council, especially as we begin this third millennium since the birth of Jesus Christ. He reminds us that the journey toward the necessary and sufficient visible unity of Christians, in the communion of the one Church willed by our Lord and Savior, Jesus Christ, requires patient and courageous efforts. Among these efforts must be a thorough study of various areas of the catholic and apostolic faith so that a true consensus of the faith can be achieved by all who consider themselves part of the universal catholic and apostolic Church. One of the primary areas pointed out as needing comprehensive study is "the Virgin Mary, as Mother of God and Icon of the Church, the spiritual Mother who intercedes for Christ's disciples and for all humanity."[10]

If we look carefully at the various components in the statement above, we would generally find agreement among orthodox Christians that Mary is the Mother of God, as we have seen this definition put forth by the Council of Ephesus in 431. It is even generally agreed by orthodox Christians that this declaration is necessary to safeguard the divinity of the Person of Jesus Christ. At the Council of Chalcedon in 451, the normative decision of Ephesus led to the Christian confession that Jesus Christ is truly one divine Person, the only-begotten Son of God, consubstantial with the Father, in two natures, both divine and human, without change, without confusion, without separation and without division.[11] And, as part of this Christological confession, orthodox Christians would generally hold to the *communicatio idiomatum* as a necessary consequence of the doctrine of the unity of the Person of Christ.[12] While the very term "Mother of God" must continually be explained, especially to contemporary Christians, there seems to be a unity of belief with St. Cyril of Alexandria that Mary is indeed Mother of God, the *Theotókos*.[13]

Correspondingly, most orthodox Christians would also agree that her divine Son, Jesus Christ, had to have been virginally conceived by the power of the Holy Spirit in the womb of Mary because the Incarnation of the Second Person of the Blessed Trinity could be no mere fruit of human sexual intercourse but rather only the work of God Himself through, with, and in Mary. This belief is confessed by orthodox, creedal Christians of various denominations every Sunday in the language of the Nicene Creed when they say that for us and for our salvation, the only Son of God, eternally begotten of the Father and of one being with the Father, came down from heaven and became flesh from the Virgin Mary by the power of the Holy Spirit. [14]

Similarly, most orthodox Christians would have no problem considering Mary as an icon of the Church. She was even constantly hailed by Martin Luther and John Calvin as the perfect example of discipleship, using the words of the Savior in St. Luke's Gospel, 11:27–28. When Mary was blessed by a woman in the crowd for bearing Jesus in her womb, the Savior replied rather blessed is she because she perfectly hears the word of God and keeps it.[15] As Calvin says: "And this is the greatest praise we know how to give her . . . that we avow Mary as our teacher and that we are her disciples."[16]

The results of a recent survey of members of Ecumenical Society of the Blessed Virgin Mary indicate that most orthodox Christians who are knowledgeable about the meaning of the various Christological and Mariological terms used above agree about the truth to which these terms point. This survey was given during the fall of 1998 and the winter of 1999 with a 70% return rate, which is generally regarded as very good in research of this type. The faith traditions represented by the respondents are Roman Catholic, Anglican, Lutheran, Orthodox, and Methodist. There was overwhelming agreement by 100% of the respondents that Mary is the Mother of God, by 96% that Jesus was virginally conceived within Mary's womb, and 100% agreement that Mary's faith, as shown in the scriptures, is a role model, or icon, for all Christians.[17]

While all this sounds promising, there remains much confusion, great disagreement and heated debate among Christians in the final area of Marian doctrine outlined by Pope John Paul II as needing further study, namely, the role of Mary as *our* spiritual Mother, i.e., as one whose continuing and eternal vocation is somehow to mediate the fruits of Redemption. In the results of the survey mentioned above, 86% of those responding held that the intercession of Mary detracts from the "one-mediatorship" of Christ while, at the same time, 89 % agreed that we can ask Mary to pray for us just as we ask our friends to pray for us.[18]

Why all the confusion and the debate about Marian mediation among Christians? For starters, many note that the meaning of the terms "Mother" and "spiritual Mother" when applied to Mary in her relationship to us are not clear. These terms do not have a univocal meaning among either Protestant or Catholic Christians. Many wonder if these terms express merely a psychological or emotional relationship of affection between Mary and us. Is she merely one who holds our hand as a friend and good example on the way to her Son, as depicted in the marble relief at the Basilica of the National Shrine of the Immaculate Conception? Or, do these terms speak of an ontological reality, i.e., something that really exists in the order of *being*? In other words, is there something about Mary's role that really exists in the order of grace that is analogous to that of biological motherhood in the order of nature? If she is our spiritual Mother in the order of grace, then how do we speak of her relationship to the various Persons of the Blessed Trinity? And, similarly, if something ontological is indeed occurring in the order of grace through the Blessed Virgin, do we make our way to her Son somehow easier for ourselves when we consciously learn how to give ourselves over to Mary as our spiritual Mother? What is meant by the term "consecration to Mary?" What are people really doing by consecrating themselves to her? What happens to people who don't knowingly consecrate themselves to Mary or acknowledge her as the spiritual Mother that she is?

These and similar questions lead us into the very heart of the renewed Marian conversation among Christians of all denominations about both the meaning of Marian mediation itself and the possibility of the Blessed Virgin's having a significant and unique role in the full and final Redemption of humankind by her Son. The various titles by which Mary has been invoked in the Catholic Church over the centuries, as reiterated in *"Lumen Gentium,"* immediately come to mind: "Advocate, Helper, Benefactress, and Mediatrix."[19] Furthermore, these terms invariably lead us back to and even imply the debate that has been going on with various degrees of intensity within the Roman Catholic Church during this century. This debate is about whether Mary should be spoken of, officially, as "Co-redemptrix, Mediatrix, and Advocate for the People of God" through a dogmatic definition of these titles. Are perhaps the issue of Marian mediation and the ongoing involvement of the Blessed Virgin Mary in the work of Redemption such a dilemma because there are deeper theological questions and divisions among Christians that this debate about Mary really raises?

The primary reason most often cited for disagreement among confessing, orthodox Christians about Mary's ongoing role in mediating the grace of Redemption, often called subjective Redemption, as well as about her role in the mystery of objective Redemption itself, is concern about her taking something away from the Person and work of Jesus Christ as the Redeemer, the one and perfect Mediator between God and humankind. This concern is usually expressed at the slightest mention of Marian mediation, sometimes even by Catholics and Orthodox Christians, as well as by Anglicans and Protestants. There is what we might call in contemporary psychological terms a schizophrenic tendency with regard to Marian mediation. Many tend to make practical use of the intercession or mediation of the Blessed Virgin in their own personal prayer, at least from time to time, while either not knowing how or actually being afraid to speak of her mediation without denying the one mediation of Christ between God and humankind. We saw this tendency expressed in the results of the survey of the members of the Ecumenical Society of the Blessed Virgin Mary as cited above. It is seen to have its roots in the Protestant Reformation that has in some way affected all Christians. The slogans of the Reformation that express the heart of this schizophrenia about Marian mediation are *sola gratia, sola fide, sola scriptura,* and *solus Christus.*[20]

The classic scriptural support for these post-Reformation concerns about safeguarding the unique mediation of Jesus Christ when speaking of Marian mediation is to be found in 1Tim. 2:5, where it is proclaimed that "there is one God; there is one mediator between God and humankind, Christ Jesus, himself human, who gave himself a ransom for all." This text from 1Timothy is usually quoted out of context. Thus, the irony is that it is often forgotten that this proclamation about the unique mediatorship of Christ follows Paul's urging the readers of this apostolic letter to make "supplications, prayers, intercessions, and thanksgivings for everyone . . . so that we may lead a quiet and peaceable life in all godliness and dignity. This is right and is acceptable in the sight of God our Savior . . . ."[21]

The Anglican theologian, John Macquarrie, is especially helpful in pointing out the deeper theological debate behind these hard line Protestant Reformation slogans and out of context references to 1Tim. 2:5. His observations bring us to what we might consider to be the truly unresolved question that lurks in the minds of all Christians when Marian mediation is considered from a theological viewpoint. Namely, what is the human role in any adequate theology of salvation? Is the human role purely a passive one, or is it, as the fathers of the Second Vatican Council asserted about Mary in *Lumen Gentium VIII*, also an active role?

While pelagianism has been rightfully condemned, how do we keep from swinging toward the Reformation view that humankind is so completely morally and spiritually bankrupt, having been rendered so totally helpless as a consequence of sin, that God must save us wholly and entirely through an act that is totally outside of us, even without us, so to speak? Macquarrie aptly makes the point that the post-Reformation dilemma which lingers behind any real consideration of Mary's mediation is finding a way to speak about the priority of divine grace that evokes and enables a full human response without rendering the human yes to grace superfluous. This is the real theological dilemma all Christians have in speaking of any role which the Blessed Virgin's *fiat* plays in both objective and subjective Redemption. And, related to this dilemma, is the need to find a way to speak of the necessity of grace while not exempting the recipient of grace from bearing "fruits worthy of repentance" (Luke 3:8).[22]

Let us take Macquarrie's thinking one step further. When it comes to the specific task of speaking of the role of divine grace and the spiritual Motherhood of the Blessed Virgin Mary, we must find a way to speak not only of the intersection of grace and the need of the human person to bear fruits of repentance. We must also find a way to speak of one particular human person's having been made so astoundingly holy by the singular grace of having been conceived without original sin that, being "full of grace" as the angelic salutation declares, she indeed continues to bear "fruit that will last . . . by which the Father is much glorified" (John 15:8; 16). How do we speak theologically of the possibility that Mary's mediation of grace, while like our own prayers of intercession for one another in some respects, may indeed be qualitatively different, in the sense that God has chosen to have the entire grace and work of the Redemption flow through her? Is there a God-given role that her eternal bearing of fruit plays in the fruit that I, you, and all of us are both nourished by and consequently empowered by grace to pass on to others, even if we are not consciously aware of this? And, furthermore, if this is so, then how do we speak of the Blessed Trinity's seeming dependence upon the "yes" of this particular human woman in bringing about not only the Incarnation but the entire work of Redemption in a way that does not render the sovereign Power of God impotent and does not reduce Mary to a mere human puppet on God's stage?

In summary, we might say that the primary challenge facing Christians today with regard to Marian mediation is finding a thoroughly orthodox way to answer the above questions about the unique human contribution of one particular human person to the work of Redemption. If we can find a way to address these questions, we will greatly aid the apologetical task of helping all Christians understand what the Catholic Faith means, theologically speaking, by the "spiritual Motherhood" of the Blessed Virgin Mary. And, if we can find a way to do this, perhaps we will allow the Blessed Virgin to become a cause for the unity of Christians rather than remain an excuse for our tiresome and scandalous divisions.

St. Louis Marie de Montfort, a Light along the Path

Since the primary stumbling block in the ecumenical conversation about the essentials of the Catholic and Apostolic Faith in regards to the Blessed Virgin Mary is the very issue of her mediation, it seems important that those of us who are engaged in the work of Marian apologetics turn again and again to that line of sacred tradition that supports a truly orthodox understanding of Mary's mediation as rooted in the scriptures, the writings of the Fathers, and the Catholic creeds. Certainly one of the prominent Marian Saints and authors who falls into this category and who deserves more patient and courageous study is St. Louis Marie Grignion de Montfort. For our present challenge, his writing is especially important because one of his primary foci is the very issue of Mary's ongoing and eternal mediation in the redemptive work of the one Mediator, Jesus Christ.

Pope John Paul II, who has written of Mary's maternal mediation in his encyclical, *Redemptoris Mater*, attributes much of his own understanding of the mystery of who Mary is in the plan of salvation to his encounter with the writings of St. Louis de Montfort.[23] Furthermore, there are even those who believe that St. Louis Marie's Marian doctrine is so significant and even paradigmatic for an orthodox understanding of the Blessed Virgin Mary that he ought to be declared a Marian Doctor of the Church. Among such persons is none other than Fr. René Laurentin, one whom many consider to be the most prominent Marian theologian of the 20th century and one who was very influential in shaping the teaching of the Second Vatican Council on Mary.[24]

As will be shown in this book, St. Louis de Montfort's basic premise is that because Mary has been uniquely chosen by God to mediate the Incarnate Son to us in the first place, she has likewise been chosen by God to mediate perpetually the grace of her Son's Redemption to all human persons in a unique way. However, St. Louis is adamant that Mary, of herself, is nothing and that all that is accomplished by God through, with, and in her is God's doing. She is indeed God's Masterpiece of creation—a mere creature—but also the only creature that God has uniquely and unequivocally made "full of grace" from the moment of her conception. And, Mary has been given to us by God precisely to lead us perfectly to her divine Son so that we too might become through, with, and in her, filled with His grace.

I have chosen to entitle this book, *Jesus Redeeming in Mary*, because of Montfort's insistence that the ongoing and eternal mystery of the Word of God's taking flesh in the womb of the Virgin Mary has resulted in the same Word's free and eternal choice to accomplish His work of redeeming us precisely through, with, and in this same Mary. It is my prayerful hope that the theological depth of what St. Louis means by the prepositions "through," "with," and especially "in" might become clearer through this look at his writings from a theological point of view. For therein seems to lie his profound contribution to helping us address the questions of many Christians about Marian mediation.

Before we move on to the body of this book, it is important for the reader to note that we will not be concerned with delineating the exact theological meaning of such Marian titles as Mediatrix, Co-redemptrix, or Advocate for the people of God. Rather, our intent here is to articulate the theological underpinnings that support the enduring tenet of the Catholic Faith about Mary's relationship to, and participation in, the redeeming work of Jesus Christ by offering theological reflection on the meaning of St. Louis Marie Grignion de Montfort's major Marian premises. And, since all authentic theological reflection about the Blessed Virgin Mary must be based upon scripture, it is my hope that our reflection on the thought of St. Louis de Montfort will help expose the deeper theological and spiritual meaning of the biblical texts and creedal affirmations concerning the Blessed Virgin that all orthodox Christians hold in common.

Finally, it is my prayer that this humble writing may contribute in some small way to one of the major ecumenical directives offered by the Second Vatican Council, namely, the mandate given to Catholic theologians in the "Decree on Ecumenism":

> When comparing doctrines, they should remember that in Catholic teaching there exists an order or "hierarchy" of truths, since they vary in their relation to the foundation of the Christian faith.[25]

When it comes to Marian doctrine, the Council's directive seems to be asking Catholic theologians to become attentive to expressing ever anew the truths about the Blessed Virgin in relationship to the Christological mystery itself. For it is only then that the splendid and full array of Marian doctrine can be seen, not as tangential, but rather as the quintessential aspect of the very Person and work of Jesus Christ, which it most certainly is!

As an Anglican Catholic theologian, committed not only intellectually to following this directive but also personally to helping many embrace the Marian dimension of Catholic Truth, it is my prayer that all who read this book might come to a "deeper realization and a clearer expression of the unfathomable riches of Christ,"[26] by seeing and honoring the Most Blessed Virgin Mary more truly.

NOTES

[2] Msgr. Michael J. Bransfield, "A Monumental Work Completed, A New Journey of Faith Begun," *Mary's Shrine* Fall/Winter 1999: 3.

[3] Josef Neuner, S.J., and Jacques Dupuis, S.J., ed., *The Christian Faith in the Doctrinal Documents of the Catholic Church* (New York: Alba House, 1998)197 (DS 251–252).

[4] *Dictionary of Mary* (New York: Catholic Book Publishing Company, 1997) 332.

[5] Michael O'Carroll, C.S.Sp., *Theotokos* (Collegeville: The Liturgical Press, 1982) 111.

[6] O'Carroll 111. The disagreements of this Council over how to articulate the two natures of Jesus Christ united in the one, divine Person of the Incarnate Word resulted in a break between Christians of the Catholic Church and those of what has come to be called the Assyrian Church of the East. A significant part of this Church did come into union with the Roman pontiff as the Chaldean Catholic Church. In 1994, a major breakthrough occurred toward both reuniting these two Churches with each other and bringing both into full communion with the Roman pontiff. A Joint Declaration was issued by Pope John Paul II and Patriarch Mar Dinkha IV of the Assyrian Church which states that since both Churches attest that Christ's divinity and humanity are united in one divine Person, they also agree that the "humanity to which the Blessed Virgin gave birth always was that of the Son of God Himself. . . . In the light of this same faith the Catholic tradition addresses the Virgin Mary as "the Mother of

God" and also as "the Mother of Christ." Jeffrey Gros, et. al., *Introduction to Ecumenism* (Mahwah: Paulist Press, 1998) 156–7.

[7] O'Carroll 113.

[8] O'Carroll 113. Michael O'Carroll attributes as his source for this sermon the following two reference works: *Patrologia Graeca* (Migne) 77 and *Acta Conciliorum Oecumenicorum*, 1, 1, 2, ed. E. Schwartz (Strassburg: 1914) 102–3.

[9] Bransfield 2–3.

[10] John Paul II, *Ut unum sint*, Vatican trans. (Boston: Pauline Books, 1995) 89.

[11] Neuner 203 (DS 302).

[12] St. Thomas Aquinas, *Summa Theologica* , trans. Fathers of the English Dominican Province, vol. IV (Westminster, MD: Christian Classics, 1948) IIIa, q.35, art. 4 2199 -2200.

[13] In an article by Charles Dickson, Ph.D., "Consensus Views on the Biblical Picture of Mary," *Queen of All Hearts* January-February 1999: 36–8, Rev. Dickson speaks of the growing consensus among Christians regarding the above orthodox understandings of the Blessed Virgin Mary.

[14] Dickson 36–8.

[15] Luther regularly praised Mary's virtues and held her up for imitation, especially as regards her exemplary living of humility, chastity, and faith. See William J. Cole, "Was Luther a Devotee of Mary?" *Marian Studies* 21 (1970): 94–202, for further conversation on Luther's praise of Mary as an icon of perfect discipleship.

[16] A quote from John Calvin, *Sermon XI on the Harmony of the Gospels*, found in the purpose statement of the Ecumenical Society of Blessed Virgin Mary in the United States, Nov. 1998.

[17] Patricia Kirby, Ed.D., *Results of a Survey on "Mary in the Christian Churches Today,"* Ecumenical Society of the Blessed Virgin Mary (Washington: Oblate College, 1999) 1–2.

[18] Kirby 3.

[19] "Lumen Gentium," *Documents of the Second Vatican Council*, ed. Austin Flannery, O.P. (Northport, NY: Costello, 1992) 419.

[20] Thomas Xavier, "A New Dogma in 1998?" *Inside the Vatican* May 1997: 60–1. The valid point is made that the idea of "Jesus alone" is in point of fact a relatively recent and novel theological position. One never hears this theological concept expounded in the writings of the Fathers or really even in the New Testament itself. It is purely a Reformation and post-Reformation idea.

[21] All scriptural quotes in this book are from *The Revised Standard Version of the Holy Bible* (New York: Oxford University Press, 1977).

[22] John Macquarrie, *Mary for all Christians* (Grand Rapids: Wm. B. Eerdmans, 1990) 98– 115.

[23] In his book, *Crossing the Threshold of Hope* (New York: Alfred Knopf, 1994) 212–213, Pope John Paul II says that thanks to St. Louis de Montfort he came to understand that true devotion to the Mother of God is actually Christocentric, profoundly rooted in the Mystery of the Blessed Trinity, and the mysteries of the Incarnation and the Redemption. Furthermore, he says that this mature form of Marian piety that he gained from discovering St. Louis de Montfort has stayed with him over the years and born theological fruit in the encyclicals, *Redemptoris Mater* and *Mulieris Dignitatem.*

[24] René Laurentin, *The Meaning of Consecration Today* (San Francisco: Ignatius Press, 1992) 54. Fr. Laurentin says that the writings and practice of Grignion de Montfort actually brought about the elimination of various Mariological exaggerations and deviations that had crept into Marian theology and piety by the times in which he lived and wrote.

[25] "*Unitatis redintegratio*" *Documents of the Second Vatican Council*, ed. Austin Flannery, O.P. (Northport, NY: Costello, 1992) 462.

[26] "*Unitatis redintegratio*" 462.

CHAPTER 1

The Patristic Understanding of Mary as the Second Eve— the Preparatory Stage for the Writings of St. Louis de Montfort

Opening Considerations

Certainly one of the first questions we must investigate as we embark upon this journey to understand Mary's role in Redemption is how the Church, commissioned in the Gospel by her Lord and Savior to make all nations into His disciples by baptizing them in the Name of the Father, and of the Son, and of the Holy Spirit (Mt. 28:19), came to be concerned at any depth about the woman designated by the Gospels simply as Mary, the mother of Jesus? In other words, what caused the early Church to begin a theological discussion about the nature and role of the woman, Mary, herself? Was it not sufficient for the Church to discuss the nature and role of Jesus Christ and to be content with thinking of Mary merely as the human mother of the Savior?

The primary reason that the early Church began to reflect theologically on Mary herself is the same reason that we are still discussing her today. This reason is that it is through, with, and in Mary's very being that God gives the incontrovertible sign promised in Isaiah 7:14 that "God is with us" in Jesus of Nazareth. "Behold a virgin shall conceive and bear a son and shall call his name Immanuel." It can be safely said that in the history of the world never has it been known for a human being to be born of a woman, virginally. It is generally agreed by Marian scholars that Mary's virginity provided the patristic age with its first vexing problem in her regard[27] and led to the Church's first insight into the questions about Mary that we are still dealing with today. Namely, by divine plan this particular woman Mary had been chosen by God to be uniquely associated with the Redeemer.

For the Church during its patristic age, it was belief in and reflection upon the virginal conception of Jesus Christ that paved the way for what is considered to be the beginning of Marian theology—the idea that the Blessed Virgin Mary is the New Eve.[28] In the words of John Henry Newman in the *Letter to Pusey* :

> What is the greatest rudimental teaching of Antiquity from its earliest date concerning her (the Blessed Virgin)? By "rudimental teaching" I mean the *prima facie* view of her person and office, the broad outline laid down of her, the aspect under which she comes to us, in the writings of the Fathers. She is the Second Eve.[29]

The New Testament evidence for Mary's virginal conception of Jesus and the accompanying patristic reflection upon her as the Second Eve is found principally in the Gospel of Matthew and the Gospel of Luke, where she is described as the virgin mother of Jesus Christ.[30] In chapter 1 of the Gospel of Matthew that discusses the lineage of Jesus, we are told that Jesus was born of Mary. We are not told that Joseph was the father of Jesus. We are merely told that Joseph was the husband of Mary (Mt 1:16). This description of Joseph is a clear break and change in the form through which the lineage is given for all the other male figures listed before Joseph. While the others are described as being the father of a particular person, Joseph is not described as being the father of anyone but merely the husband of Mary, of whom Jesus was born, who is called the Christ (Mt 1:1–16).

As we continue reading in Chapter 1 of the Gospel of Matthew about the account of the birth of Jesus Christ, we see that "when his mother Mary had been betrothed to Joseph, before they came together she was with child of the Holy Spirit; and her husband Joseph, being a just man and unwilling to put her to shame, resolved to divorce her quietly" (Mt. 1:18b–19). Matthew's Gospel goes on to tell us that an angel of the Lord speaks to Joseph in a dream to allay his fears about Mary's pregnancy, telling him "for that which is conceived in her is of the Holy Spirit" (Mt. 1:20). The Gospel account goes on to say that all this took place to fulfill the promise of the Lord given through the prophet Isaiah in Is. 7:14, "Behold a virgin shall conceive and bear a son, and his name shall be called Emmanuel" (Mt 1:23).

In the Gospel of Luke, we hear that "the angel Gabriel was sent from God to a virgin betrothed to a man whose name was Joseph" and that the angel tells her "you will conceive in your womb and bear a son, and you shall call his name Jesus" (Lk. 1: 26–27; 31). We hear Mary asking the angel in response to this announcement, "How can this be, since I have no husband? And the angel said to her, "the Holy Spirit will come upon you, and the power of the Most High will overshadow you; therefore the child to be born will be called holy, the Son of God" (Lk.1: 34–35). We also hear Mary freely choosing to respond in perfect obedience to the announcement by the angel about God's will for her. "Behold, I am the handmaid of the Lord; let it be to me according to your word" (Lk. 1:38).

In addition to the above Gospel accounts on Mary's free and total consent to the will of God for her as announced by an angel and her consequent virginal conception of Jesus, by the power of the Holy Spirit, the New Testament also contains St. Paul's teachings in Romans 5 and 1 Corinthians 15 on the Christ-Adam typology. "Death reigned from Adam to Moses, even over those whose sins were not like the transgression of Adam, who was a type of the one who was to come. But the free gift is not like the trespass. For if many died through one man's trespass, much more have the grace of God and the free gift in the grace of that one man, Jesus Christ, abounded for many" (Rom. 5:14–15). "For as by a man came death, by a man has come also the resurrection of the dead. For as in Adam all die, so also in Christ shall all be made alive" (1Cor. 15: 21–22).

This revelatory typology of St. Paul on Christ as the Second Adam, coupled with the Gospel accounts of Mary's virginity and the virginal conception of Jesus, served to fuel the inevitable patristic comparison of Mary to Eve. An historical survey of patristic sources reveals that theological reflection upon the full meaning of Mary's virginal conception of Jesus coincided with reflection upon her role as the Second Eve. In fact, simultaneous reflection upon these two aspects of Mary herself coupled with reflection upon Mary as the *Theotókos* complemented one another as the Fathers combated the half truths rampant in the early Church's efforts to delineate a truly orthodox Christology and Trinitarian theology.

The Marian Theology of the Early Fathers of the Church

Belief in the virginal conception of Jesus Christ as doctrine is found widely in the second century in the official creeds, such as that of Hippolytus (c. 217) and its most widely known antecedents, *Romanum Vetus* and *Textus Receptus*. In addition, St. Ignatius of Antioch (c. 35 – c. 107), Aristides (2nd cent.), St. Clement of Alexandria (c. 150 – c. 215), St. Justin Martyr (c. 100–165) , and St. Irenaeus (c. 130 – c. 200) all testify to Mary's virginal conception of Jesus. Of these early voices who uphold the virginal conception, Justin and Irenaeus are considered to be the first two exponents of Marian theology, i.e., interpreters of Isaiah 7:14 in a Marian sense, as well as the pioneering voices of the Eve-Mary parallel.[31] Before taking a close look at the writings of these last two key Church Fathers, it is important to note that it is believed that the remote origins of the Eve-Mary parallel may date as far back as Papias, Bishop of Hierapolis in Asia Minor, at the turn of the first century (before 110).[32]

St. Justin Martyr, an early Christian apologist born of pagan parents and converted to Christianity c. 130, taught at Ephesus for a time where he engaged in his Disputation with Trypho the Jew c.135.[33] In his *Dialogue with Trypho* he graphically puts forth what may well have been inspired by an oral tradition dating from at least the time of Bishop Papias:

> The Son of God…became man by the Virgin, in order that the disobedience which proceeded from the serpent might receive its destruction in the same manner in which it derived its origin. For Eve, who was a virgin and undefiled, having conceived the word of the serpent, brought forth disobedience and death. But the Virgin Mary received faith and joy, when the angel Gabriel announced the good tidings to her that the Spirit of the Lord would come upon her, and the power of the Highest would overshadow her: wherefore also the Holy Thing begotten of her is the Son of God; and she replied "Be it unto me according to thy word." And by her has He been born, to whom we have proved so many Scriptures refer, and by whom God destroys both the serpent and those angels and men who are like him; but works deliverance from death to those who repent of their wickedness and believe upon Him.[34]

While Justin is primarily concerned with Christ in this work and consequently only announces the Eve-Mary parallel, without making an effort to examine at any depth the exact nature of the Virgin Mary's redemptive role, he does say that by divine design the pattern of human redemption parallels humankind's fall. This is revealed precisely in the fact that both the fall and the Redemption were brought about through the *agency of a virgin*. As we compare these two virgins, we cannot help but draw the conclusion that the good fruit of Mary's co-operation with God contrasted sharply with the bad fruit of Eve's cooperation with the serpent, Satan. And, it is this very contrast that has made all the difference for the human race! Mary's joy, faith, and willing *obedience* in response to God's command have brought forth the One who gives *life* by destroying the serpent and the power of evil in those who repent and believe in Him. In contrast, Eve's *disobedience* of God has brought forth nothing but *death*.

In light of the Genesis account of the fall of humankind, the reader of Justin will also conclude that just as the effects of Eve's fall were brought about in relationship to and subordination to Adam, so also will the effects of Mary's redemptive choice be brought about in relationship to and subordination to Christ. However, there is one additional detail about our first parents that Genesis reveals as God's having reversed in our second parents. In the case of Adam and Eve, Eve received her flesh through the rib of Adam (Gen. 2:22). In the case of Christ "the Holy Thing was begotten of her." Thus, Justin alludes to another important element in the Church's ongoing reflections upon the person of Mary and her role in Redemption. In the mystery of the new Creation, the Second Adam takes flesh from the Second Eve. Thus, the Second Eve's subordination to the Second Adam in no way intends gender inequality, as some feminists wrongly conclude, but rather the re-subordination of the entire human race to God through the Virgin Mary's loving and total obedience to God the Son, Who became incarnate from her flesh by the Power of the Holy Spirit.

With Mary's virginal conception of the Redeemer and the redemptive reversal of the Eve-Mary parallel in mind, we now move on to consider the thought of St. Irenaeus, Bishop of Lyons. As a native of Smyrna, it is recorded that Irenaeus was taught by St. Polycarp, Bishop of Smyrna (c.69 – c.155),[35] providing him with a direct link to the apostles themselves. Irenaeus is generally considered to be the first great Catholic theologian and forms an important bridge between the East and the West in the history of Christian thought. It is in the writings of Irenaeus, who knew and used Papias' work and who may have developed what he discovered in Justin, that we find the Eve-Mary parallel integrated for the first time with a theology.[36] We find his giving the Virgin Mary a distinctive role in redemption clearly elaborated in his principal work, *Against Heresies*, written between 182 and 188. This monumental exposition and defense of the Catholic faith was written by Irenaeus to mount a detailed attack against Gnosticism, especially the system of Valentinus, and the millenarianism popular in Montanist circles in the last quarter of the 2nd century. *Against Heresies* is considered to be among the most important theological writings of the early Christian Church.[37]

There are two key principles which characterize Irenaeus' overall theological insight and which especially undergird his approach to the Blessed Virgin. These are *recapitulatio* and *recirculatio*, translated as recapitulation and recirculation. By recapitulation, Irenaeus saw that the paradoxical imperative of God's design is that fallen human nature must be lifted and restored to God by the same nature that was responsible for its having fallen in the first place. This imperative is resolved in the Eternal Word of God made flesh, who totally identifies Himself with humanity by becoming its second Head (*caput*). By recirculation, Irenaeus saw that it is also God's plan that the process of restoration must correspond inversely to that of the fall, somewhat as a knot is untied.[38] This means that the knot fashioned of Eve's and Adam's disobedience, with all its consequences for man, woman, and the whole created order, can only be untied by the obedience of both the Virgin Mary and the Word made flesh.

Irenaeus gives us three profound passages that demonstrate his key insights into God's plan of Redemption. The first is as follows:

> For as by one man's disobedience sin entered, and
> death obtained [a place] through sin; so also by the

obedience of one man, righteousness having been
introduced, shall cause life to fructify in those persons who in times past were dead. And, as the pro-
toplast himself, Adam, had his substance from
untilled and as yet virgin soil ("for God had not
yet sent rain and man had not yet tilled the
ground" Gen. 2:5), and was formed by the hand of
God, that is by the Word of God, for "all things
were made by Him" (John 1:3), and the Lord took
dust from the earth and formed man; so did He
who is the Word, recapitulating Adam in Himself,
rightly receive a birth, enabling Him to gather up
Adam [into Himself], from Mary, who was as yet a
virgin. . . . Those, therefore, who allege that He
took nothing from the Virgin do greatly err,
[since,] in order that they may cast away the
inheritance of the flesh, they also reject the analogy [between Him and Adam] . . . For if He did
not receive the substance of the flesh from a
human being, He neither was made man nor the
Son of man; and if He was not made what we
were, He did no great thing in what He suffered
and endured . . . . The Apostle Paul, moreover, in
the Epistle to the Galatians, declares plainly, "God
sent His Son, made of a woman" (Gal. 4:4).[39]

It is instructive to note that in the last sentence above that
Roberts' and Donaldson's translation of Gal. 4:4 does not say
"born of a woman" but rather "made of a woman." The use of the
word "made" seems appropriate here as Irenaeus is emphasizing
that the Son of God took a real human nature from the Virgin
Mary. In other words, she is no mere passive vessel whom God the
Son merely passed through on His way to earth. Rather, Irenaeus
shows Mary to be integral to the Incarnation—and hence salvation itself—precisely because she is the woman in, and from

whom, the Eternal Word took that very human nature needed to save us.

In speaking further of the significance of Mary's role, Irenaeus goes on to say:

> In accordance with this design, Mary the Virgin is found obedient, saying, "Behold the handmaid of the Lord; be it unto me according to thy word" (Luke 1:38). But Eve was disobedient; for she did not obey when as yet a virgin. And even as she, having indeed a husband, Adam, but being nevertheless as yet a virgin (for in Paradise "they both were naked, and were not ashamed," inasmuch as they, having been created a short time previously, had no understanding of the procreation of children; for it was necessary that they should first come to adult age, and then multiply from that time onward), having become disobedient, was made the cause of death, both to herself and to the whole human race; so also did Mary, having a man betrothed [to her], and being nevertheless a virgin, by yielding obedience, become the cause of salvation, both to herself and the whole human race. And on this account does the law term a woman betrothed to a man, the wife of him who had betrothed her, although she was as yet a virgin; thus indicating the back-reference (*recirculationem*)[40] from Mary to Eve, because what is joined together could not otherwise be put asunder than by inversion of the process by which these bonds of union had arisen; so that the former ties be canceled by the latter, that the latter may set the former again at liberty. . . . And thus also it was that the knot of Eve's disobedience was loosed by the obedience of Mary. For what the virgin Eve had

bound fast through unbelief, this did the virgin Mary set free through faith.[41]

And, last but not least, in the following passage we hear Irenaeus make specific mention of Mary's role in salvation itself:

> That the Lord then was manifestly coming to His own things, and was sustaining them by means of that creation which is supported by Himself, and was making a recapitulation of that disobedience which had occurred in connection with a tree, through the obedience which was [exhibited by Himself when He hung] upon a tree [the effects] also of that deception being done away with, by which that virgin Eve, who was already espoused to a man, was unhappily misled, was happily announced, through means of the truth [spoken] by the angel to the Virgin Mary, who was [also espoused] to a man. For just as the former was led astray by the word of an angel, so that she fled from God when she had transgressed His word; so did the latter, by an angelic communication, receive the glad tidings that she should sustain (*portaret*) God, being obedient to His word. And if the former did disobey God, yet the latter was persuaded to be obedient to God, in order that the Virgin Mary might become the patroness (*advocata*) of the virgin Eve. And thus, as the human race fell into bondage to death by means of a virgin, so is it rescued (*salvatur*)[42] by (the means of)[43] a virgin; virginal disobedience having been balanced in the opposite scale by virginal obedience. For in the same way the sin of the first created man (*protoplasti*) receives amendment by the correction of the First-begotten, and the coming of

the serpent is conquered by the harmlessness of
the dove, those bonds being unloosed by which we
had been fast bound to death.[44]

These three key major Marian passages from *Against Heresies*
show us that for Irenaeus the Virgin Mary is clearly the Second
Eve in the divine plan and as such has a distinctive and unique
role in the work of Redemption. Mary's free and total cooperation
with God is shown by Irenaeus to be the human contribution
God required to bring humankind back from the spiritual death,
caused by our first parents' disobedience, into the fullness of life
that could only be obtained by the divine Son, Incarnate from
this Second Virgin's flesh. Thus, God chooses to depend upon
Mary's free and obedient yes to inaugurate God's own redemptive
plan to recirculate the no of Eve and recapitulate humankind's
covenant with God. Her obedience is hailed by Irenaeus as the
instrumental cause of salvation for her and for the entire human
race, even to the extent that Irenaeus calls Mary the patroness or
advocata of the disobedient virgin Eve and all her children. How
can this be?

By the Power of the Holy Spirit, her yes makes her the virginal ground through, with, and in whom the Eternal Word's
human nature comes into existence so that He can actually be
the second head of our race and reconcile us with God. As a virgin, Mary chooses to give herself solely and entirely to God and
does not flee from God, as did Eve. She chooses to surrender to
God her physical reality, the total assent of her mind, and the free
consent of her will. Her total cooperation with God's will and
acceptance of the divine Self-offer take place on both the material and the spiritual levels of her very being. Unlike the first Eve,
there is no self-interest in Mary. God encounters in this Second
Eve a woman who holds nothing back from Him. Through her
surrender, the Eternal Word of God makes her clay His very own
and sets the captive human race free from the bondage of Satan
and sin. It is precisely because her consent and consequent gift of

self are so total, in contrast to Eve, that she thereby becomes the purely human instrument which effectively re-establishes humankind's response to God on both the physical and the spiritual levels of human existence alongside and in subordination to the Redeemer, who is not purely human but rather the divine Person of God the Son in the flesh.

Because her yes precedes and makes possible the obedience of the Second Adam—whose very intent is to fructify those who were dead—Irenaeus helps us see that the consent of the Blessed Virgin Mary to the Incarnation clearly has a soteriological or redemptive character, while always subordinate to and finding its ultimate fulfillment in the consent of her divine Son. When we later delve into the writings of St. Louis de Montfort, we will see why this soteriological character which marks Mary's *fiat* is such an important conclusion to take with us from the writings of St. Irenaeus. Let us also take from our reading of St. Irenaeus the clear insight that the particular human element required by God to bring about the redemptive Incarnation of the Eternal Word Himself was none other than the twin elements of Mary's virginal heart and virginal body. By the divine plan, both had to be freely offered to God in the total obedience of love for the Eternal Word's redemptive Incarnation to be accomplished by the Power of the Holy Spirit. This is important not only for understanding Mary herself but also for understanding the free and total surrender God requires of each human person in order for grace to be efficacious.

The Eve-Mary Parallel in the Fathers after Irenaeus

If we continue looking at the history of the development of the Eve-Mary parallel in the early Church, we keep discovering the theme of Eve's virginity, disobedience, and consequent death for the human race balanced and even reversed by the virginity, obedience, and life-giving fruit of Mary. We find this in the writings of Tertullian, c. 210, in his work *De carne Christi*; in the epistles and sermons of St. Ambrose during the final quarter of the 4th century when he calls Eve the mother of the human race but Mary the Mother of salvation; and in the epigrammatic words of St. Jerome in the 5th century, "Death through Eve, life through Mary."[45] Traces of this parallel are likewise found in the writings of St. Augustine and Peter Chrysologus in the 5th century.

Caelius Sedulius especially echoes Irenaeus' insights into Mary's active role in the divine plan of Redemption in his lyrical Latin poem, *Carmen*, written c. 440–450.

> As the tender rose springs up among prickly
>   thorns
> But does not offend in any way, since its beauty
>   obscures its thorny branches,
> So holy Mary, the new virgin descending
>   from the branch of Eve,
> Makes pure the old virgin's offense.
> Just so the old nature languished, corrupted
> Under the sentence of death. Once Christ was
>   born,
> Man could be born anew and cast off his old
>   nature's stain.[46]

When it comes to the continuation of the Eve-Mary parallel in Eastern patristic thought after Irenaeus, we find that it was not conspicuous in the thought of the early Alexandrians. In fact, it was almost a century and a half after Irenaeus before this theme reappears in the Syrian Church in the writings of the Persian, Aphraates, in 337. Among the Eastern writers after Irenaeus, St. Ephraem stands out as being particularly aware of the implications of the Eve-Mary analogy , as evidenced in the following excerpt from his work, *Hymns on the Church*, written during the 4th century:

> Behold the world! To it were given two eyes:
> Eve was the left eye, the blind eye; the right eye,
>   the luminous eye is Mary.

Because of the eye that grew dark, the whole
world became dark.
Then men, groping in the shadows,
will consider every stone on which they stumble
to be a god.
They have called lies the truth.
But when the world once more begins to shine,
by the other eye
and the light of heaven taking up a dwelling in
the cavity of this eye,
then men will rediscover unity, perceiving that
what they had found
was the downfall of their lives.[47]

The Eve-Mary parallel can also be perceived in the 4th century theology of St. Cyril, Bishop of Jerusalem; Epiphanus, Bishop of Salamis; St. Gregory, Bishop of Nyssa; and St. John Chrysostom. Chrysostom tells us, "A virgin cast us from paradise; through a virgin we have found life eternal."[48] Cyril of Jerusalem uses the birth of Eve from Adam's side as a parallel to the birth of Christ from the Virgin. His words in *Lecture XII* are quite clear. "Eve was begotten of Adam, and not conceived of a mother, but as it were brought forth of man alone. Mary, therefore, paid the debt of gratitude, when not by man but of herself alone in an immaculate way she conceived of the Holy Spirit by the power of God."[49] In short, by the close of the 4th century, the belief and idea that the Virgin Mary was the counterpart of Eve had been incorporated into the soteriology of the Syrian Church and had become common in the theology of the Greek-speaking Church.[50]

In the 5th century, the anti-Nestorian rhetoric and homilies of such persons as St. Cyril of Alexandria, Proclus of Constantinople, Theodotus of Ancyra, Antipater of Bostra, and Chrysippus of Jerusalem testified to the role Mary played in salvation. In the writings of this group, we find such exclamations about the Blessed Virgin as: "Eve has been redeemed through you," and "Of all these miracles performed by Christ, the cross, resurrection of Christ and of the dead who is the cause? Who else save her who gave birth to Him who performed these wonders?"[51] She is "the nuptial chamber wherein the Logos wedded the flesh, the burning bush of nature, which did not burn in the fire of divine travail, the handmaid and Mother, the Virgin and heaven, the only bridge between God and man. . . ."[52]

These insights of Irenaeus and Ephraem about the Virgin Mary's role in Redemption are continued in the 6th and 7th century in the East without being significantly advanced. However, one of the great contributions of patristic times in the East to the body of literature on Mary's role in Redemption is a liturgical hymn of Marian praise and prayer known as the Akathist Hymn, or the *Akathistos* ("the hymn sung standing"). While the common Marian tradition of Byzantine Christians encompasses several liturgical offices, in addition to the regular commemorations and praise of the Blessed Virgin which occur frequently in the Eucharistic Liturgies as well as in the daily offices, the Akathist Hymn is considered to be the crown of Eastern Christianity's tribute to Mary in her unique role as Bearer of the Incarnate Son of God.[53]

Although the research of scholars has not positively identified the date of the composition or the poet of the Akathist, it is usually attributed to the Patriarch Sergius of Constantinople (610–673) or to his contemporary, the Deacon George of Pisidia. The opening chant of the Akathist indicates that the hymn was most probably composed in thanksgiving for the miraculous deliverance of the city of Constantinople from some foreign onslaught. According to the testimony of historical witnesses, it is certain that the Akathist was first used in services of thanksgiving for the protective action of the *Theotókos* during military attacks against Constantinople in the 7th century. It does appear that the Akathist was included at a relatively early date in the Byzantine *Triodion*, a section of the Byzantine Church's breviary, for recitation on Saturday of the fifth week of Lent. This day is

still designated in many of the Eastern Orthodox churches as
"Akathist Saturday."[54]

The following excerpts from the Akathist represent merely a
brief selection of the many refrains of praise for the Blessed Virgin that resound in this extraordinary work. Special attention has
been paid to selecting those refrains which seem to echo and
elaborate what we have already heard Irenaeus and the other
Fathers say about Mary's having a definitive role in Redemption:

Part One

An archangel sent from heaven said to the Virgin:
"Hail!" As he saw You, O Lord, assuming human
form, he was amazed, and with the voice of a
    spirit,
he cried to her such things as these:

Hail, for by you joy will shine forth!
Hail, O you through whom the curse is erased!
Hail, Revocation of Adam's fall!
Hail, Redemption of the weeping Eve! . . .
Hail, O you through whom the Creator is made
    an infant!
Hail, for through you is adored the Maker! . . .

Hail, Heavenly Ladder by which God has come
    down!
Hail, Bridge by which those of earth are borne to
    Heaven! . . .

Hail, acceptable Incense-cloud of intercession!
Hail, O universal Forgiveness![55]

Part Two

Shepherds heard the angels hymning the
    presence
of Christ in the flesh, and, they themselves
    running
like sheep to a Shepherd, saw Him as a spotless
Lamb feeding at the breast of Mary. Her they
    extolled,
and said: . . .

Hail, Opener of celestial portals! . . .
Hail, O you through whom Hell was despoiled!
Hail, O you through whom we are robed in
    glory! . . .

Hail, O you who free from the filth of
    transgression!
Hail, O you who deliver from the fire of
    passions! . . .

Hail, Uplifting of mankind! . . .
Hail, sustaining Food replacing the manna![56]

Part Three

The Maker of all revealed a new creation,
    manifesting
Himself to us who by Him were created:
    Flowering
forth from a womb as it was, incorrupt, so that,
    seeing
this miracle, we might praise that same Virgin
    singing: . . .

Hail, O you who are the birth-giver of the
    captives' Redeemer!
Hail, Mediatrix before the righteous Judge! . . .
Hail, O you through whom sin is forgiven!
Hail, O you through whom Paradise is
    opened! . . .
Hail, Ship carrying those desiring salvation![57]

Part Four
You are the fortress of virgins, O God-bearing
Virgin, and of all who run to you; for He Who
founded both Heaven and earth prepared you,
    and
took up His dwelling in you, and taught us all to
salute you, O Immaculate: . . .

Hail, Gateway leading to salvation! . . .
Hail, for you bring rebirth to those conceived in
    sin! . . .
Hail, O you who purify us of the mire of sin! . . .
Hail, Fragrance of the sweetness of Christ! . . .

Hail, Dwelling Place of God the Word! . . .
Hail, Ark of the Holy Spirit's gilding! . . .
Hail, Remedy for my body!
Hail, Redemption for my soul![58]

In closing our look at what the early Church had to say about
the Blessed Virgin as the Second Eve, the woman who served as
an associate of the Second Adam Who is the divine Redeemer
Himself, St. John Damascene seems to sum up all that has gone
on before in both Eastern and Western patristic thought. He
attributes to Mary the benefits of salvation almost without distinction from the role played by her Son in his second homily on
the Dormition of the Blessed Virgin:

Through her, the long warfare waged with the Creator has ended. Through her, the reconciliation between us and him was ratified. Grace and peace were granted to us, so that men and angels are united in the same choir, and we, who had been deserving of disdain, have become sons of God. From her we have harvested the grape of life; from her we have cultivated the seed of immortality. For our sake she became Mediatrix of all blessings; in her God became man, and man became God.[59]

The Theological Significance of Patristic Sources

What weight should we give to the writings of the early Church Fathers in the development of Christian doctrine? More specifically for our purposes, how do we assess the value and meaning of the writings of St. Irenaeus and the generations of those who echo his thought as regards the Blessed Virgin Mary's role in Redemption?

The content of patristic thought holds a primary place in the history of theology because of its proximity to the apostolic tradition. In the case of St. Irenaeus, this is especially true because of his intimate acquaintance with the teachings of St. Polycarp, who is known to have been a disciple of St. John the Evangelist.[60] In his *Dictionary of Theology* written jointly with Herbert Vorgrimler, Karl Rahner, S.J., has the following to say about the importance of the Fathers of the Church: "According to the definition of Vincent of Lerins (mid 5th century), the Fathers are those writers of Christian antiquity who each in his own time and locality were accredited doctors of the one faith in communion with the Church."[61] The Catholic Church recognizes these early Christian writers as Fathers specifically because they are distinguished by their authoritative and orthodox doctrine, which does not imply infallibility and does not exclude actual errors in particular matters. They are also recognized as Fathers in the Faith because of their personal holiness.[62]

As regards this and any explanation of the Catholic Faith, the writings of the Fathers must be read as authentic witnesses to what Christians believed during the centuries immediately following the period of the New Testament itself, a period to which we must refer if we truly desire to hear the authoritative voice of the Holy Spirit in sacred tradition. Consequently, the writings of the Fathers can serve both as an authoritative theological base line and as an inexhaustible well spring for the theological reflection of all Christians. This common source of authority seems especially necessary in those areas of Christian doctrine where we are still seeking to come to some consensus about the truth revealed and entrusted to all Christians, such as in the area of Marian doctrine.

This having been said, there is one issue that must be dealt with when considering the weight to give the Fathers in seeking to understand Mary's role in Redemption, as well as in any other truth of the Catholic Faith. This issue is whether a later or current understanding of a doctrine must be specifically stated and affirmed in the writings of the Fathers or whether it is sufficient to locate the germ of any later understanding there. If we hold the Catholic Church herself to be the guardian of the deposit of the faith in any age, then we must answer that the writings of the early Fathers themselves do not have to be the deposit of the faith either in themselves or in total.

Furthermore, if our purpose in looking at the Fathers is to seek an evermore accurate expression of truth in the light of revelation, then it seems sufficient to discover in the Fathers mere indications of what the Holy Spirit chooses later to bring to light through what the Catholic Faith calls an *authentic* development of doctrine. (We will discuss what is meant by *authentic* development of doctrine later in this chapter.) Thus, it seems neither necessary nor realistic to find in the writings of the Fathers the fullness of expression of any Christian doctrine. However, because the writ-

ings of the Fathers are indeed a very significant aspect of the
deposit of the faith, due to their proximity to the apostolic age, it
is important to find in the writings of the Fathers of the Church
the seed for what the Holy Spirit later enables us to see and articulate, explicitly, as truth in the light of the scriptures.

As regards what Irenaeus and the Fathers who echo him have
to say about the Blessed Virgin's role in Redemption, my study
has convinced me that Irenaeus did not limit Mary's cooperation
in human salvation to merely saying yes to producing the
Redeemer, as if the Trinity were merely using her to prepare the
stage for the real work of Redemption which Christ alone would
accomplish through His suffering and death on the Cross. As we
saw earlier in this chapter, even a cursory look at the writings of
St. Irenaeus indicates that he viewed both Mary's obedience and
the physical gift of herself as integral aspects of humankind's salvation and, in so doing, he associates the Blessed Virgin directly
and immediately with the Incarnation whose very intent was
Redemption itself. In the very act of her free and total self-gift to
God, Mary begins the 'recapitulation and recirculation' God's
divine plan required for humankind's being reunited with God—
the end and purpose of Christ's redemptive work.

Thus, I concur unreservedly with the substantial number of
Catholic Marian scholars who conclude that in speaking of the
economy of salvation, St. Irenaeus "represents Mary as the New
Eve being by God's will and plan intimately associated with
Christ the New Adam, as one single and total principle of salva-
tion, as Eve was in fact, associated with Adam as one single and
total principal of the Fall. . . . Irenaeus seems to place Mary's
Mediation of grace and salvation, not just between Christ and
humanity redeemed by Him, but together with Christ between
God offended by sin and humanity needing Redemption."[63]

Finally, as regards the significance of what the Fathers of the
Church have to say about the Blessed Virgin Mary's role in
Redemption, it is important to see how the fathers of the Second
Vatican Council summarized the truth they perceived should be

passed on from the writings of St. Irenaeus and other Church Fathers in Chapter 8 of *"Lumen Gentium"*:

> Committing herself whole-heartedly and impeded by no sin to God's saving will, she (Mary) devoted herself totally, as a handmaid of the Lord, to the person and work of her Son, under and with him, serving the mystery of the redemption, by the grace of Almighty God. Rightly, therefore, the Fathers see Mary not merely as passively engaged by God, but as freely cooperating in the work of man's salvation through faith and obedience. For, as St. Irenaeus says, she "being obedient, became the cause of salvation for herself and for the whole human race." Hence not a few of the early Fathers gladly assert with him in their preaching: "the knot of Eve's disobedience was untied by Mary's obedience: what the virgin Eve bound through her disbelief, Mary loosened by her faith." Comparing Mary with Eve, they call her "Mother of the living," and frequently claim: "death through Eve, life through Mary."[64]

The Continuation of the Eve-Mary Parallel after Patristic Times

What happened to the Eve-Mary analogy between the end of patristic times and the 17th century, which finally gave birth to St. Louis Marie de Montfort? In speaking of patristic times, we are referring to what is generally considered that period of Christian antiquity before the death of St. Isidore of Seville in the West (c. 636) or St. John Damascene in the East (c. 749).[65]

When this question was taken up by the Second National Convention of the Mariological Society of America at its meeting in Worcester, Massachusetts in January, 1951, Fr. Lawrence J.

Reilly of St. John's Seminary in Brighton, Massachusetts was given the task of providing an historical survey of the continuation and growth of this doctrine's articulation. In so doing, he notes that from the 9th to the 16th century, there is a marked transition. While it is true that some of the authors of this time period continued "to treat of Mary's free cooperation in the Incarnation, looked at from the point of view of its redemptive character, nevertheless a more profound consideration of the soteriological nature and salvific purpose of Mary's association with her divine Son, the Redeemer, on Calvary, very gradually begins to be made."[66]

St. Peter Damian, reformer and Doctor of the Church, (1007–1072),[67] serves as a good example of the deepening reflection on the soteriological aspect of the Virgin Mary's relationship to her Son. The following excerpts are from three of his sermons on the Blessed Virgin: Sermo *de Nativitate perpetuae Virginis Mariae; Sermo 46, Homilia in Nativitate Beatissimae Virginis Mariae; and Sermo 11 de Annuntiatione Beatissimae Virginis Mariae:*

> Through a woman a curse was spread over the earth; through a woman a blessing was returned to it. Through a woman the bitter drink of death was offered; and through a woman also the sweet drink of life was given. Flowing profusely, the new benediction killed the contagion of the ancient curse.

> Immediately that heavenly assembly is called forth, and, according to the prophet, God begins His counsel, speaks with the angels of their restoration, and of the redemption of men . . . and they are amazed and marvel beyond joy at the manner of the redemption. And immediately out of the treasury of divinity the name of Mary is taken, and it is decreed that all this is to be done through her and in her and with her: just as with-

out Him nothing was made, so without her nothing was remade.

> . . . we are debtors to the most blessed Mother of
> God, and . . . after God we should thank her for
> our redemption.[68]

St. Peter Damian even goes so far as to say: "Through this most
blessed virgin not only was life restored to men which formerly
was lost, but even the beatitude of the angels was increased."[69]

St. Fulbert, Bishop of Chartres (c. 960–1028),[70] emphasizes
another theme that begins to appear increasingly during this time
frame alongside the stress on the soteriological aspect of the Virgin's role, namely Mary's spiritual maternity of the baptized. In
Sermo 5, De nativitate Mariae Virginis, Fulbert tells us that there
are many examples of the just among us obtaining more quickly
through the intercession of the Mother of the Lord whatever they
ask of Him. Likewise, we have many instances of sinners obtaining mercy more often through the intercession of the Blessed Virgin. He ends a rousing plea to Mary by men and women from all
conditions and walks of life in *Sermo 6, In ortu almae Virginis* with
the following couplet:

> On thy birthday, dear Mother, come to our aid,
> Increasing our virtues and wiping out sin.[71]

We find these thoughts on the Blessed Virgin's role in salvation, coupled with a view of her as our spiritual Mother, echoed
and cleverly developed in *Oratios 51, 52*, and *54*, respectively, of
St. Anselm, Archbishop of Canterbury, (1033–1109):[72]

> Thou art the salvation of sinners, O Son, and
> thou, O Mother.[73]

> Every nature has been created by God, and God

was born of Mary. God created all things, and
Mary gave birth to God. God, Who made all
things, made Himself from Mary; and so, all things
which He had made, He remade. He who was able
to make all things from nothing was not willing to
remake them, when they were violated, without
Mary. God then is the father of created things, and
Mary the mother of recreated things. God is the
father of the constitution of all, and Mary is the
mother of the restitution of all. God generated
Him through whom all things are made, and Mary
bore Him through whom all things are saved. God
generated Him without Whom there is nothing at
all; and Mary bore Him without Whom nothing is
well off at all.[74]

Through thee we have access to the Son Who
redeemed the world through thee.[75]

The noted disciple of St. Anselm, Eadmer (1060 – c.1128), who
actually wrote the famous *Tractatus de conceptione S. Mariae* which
was originally attributed to St. Anselm,[76] was the first to speak in
explicit terms of the reparative merits of the Blessed Virgin Mary.
He says in another of his works on Mary, *Liber de Excellentia Virginis
Mariae*, that "she merited to become in a most worthy manner the
Reparatrix of the lost world. . . . Just as God in making everything
by His Power is the Father and Lord of all things, so the Blessed
Mary in repairing everything by her merits is the Mother and Lady
of all things."[77] It is significant to note that both St. Anselm and
Eadmer explicitly lift up this vital connection between Mary's
salvific role and her being the Mother through whom all is repaired
or recirculated, to use the terminology of St. Irenaeus.

Around the end of the eleventh century or the beginning of
the twelfth, we see these soteriological and maternal themes
increasingly appearing in Marian hymns, such as, *Alma Redemp-*

toris Mater, the *Ave Maris Stella*, and the *Salve Regina*,[78] which is still one of the most widely used prayers to the Blessed Virgin:

> Hail, holy Queen, Mother of Mercy;
> hail, our life, our sweetness, and our hope.
> To you do we cry, poor banished children of Eve.
> To you do we send up our sighs,
> mourning and weeping in this valley of tears.
> Turn then, most gracious Advocate,
> your eyes of mercy toward us.
> And after this our exile
> show unto us the blessed fruit of your womb,
>   Jesus.
> O clement, O loving, O sweet Virgin Mary.[79]

The *Salve Regina* was introduced into the liturgical worship of the Abbey of Cluny about 1135. Later the Cistercians made use of this prayer, followed by the Dominicans. It became the last evening chant of many religious communities during the 13th century and was included in the Divine Office in the 14th century.[80] In this prayer, we see expressed very clearly the belief that while Jesus Christ is the fruit of her womb, Mary herself is a Mother who mediates mercy, grace, and intercession. She is seen as an advocate with power to save all. Prayers such as this served to fuel the saying: "What God can do by commanding, you can do by praying, O Blessed Virgin."[81]

This brings us to one who is considered to be the Marian doctor, *par excellence*, and equal to the greatest of the Fathers of the Church, St. Bernard, Abbot of Clairvaux (1090–1153).[82] In a prayer credited to St. Bernard, c. 1153, we hear him elaborate on the themes of the *Salve Regina* as he calls the Blessed Virgin not only the Mother of Jesus but the Mother of salvation. She is Mediatrix and Advocate not only of grace but also of our very relationship with the Savior because it is none other than she, who mediated Jesus to us in the first place:

O blessed Lady, you found grace, brought forth
Life, and became the Mother of salvation. Obtain
the grace for us to go to the Son. By your mediation, help us to be received by the one who
through you gave himself to us.

May your integrity compensate with him for the
fault of our corruption; and may your humility,
which is pleasing to God, implore forgiveness for
our vanity. May your great charity cover the multitude of our sins; and may your glorious fecundity
confer on us a fecundity of merits.

Dear Lady, our Mediatrix and Advocate, reconcile
us to your Son, recommend us to him, and lead us
to him. By the grace you found, by the privilege
you merited, by the Mercy you brought forth,
obtain for us the following favor, O blessed Lady.

May the one who, thanks to you, came down to
share our infirmity and misery make us share,
again thanks to you, his glory and beatitude: Jesus
Christ, your Son, our Lord, who reigns in heaven
and is blessed forever![83]

Perhaps one of the reasons St. Bernard was so devoted to the
Blessed Virgin and understood so profoundly the essential role
she played in Redemption is his firm belief, with St. Augustine,
that Redemption cannot be accomplished without the collabora-
tion of grace and free-will. In his treatise, *De gratia et libero arbi-
trio*, St. Bernard writes: "Remove free will, and there is nothing to
be saved; remove grace, and there is left no means of saving. The
work of salvation cannot be accomplished without the cooperation of the two."[84] In the above prayer, he credits Mary with the

ability to make up for, as it were, the imperfections in our own free will. Mary can substitute her integrity for our corruption. She can substitute her perfect cooperation with grace for our imperfect cooperation. Her perfect humility can make up for our vanity. Her perfect love of God and submission to His Will can cover for the multitude of times we have failed to perfectly love and submit to Him. Her glorious and perfect fecundity can be the substitutionary means through which we receive the merit of sharing the glory and beatitude of her Son.

Not surprisingly, St. Bernard is considered to be the first theologian to refer explicitly to the redemptive satisfaction of the Blessed Virgin. In his *Homilia II super Missus est*, we hear him exclaim: "Run, Eve, to Mary; run, mother, to daughter. The daughter answers for the mother; she takes away the opprobrium of the mother; she makes satisfaction to Thee, Father, for the mother. . . . O woman singularly to be venerated. . . . Reparatrix of parents."[85] In another famous Marian prayer, the *Memorare*, which St. Bernard did not write as once believed but rather made popular, we hear the underlying themes of his famous sermon entitled, *Sermo de Aqueductu*.[86] God chose to give Mary a first fullness of grace, Jesus Christ Himself, in order that she might share Him with us. God also chose to give Mary a second fullness, which is the result of the first, the fullness of graces that we receive through her intercession and mediation on our behalf. Thus, we should invoke her with the greatest of confidence. St. Bernard's constant assurance was that if the Blessed Virgin prayed for us, we would be saved. "Just as the Father cannot help but hear the Son, so the Son cannot help but hear his Mother."[87]

> Remember, O most gracious Virgin Mary,
> that never was it known
> that anyone who fled to your protection,
> implored your help and sought your intercession,
> was left unaided.

Inspired with this confidence,
I fly to you, O Virgin of Virgins, my Mother;
to you do I come,
before you I stand, sinful and sorrowful.
O Mother of the Word Incarnate,
despise not my petitions,
but in your mercy hear and answer me.[88]

It is St. Bernard who is credited with initiating the famous expression which has permeated Marian thought since him, namely, God Himself wants us to honor her, "who willed us to have everything through Mary."[89]

Before leaving our consideration of the development of Marian thought in the 12th century, it is important to note that Rupert, abbot of Deutz, (1075 – c.1130)[90] is credited with being the first in the Western Church[91] to testify that the words of Christ on the Cross to St. John, "Mother, behold the son; son behold thy Mother," applied to more than St. John himself. Rupert holds that because the Blessed Virgin truly bore the pain of the Cross with her Son while she stood by the Cross, she gave birth to the salvation of us all and she is clearly the Mother of us all.[92]

During the 13th century we see this theme of the Blessed Virgin's redemptive cooperation in the Passion of her Son intensifying. Pseudo-Albert is among those who elaborate on this theme in questions 150 and 51 of the *Mariale super missus est.* [93] "He willed that she be a sharer in the penalty of the Passion, in so far as she might become the Mother of all through re-creation even as she was the adjutrix of the Redemption by her co-passion." "She by her spontaneous consent in His Passion, offered Him up for us all: through this most adequate and most pleasing Victim once offered up, she reconciled the whole human race to God."[94] Not surprisingly, Mary's association with the Redeemer is given a new and striking formulation. The Virgin begins to be called the associate of Christ (*Socia Christi*) through the use of an expression taken from Genesis 2:21, "a helpmate like to him." The *Mariale* is credited with offering us this additional trait of the Eve-Mary parallel that had been previously neglected.[95] It is not surprising that, finally, in the 14th century the word "Co-redemptrix" first appears. It is found "in an anonymous *Tractatus de praeservatione glorioissimae Virginis Mariae*, written by a Franciscan theologian before the year 1323."[96]

This line of thinking about the Blessed Virgin's share in the redemptive merits of her Son's Passion through her co-passion continues throughout the 14th century and on into the 15th century through such voices[97] as Blessed John Tauler (1300–1361),[98] Jean Gerson (1363–1429),[99] St. Antoninus, Archbishop of Florence (1389–1459),[100] and Denis the Carthusian (1402–1471).[101] A significant 15th century proponent of Mary's mediation was the Franciscan reformer, St. Bernardine of Siena (1380–1444).[102]

In *Sermo 5* of the De La Haye edition of the works of St. Bernardine, we hear him call Mary "the mother of all who love Christ by infusion of invisible grace." "She [Mary] had in her womb, that is, in her intimate maternal affection, the Son of God and the whole mystical Christ; that is, the head with the whole body of the elect." By giving God her free and complete assent to the Incarnation, she desired and procured the salvation of all the elect, "so that from that moment she bore them all in her womb, as a mother in the truest sense bears her children."[103] He goes on to say that, at the foot of the Cross, John the Beloved disciple represents the souls of all the elect, of whom the Blessed Virgin has become the Mother in the order of grace. John and all these souls receive through Mary the supernatural life of sanctifying grace, which is life in a truer and higher sense than natural life.[104] St. Bernardine puts these profound words on the lips of the Lord as He hung on the Cross in his interpretation of John 19:26–27: "Most sweet Mother, you have access to the chamber of my heart, so that coming in to Me and going out to your sons you can carry out what you will and dispense it to your sons."[105]

St. Antoninus, Archbishop of Florence (1389–1459),[106] elaborates further on what it means that the Virgin Mary is the

Mother of all in the order of grace by speaking of how this is true even for the saints who lived and died prior to the historical event of the Incarnation. In his *Summa Theologica* he explains that "it makes little difference that many saints have preceded her in this mortal life. If there is question of the order of nature, a son cannot exist in time before his mother; but it is different in the order of grace. All the saints who have preceded Christ were saved by their faith, explicit or implicit, in the Incarnate Word who one day was to be born of the Virgin; and it is in view of His plenitude that they received grace. In the same way as spiritual regeneration by grace proceeds, for the saints of the New Testament, from their living faith in the Word made man in the womb of Mary, so the saints of the Old Law owe their regeneration to their faith in the Incarnation of the Word; the Incarnation of which Mary was the free instrument. Hence the Blessed Virgin is without exception or restriction a Mother for all men who are regenerated by grace."[107]

In speaking of the Blessed Virgin's universal mediation of grace, the 14th century in the East produced what is often considered to be the summit of Byzantine Marian theology, namely the theology of the Palamites. "The mediation of the *Theotókos* was part of their vision of the cosmic Christ, the center and purpose of creation. The Incarnation was brought about in her and by her; the Person of Christ is inseparable from that of His Mother."[108] In Homily 14, St. Gregory of Palamas (1296–1359)[109] proclaims that the Mother of God "is the source and root of the race of liberty" and that "the Virgin Mother alone dwells on the frontier between created and uncreated natures, and those who know God recognize also in her the habitation of the Infinite."[110] In speaking about the importance of the Palamites for our understanding of the role of Mary in God's salvific plan, the famous contemporary Marian theologian, Michael O'Carroll, says that when "the theology of the Palamite theologians is fully assimilated by the Latins, the idea of Mary's primacy, absolute and universal as that of Christ, but subordinate to and totally dependent on Him, will be more readily acceptable."[111]

And, finally, as we consider the 16th century, we notice that not even the stresses of the Protestant Reformation could dampen the conviction of the Catholic world that the Blessed Virgin has been given a key role in humankind's restoration, alongside that of her Son. A key papal theologian who "wielded tremendous influence" at the Council of Trent, Alphonsus Salmeron, S.J., (d. 1585), seems both to summarize and crystallize the insights of the many centuries between St. Irenaeus and himself:

> The Mother stood by the cross in order that the reparation of the human race might offset the ruin of the world. For, as ruin followed from the fact that a woman approached and ate of the tree of the knowledge of good and evil and thereby died and passed it on to man to eat in death, so here, on the contrary, . . . the Man first tasted of the bitter wood of the Cross and then gave to the woman to taste. And as in the first case disaster befell the world from the work of the two (but especially of the man), so also salvation and Redemption came from two (but particularly from Christ). For whatever virtue Mary has, she received from Christ-not merely by reason of a sort of fitting aptness, but also by reason of the excellent virtue of Christ in redeeming. This virtue He willed to communicate to His Mother (whose work He did not need) as Co-Redemptrix, not only without detraction from Himself, but with great glory to Himself.[112]

As regards the views of the Protestant reformers, the thought of Martin Luther, (1483–1546),[113] is representative of what the reformers generally had to say about Marian mediation and the Blessed Virgin's active participation and co-operation in the redeeming work of her Son. The following thoughts are taken from various sermons preached throughout Luther's life on Marian feasts, which are the primary source for his thought regarding Mary. What we hear Luther express below is not surprising to us. His comments reflect not only his thought about Mary, but also the reformers' common skepticism about the role of any human cooperation in the work of Redemption. As discussed in our introductory chapter, Marian mediation and any role attributed to her in Redemption is unfortunately seen by them as a direct contradiction of their view of salvation which is described as *solus Christus* and *sola gratia:*

> We have no other mediator, not Mary, not the apostles, but only Christ.
>
> The papists have made Mary into an idol, saying that Mary was given us as our mother. Flee from this; remain in Christ crucified.
>
> I am nothing but the material in which God works [says Mary]. I have accomplished nothing in this event, and so let no one praise or honor me because I am the mother of God. Let God and his work be honored and praised in me.[114]

We do find some surprising comments from Luther about Mary as our mother. However, his negative view of Marian mediation seems to render such comments to be purely devotional, at best, with no theological intent:

> Mary is the Mother of Jesus and the mother of us all.
>
> If Christ is ours, we must be where he is; and all that he has must be ours, and his mother is therefore also ours.
>
> We are the children of Mary.[115]

Authentic Development of Doctrine
in Marian Theology

Before concluding this chapter, it is necessary to consider some methodological concerns raised by our study of the Fathers and the various voices after patristic times that testify to Mary's role in Redemption. While we have considered the relationship of the writings of the Fathers to those voices in sacred tradition who later continued their line of thought, we have not yet asked the primary questions that are often raised by many Protestant Christians in considering the writings of the Fathers and those who followed them as a source of authority. And, since the thought of St. Louis de Montfort can be seen as a continuation in this line of sacred tradition concerning the Blessed Virgin, it is important that we ask and answer these questions.

Why can we not just stick with the literal words of scripture about Mary? Why does the Catholic Faith find it necessary to get involved with what it calls "sacred tradition," as passed on in the writings of the Fathers and those who further develop their thought? Furthermore, why be bothered with what the Catholic Faith calls "development of doctrine?" Are there guidelines for an *authentic* development of doctrine that is based on the text of scripture? What makes an *authentic* development of doctrine different from a mere theological opinion? In light of modern exegetical methods that primarily focus on the words of the biblical text themselves to find meaning, on what grounds can we grant authority to what sacred tradition says about the Blessed Virgin Mary?

To see the extent to which these questions have become problematic for the contemporary investigation of what we can say about Mary in light of divine revelation, let us consider the conclusions of the interdenominational task force that grew out of the 1965 National Lutheran-Catholic Dialogue to determine what the scriptures say about Mary. This important task force, which included many well known Catholic biblical scholars such as Raymond Brown, Joseph Fitzmyer, and Paul Achtemeier, was set up precisely because Mariology is an "important and controversial subject in the interconfessional discussion,"[116] as we discussed at length in our own introduction above. The concern of the task force was to determine the New Testament portrait of Mary that could be "derived only from what the texts say or from what they can legitimately be taken to imply,"[117] with the hope of finding a biblical common ground for Christians in the conversation about Mary.

As a result of its study, the task force was not able to make any conclusions that pointed to Mary as the Mother of God or the *Theotókos*. The most that could be said in this regard was that the Son of God was "born of a woman," pointing to the true humanity of Jesus.[118] In addition, it concluded that "the question of the historicity of the virginal conception could not be settled by historical-critical exegesis, and that one's attitude towards church tradition on the matter would probably be the decisive force in determining one's view whether the virginal conception is a theologoumenon or a literal fact. . . . (And), while the virginal conception is based on New Testament evidence, the doctrine of Mary's perpetual virginity goes beyond anything said of her in the Scriptures."[119]

The principal view of Mary that the task force could unanimously endorse, as a result of looking at the scriptures through the lens of historical criticism alone, was that she was humbly obedient to God and His word and can thus be rightfully considered to be the handmaid of the Lord.[120] The task force determined that anything else we can say about Mary, from their perspective, is in light of the scriptures as interpreted by the tradition of the Fathers and those who came after them. Significantly, the majority of the members of the task force did conclude that while the scriptures themselves don't specifically speak of Mary as the Second Eve or the Mother of the disciples in the order of grace, they could be seen as making "an opening . . . for the process of further Marian symbolizing within the church."[121] Since the thought of St. Louis de Montfort builds on all that preceded him in sacred tradition, it is necessary that we consider why the Catholic Church, along with the theologians who support the Catholic Faith, constantly find it necessary to go beyond the scant light that historical-criticism offers with regard to understanding who Mary is in the light of revelation and look to sacred tradition as an authentic source of authority.

First, let us be clear about what we mean in this study by the term "sacred tradition." A particularly helpful definition of sacred tradition was generated through the numerous post-Vatican II efforts of Roman Catholics and Anglicans who have been considering what would be required for Anglicans to come into full communion with the Roman Catholic Church:

> [Sacred] tradition, which is grounded in the original deposit of Christian faith given by God to the apostles, is the continuous stream of explanation and elucidation of that faith. Thus [sacred] tradition is more than a body of doctrine, though the creeds are a prime example of the role of [sacred] tradition in expressing the faith of the Church in its early centuries. The Church's [sacred] tradition is revealed by the interaction of a complex of interrelated components, including Scripture, the creeds, the teachings of the councils of the Church, the teaching role of the bishops, sacraments and liturgy, and the reception of doctrine by the whole Church.[122]

Using the definition above, we might say that this "interaction of a complex of interrelated components, including Scripture, the creeds, etc." which we call sacred tradition is authoritative because it comes about under the inspiration of that same Holy Spirit who caused the words of the biblical text to be written. And, the theological term that is often used to speak about the inspired process which gives birth to sacred tradition, that "continuous stream of explanation and elucidation" *which may not contradict* either the implicit or explicit meaning of the original apostolic witness as recorded in the scriptures, is development of doctrine.

By an authentic development of doctrine, neither the Magisterium of the Catholic Church nor orthodox Catholic theologians have ever meant to imply, in any way, a post-modern deconstructionist proliferation of 'truths' generated by the thought of different individuals from varying psycho-sociological or cultural backgrounds. This post-modern proliferation of pluriform ideas resulting from incessant dialog has left us merely with many more or less valid opinions to the point that many contemporary persons, including some who call themselves Christians, can tragically say little, if anything, about objective, revealed truth at all!

On the contrary, an authentic development of doctrine refers to the unfolding, over time, in our limited human understanding of the *meaning* of the objective revealed truth of the Apostolic Faith as recorded in scripture, a meaning that has been entrusted to the whole Catholic Church by the Holy Spirit in the words of the revealed text all along. Thus, for orthodox Catholics, development of doctrine does not mean that the doctrine itself grows or changes but that our human capacity and readiness to both receive and articulate the depth of God's Self-revelation in Jesus Christ grows and changes with time under the guidance of the Holy Spirit.

In his dictionary of theology, Karl Rahner gives us three instances where the Catholic Church has historically found it necessary to engage in an authentic development of doctrine. The Church is seeking to define theological "propositions as divinely revealed which either (1) existed before but were not always taught *as* divinely revealed, or (2) state the substance of the affirmation of previous tradition in quite a different terminology, one which is only in the process of developing, whereby the Church more explicitly protects that sense of the revealed

truth which has always been known, against heretical misinter-
pretations, or (3) for which even tradition does not at once and
directly furnish explicit propositions that are obviously equivalent to the definition and that can be proved to date back to the
Apostles."[123] These three instances are critical for the ongoing
life of the Church in its mission to proclaim the truth to each
new generation because "on the one hand revelation must be
closed with the first generation," i.e., "with the death of the last
apostle." While on the other hand, the Church can and must
indeed be open to "reach a clearer understanding of revelation"
without receiving a new revelation.[124]

This having been said, we can say that the essential problem
before the Church in the development of doctrine is to demonstrate that a particular 'developed' exposition of the faith is iden-
tical with the apostolic exposition that was made in Jesus Christ.
This is of critical importance because the revealed truth
entrusted to the Church was concluded with the death of the last
Apostle as noted above. Thus, if the Church has as her primary
vocation "to bear witness to what she heard from Christ in the
apostolic generation and recognized then as belonging to her
deposit of faith,"[125] concern for the authentic development of
doctrine must be paramount in the mind and heart of the
Church, as well as in the minds and hearts of those theologians
who truly serve the purpose of proclaiming the good news of Jesus
Christ to human persons in their "ever new, changing historical
reality. . . . (T)his situation must never be thought of as just the
result of a secular historical development, but is itself the result
of Christ's government of his Church, as he gradually leads her,
sometimes by new ways, through a changing reality to his own
single truth. . . . The decisive feature of such a change is not
'progress' in the sense of acquiring a sort of plus-quantity of
knowledge . . . but . . . the change, the new look, of the same reality and truth, appropriate to just this age of the church: it is
change in, not of, identity."[126]

While it finally belongs to the Church's Magisterium to

declare solemnly a developing doctrine to be a dogma, meaning that the doctrine merits and requires the assent of faith on the part of the faithful, Rahner reminds us that this development and declaration have "never proceeded without the labour of theologians."[127] Thus, we would have to conclude with Rahner that theologians committed to serving the expression of truth in the light of revelation have a responsibility to help the Magisterium in determining if there is a rationally justifiable connection between "old" and "new" propositions, such that the later proposition can be *clearly* shown not to be a new revelation at all. The primary task for theologians working in an area where there has been substantial growth in the human capacity to understand, as is certainly the case where Marian doctrine is concerned, is showing to what extent a truth that is later articulated, and thereby made explicit, has been implicit in the whole deposit of faith from the beginning.[128] In looking at the Fathers and those who have followed them, we have been trying to trace the ongoing understanding and articulation of the doctrine of Mary as the Second Eve, with its various components and ramifications, since apostolic times.

Rahner's explanation also leads us to the important conclusion that theologians must seek not only to safeguard this deposit of faith along with the Church's Magisterium but also to articulate and expound it, ever anew and ever more fully, such that the fullness we have all received through Jesus Christ might be made known and proclaimed from the roof tops, generation to generation. "I have yet many things to say to you, but you cannot bear them now. When the Spirit of truth comes, he will guide you into all the truth; for he will not speak on his own authority, but whatever he hears he will speak, and he will declare to you the things that are to come. He will glorify me, for he will take what is mine and declare it to you" (John 16:12–14). The *Catechism of the Catholic Church* offers a quote from St. Irenaeus himself in *Against Heresies*, Book 3, chapter 24, which supports this view:

> We guard with care the faith that we have
> received from the Church, for without ceasing,
> under the action of God's Spirit, this deposit of
> great price, as if in an excellent vessel, is con-
> stantly being renewed and causes the very vessel
> that contains it to be renewed.[129]

When it comes to Marian doctrine, history shows us that the
Catholic Church has found it necessary not only to support such
growth in our doctrinal understanding but also to define solemnly
as dogma four specific doctrines about Mary. Two of these doctrines were solemnly declared to be dogma by ecumenical coun-
cils prior to the 17th century, where we situate the writings of St.
Louis de Montfort. These two doctrines are that Mary is the
Mother of God and that she was a virgin before, during, and after
the birth of Jesus Christ. As noted earlier in this chapter, our
human understanding and articulation of the fact that Mary is
both the Mother of God and perpetually virgin is constantly
intertwined with understanding her as the Second Eve.

We have seen that the declaration of Mary as the Mother of
God occurred at the Council of Ephesus in 431. At the Lateran
Council of 649, the Catholic Church upheld that Mary conceived
Jesus as a virgin by the power of the Holy Spirit and that she
remained a virgin both in the birth of her Son and for the remainder of her earthly existence.[130] The virginal conception of Jesus
safeguards and guarantees the transcendence of the divine Person
who became Incarnate by the power of the Holy Spirit through,
with, and in Mary. Furthermore, her perpetual virginity signifies
her perfect receptiveness, total consecration, and perpetual self-
gift to God in response to God's unique Gift of Self to her, and to
all of us through her. Mary's perfect virginity was affirmed from the
end of the second century by a majority of the Fathers, the same
century in which we first hear of the Eve-Mary analogy.[131]

The other two Marian doctrines that have at this point in
time been formally declared as dogma are the doctrines of Mary's

Immaculate Conception and her glorious Assumption.[132] While we have not elaborated upon the history of their articulation because we have been specifically tracing the history of the doctrine about Mary's mediation, they were believed to be true by orthodox Catholic Christians long before the Church's solemn definition of them as dogma in the 19th and 20th centuries. Furthermore, while St. Louis de Montfort did not have the benefit of their having been defined as dogma, it is clear from his writings that he believed them to be nonetheless true.

By accepting these four Marian doctrines as truth in the light of revelation, one is not merely deferring to the authority of the Catholic Church, though from my perspective as an Anglican Catholic it is not problematic to accept those solemn definitions which unfold the depth of meaning in the Christian Faith outlined in the Catholic Creeds.[133] The choice to accept the Catholic Church's explanation and formal definition of the four Marian doctrines as revealed truth is rather an intellectually honest fork that Ray Brown, et. al., have put forth as a credible possibility in dealing with the New Testament passages on the Blessed Virgin. In intentionally choosing to view the scriptures in light of the substantive evidence of sacred tradition which expounds clearly that Mary is immaculately conceived, perpetually virgin, Mother of the divine Redeemer, and assumed body and soul into heaven at her death, we stand squarely with Catholic Christians throughout the universal Church who hold that the scriptures must be interpreted by the light of that same Holy Spirit Who caused them to be written. This means that we recognize the limits regarding what human reason alone can deduce as meaning from the words of the texts themselves. And, as Catholics, we choose instead to receive that fullness of truth that is not discoverable with the scant light of historical-criticism but requires the light of faith to enlighten reason.

Finally, by standing with what Catholic Christians affirm as true about Mary in these 4 doctrines collectively, we are affirming the theological consequences of the Church's 2nd century understanding that Mary is the Second Eve. As we will continue to discuss later, this means that the Blessed Trinity chose to grace Mary uniquely with the gift of a preservative Redemption from the very moment of her conception in preparation for her fully human yes to being the Mother of the Incarnate Son. Her Immaculate Conception, by the very nature of the privilege itself, freed Mary from the wounding caused by the sin of Adam and Eve. This means that she was exempt from *all* the consequences of original sin as revealed in Genesis 3, including disruption of mutual partnership between the sexes, sexual lust, pain at childbirth, and corruption at death.

A Consideration of the Fathers' and St. Louis de Montfort's Method of Interpreting the Biblical Text

In the wake of our above conversation about the necessity of allowing for an authentic development of doctrine in understanding Marian mediation, there arises yet one final question that requires our attention before looking at the writings of St. Louis de Montfort. What can we say about how the Fathers of the Church, St. Louis de Montfort, and many others used and interpreted the biblical texts concerning the Blessed Virgin Mary in light of our contemporary exegetical methods? This question is significant because methods of interpreting scripture frequently neglected today formed the basis for what sacred tradition offers us as an authentic unfolding of the meaning of revealed truth. In other words, if they did not use the methods of contemporary text criticism, what methodology did they use? How much credence should we give to it?

Perhaps the best way to answer this question is to reflect upon the importance the contemporary person gives to the scientific, empirical approach to interpreting scripture. Because of our scientific approach to knowledge of all kinds, the contemporary mind tends to give credence and purport truth principally to that which we can prove to be true from empirical evidence. When it comes to the interpretation of the biblical text, we thus tend to give the greatest authority to what we might speak of as the *literal, plain, or historical sense* of scripture. In this sense of scripture, we might say that meaning is determined by what is literally conveyed by the words of scripture themselves. Not surprisingly, the contemporary tendency is to give credibility only or principally to that meaning which can be discovered by following the rules of historical-criticism or similarly empirical text critical methods. While these methods certainly have validity, the contemporary scientific mind often forgets that there is also significant truth to be found in what sacred tradition has spoken of as the *spiritual sense* of scripture. Much of what the Fathers and those who followed in their wake, including St. Louis de Montfort, have to say about Mary in the light of the biblical text is based upon reading and praying over the words of scripture with a particular attentiveness to that aspect of the truth which can only be derived from seeking the spiritual sense of scripture.

In speaking about the relationship of the literal or plain sense of scripture to the spiritual sense, St. Thomas Aquinas reminds us that the spiritual sense must always be founded upon the literal sense.[134] In fact, the more meaning we derive from the literal or plain sense of the words of scripture, the greater the fuel that can be brought to penetrating the depth of the text's meaning using the spiritual sense. In seeking to comprehend divine truth in light of the revealed text, we must be concerned about the literal meaning of the words of scripture themselves and what the human authors intended to convey by these words. However, we must also be open to discovering the depth of spiritual meaning that God Himself wants to reveal to us through the literal words of the text and the intentions of the human authors.

In discussing the true nature of the scriptures, St. Thomas tells us that "the author of Holy Writ is God, in whose power it is to signify His meaning, not by words only (as man also can do), but also by things themselves. So, whereas in every other science things are signified by words, this science has the property, that the things signified by words have themselves also a signification. Therefore the first signification whereby words signify things belongs to the first sense, the historical or literal. That signification whereby things signified by words have themselves also a signification is called the spiritual sense, which is based on the literal and presupposes it. Now this spiritual sense has a threefold division."[135]

The *Catechism of the Catholic Church* offers a very helpful summary of the threefold division of the spiritual sense of scripture as discussed by St. Thomas:

> Paragraph 117: The *Spiritual Sense.*
> Thanks to the unity of God's plan, not only the text of Scripture but also the realities and events about which it speaks can be signs.
>
> The *allegorical sense*. We can acquire a more profound understanding of events by recognizing their significance in Christ; thus the crossing of the Red Sea is a sign or type of Christ's victory and also of Christian Baptism.
>
> The *moral sense*. The events reported in Scripture ought to lead us to act justly. As St. Paul says, they were written "for our instruction."
>
> The *anagogical sense* (Greek: *anagoge*, "leading"). We can view realities and events in terms of their eternal significance, leading us toward our true homeland: thus the Church on earth is a sign of the heavenly Jerusalem.[136]

If we keep in mind that seeking to be attentive to especially the allegorical and anagogical senses of scripture is not only legitimate but also necessary to acknowledge God's deeper truth about Mary, we begin to discover how it is that the Fathers, and those following in their steps, could read various passages of both the Old and the New Testament as clearly pointing to Mary as the Second Eve. Like them, we will begin to see Mary as the second virginal ground overshadowed by the Holy Spirit as in creation, the human virginal ground whom God Himself approached for consent and cooperation in recreating the human race through the Incarnate Word, the Second Adam. We will also come to see the Blessed Virgin Mary, the Second Eve, as the other "woman" God promised to send in Gen. 3:15. She is the promised woman whose radical obedience to God, in love, from the moment of the Annunciation through her firm stance at the foot of the Cross, would forever be at enmity with the devil's continuous attempt to keep the human race from sharing the life of the Triune God. We will also hear Mary's divine Son's address to her as "woman" from His Cross as not merely expressing His concern about her housing arrangements after His death. We will hear His words as eternally commissioning this Second Eve and promised woman of Gen. 3:15 to be the spiritual Mother of all who are reborn and sanctified in Him by the power of the Holy Spirit.

And, last but by no means least, when we seek once again to be as attentive to the spiritual sense of scripture as we have been in our day to the literal sense, we will discover with the Fathers and St. Louis that we cannot discover the spiritual sense of scripture in regards to the Blessed Virgin, or anything or anyone else, through merely the use of our own empirical powers. We will learn that the deeper spiritual meaning of the text will be opened to us only to the extent that we, like them, have prayed with a sincere heart for the Holy Spirit to enlighten our dulled sight through the ongoing purification and sanctification of our lives. And, like the Fathers whose teaching we revere as authoritative because of the holiness of their lives, like St. Louis de Montfort and many other saints and mystics, we too will find ourselves returning again and again to the necessity of daily dying to ourselves in order to purify our love for God and put to flight the "works of the flesh" (Gal. 5:19–21).

Unless we are experiencing the spiritual ascent of loving God with our whole heart, mind, body, and strength through our loving participation in the wisdom of the Cross in union with Jesus Christ, we will not become empty enough to receive the supernatural gift of wisdom, required for the Holy Spirit to open to us the font of understanding hidden in the spiritual sense of the scriptures. Following the Blessed Virgin's example, we too must realize that virginity of heart is still the essential prerequisite for those who truly desire to know God and the depth of His Self-revelation in Jesus Christ, a knowledge that is handed on from generation to generation by the Holy Spirit through meditation on the spiritual meaning of the biblical text.

Perhaps an appropriate way to close our discussion of how the Fathers, St. Louis de Montfort, and many others have interpreted the biblical text is recalling St. Augustine's classic treatise on the correct interpretation of scripture, *De Doctrina Christiana*. In this timeless work, he poignantly speaks of the fundamental and necessary union between loving God and knowing (understanding) the truth of God's Self-revelation in scripture. "Therefore, since that truth is to be enjoyed which lives immutably, and since God the Trinity, the Author and Founder of the universe, cares for His creatures through that truth, the mind should be cleansed so that it is able to see that light and cling to it once it is seen."[137] The road that we must take for this cleansing is not a road from place to place but a road of the affections.[138] The *authentic* interpreter of the biblical text must daily strive to love the God Whose revelation he or she seeks to discover,[139] for the knowledge gained to be authoritative in the fullest sense:

> Therefore, when anyone knows the end of the commandments to be charity "from a pure heart, and a good conscience, and an unfeigned faith" (1 Tim. 1:5), and has related all of his understanding

of the Divine Scriptures to these three (faith, hope, and charity), he may approach the treatment of these books with security. For when he says "charity" he adds "from a pure heart," so that nothing else would be loved except that which should be loved. And he joins with this "a good conscience" for the sake of hope, for he in whom there is the smallest taint of bad conscience despairs of attaining that which he believes in and loves. Third, he says "an unfeigned faith." If our faith involves no lie, then we do not love that which is not to be loved, and living justly, we hope for that which will in no way deceive our hope.[140]

NOTES

[27] Walter J. Burghardt, S.J., "Mary in Eastern Patristic Thought," *Mariology*, ed. Juniper B. Carol, O.F.M., vol. 2 (Milwaukee: Bruce Publishing Co., 1957) 100.

[28] Michael O'Carroll, C.S.Sp., *Theotokos* (Collegeville: The Liturgical Press, 1982) 358.

[29] Sister Eileen Breen, F.M. A., ed., *Mary: The Second Eve from the writings of John Henry Newman* (Rockford, IL: Tan Books, 1982) 2.

[30] Ignace de la Potterie, S.J., *Mary in the Mystery of the Covenant*, trans. Bertrand Buby, S.M. (New York: Alba House, 1992) 96–107. Potterie makes a very good case for the Gospel of John's also pointing to the virginal conception and even the virginal birth of Jesus. If we read the Prologue of the Gospel of John according to the manuscripts dating from before the second century, we find that the words of John 1:13 differ from the way we see them translated in standard editions of the scripture. The English translation for all manuscripts dating from the first century for verse 13 of John's Prologue declares: "He is born not of blood, nor of the urge of the flesh, nor of the will of man, but of God." Because the major Christological difficulty of the second century was combating the heresy of the Docetists and the doctrine of the Gnostics, the term "not of blood" when applied to Christ was seen as too difficult to explain by many of the fathers, including Irenaeus, and thus it is believed that the second century manuscripts changed

the pronoun from the singular form 'he" to the plural form so that the birth of those who are made adopted children of God became referenced in verse 13 rather than the birth of Jesus. Thus, our standard translations based on second century textual witnesses refer being born not of blood, nor of the will of the flesh nor of the will of man back to the term children of God in the previous verse through use of the pronoun 'who'.

[31] O'Carroll 358.

[32] Burghardt, "Mary in Eastern Patristic Thought" 88–9. This determination is based on a fragment of *De fabrica Mundi* written by Victorinus of Pettau which is recognized by Dom Chapman as being probably dependent upon at least the oral tradition of Bishop Papias. The text of Victorinus which points to this strong possibility is in a section where the seven days of creation are paralleled by seven days of redemptive activity. The text states, "the Angel Gabriel brought the good tidings to Mary on the day whereon the dragon seduced Eve."

[33] F. L. Cross and E. A. Livingstone, ed., *The Oxford Dictionary of the Christian Church* , 2nd ed. (Oxford: Oxford University Press, 1985) 770.

[34] Justin, "Dialogue with Tryphus," chapter 100, *Ante-Nicene Fathers*, ed. Alexander Roberts, D.D. & James Donaldson, LL.D., vol. 1 (Peabody, MA: Hendrickson, 1995) 249.

[35] Cross 1107.

[36] Burghardt, "Mary in Eastern Patristic Thought" 89.

[37] Cross 713–14.

[38] Walter J. Burghardt, S.J., "Mary in Western Patristic Thought" *Mariology*, ed. Juniper B. Carol, O.F.M., vol. 2 (Milwaukee: Bruce Pub. Co., 1954) 111.

[39] Irenaeus, "Against Heresies," *Ante-Nicene Fathers*, ed. Alexander Roberts, D.D. & James Donaldson, LL.D., vol. 1 (Peabody, MA: Hendrickson, 1995) 454.

[40] Original Latin for word translated as "back-reference" in this translation is quoted as being *recirculationem* in Burghardt, "Mary in Western Patristic Thought," 112.

[41] Irenaeus 455.

[42] Original Latin for word translated as "rescued" in this translation is quoted as being *salvatur* in Burghardt, "Mary in Western Patristic Thought" 112.

[43] This phrase, "by the means of," is found in the translation supplied by Burghardt, "Mary in Western Patristic Thought," 112.

[44] Irenaeus 547.

[45] Burghardt, "Mary in Western Patristic Thought" 113–4.

[46] Luigi Gambero, S.M., *Mary and the Fathers of the Church*, trans. Thomas Buffer (San Francisco: Ignatius Press,1999) 284.

[47] Gambero 116.

[48] Burghardt, "Mary in Eastern Patristic Thought" 93–4.

[49] Bertrand Buby, S.M., *Mary of Galilee Volume III* (New York: Alba House, 1997) 213 -14.

[50] Burghardt, "Mary in Eastern Patristic Thought" 94.

[51] Burghardt, "Mary in Eastern Patristic Thought" 95–7.

[52] *The Life of the Virgin Mary, the Theotokos*, Holy Apostles Convent, trans. and ed. (Buena Vista, CO: Holy Apostles Convent and Dormition Skete, 1989) 510.

[53] *The Office of the Akathist*, trans. Edward F. James (Bay Shore, NY: Montfort Publications, 1986) 4.

[54] *The Office of the Akathist* 5.

[55] *The Office of the Akathist* 10–2.

[56] *The Office of the Akathist* 12–4

[57] *The Office of the Akathist* 15–7.

[58] *The Office of the Akathist* 17–9.

[59] Gambero 405.

[60] P. Sylvester O'Brien, O.F.M., "The Universal Mediation of Mary in St. Irenaeus," *Alma Socia Christi Acta Congressus Mariologici-Mariani Romae Anno Sancto MCML Celebrati*, Vol. II Rome: Academia Mariana,1952) 93.

[61] Rahner, *Dictionary* 174

[62] Rahner, *Dictionary* 174

[63] O'Brien 94.

[64] "Lumen Gentium," *Documents of the Second Vatican Council*, ed. Austin Flannery, O.P. (Northport, NY: Costello,1992) 416.

[65] Cross 504; 717; 748.

[66] Lawrence J. Riley, S.T.D., "Historical Conspectus of the Doctrine," *Marian Studies* 2 (1951): 47.

[67] Cross 1072.

[68] Riley 47–8.

[69] William R. O'Connor, "The Spiritual Maternity of Our Lady in Tradition," *Marian Studies* 3 (1952): 153.

[70] Cross 541.

[71] O'Connor 153–4.

[72] Cross 60.

[73] Riley 48.

[74] O'Connor 154–5.

[75] Riley 48.

[76] Cross 437.

[77] Riley 48.

[78] O'Connor 154.

[79] Anthony M. Buono, *The Greatest Marian Prayers* (New York: Alba House, 1999) 50.

[80] Buono 49–50.

[81] Buono 52 -3.

[82] Cross 162.

[83] Buono 122.

[84] Cross 162.

[85] Riley 48–9.

[86] Rene Laurentin, *A Short Treatise on the Blessed Virgin Mary*, trans. Charles Neuman, S.M. (Washington, NJ: AMI Press, 1991) 114. Fr. Laurentin points out that while St. Bernard is responsible for the image of the aqueduct that channels grace as a way to speak of Mary's mediation, he is not responsible for the image of Mary as the neck of the Church, as is often held. The image of Mary as "the neck of the Church" between Christ who is above her and the members below her is found for the first time in a work by Hermann of Tournai (d.1137) entitled *Collum Ecclesiae*.

[87] Buono 83–4.

[88] Buono 81–2.

[89] Hilda Graef, *Mary: A History of Doctrine and Devotion*, vol. 1 (New York: Sheed and Ward, 1963) 238.

[90] Cross 1208.

[91] Laurentin 112. In the East, Origen and George of Nicomedia are the only known witnesses of this spiritual sense of this Johannine passage for the first ten centuries and their views are very restrained and not fully developed. In the West, there is one earlier mention than that of Rupert of Deutz, which is not quite as specific as that of Rupert. Anselm of Lucca (d. 1086) in his *Oratio* tells us that Jesus said " 'Behold your mother' so that this glorious mother might intercede with so great tenderly affection for all who rightly believe . . . and might keep them as adopted children."

[92] O'Connor 159–60.

[93] Laurentin 117–9. This work was attributed to St. Albert the Great, Dominican and Doctor of the Church (c.1200–1280) until 1954 when two scholars demonstrated almost simultaneously that this work could not have been written by St. Albert. While being unknown, the genuine author is placed in the second half of the thirteenth century. This discovery that the *Mariale* had been falsely attributed to St. Albert the Great came as a great shock to Marian scholars, as great, for example, as it would be to literary

circles if the thesis denying to Shakespeare his dramas were scientifically justified.

[94] Riley 51.

[95] Laurentin 117–8.

[96] Riley 52. The famous hymn, the *Stabat Mater*, which emphasizes Mary's position at the foot of the Savior's cross is probably of Franciscan origin as well, being variously ascribed to St. Bonaventure and to the poet Jacopone da Todi. See Hilda Graef, *The Devotion to Our Lady* (New York: Hawthorn Books, 1963) 58.

[97] See Riley 52-5 for information on what these persons had to say specifically.

[98] Cross 1341.

[99] Cross 561.

[100] Cross 67.

[101] Cross 407.

[102] Cross 163.

[103] O'Connor 164–5.

[104] O'Connor 165–6.

[105] O'Connor 166–7.

[106] Cross 67.

[107] O'Connor 167.

[108] *The Life of the Virgin Mary* 515.

[109] Cross 600.

[110] *The Life of the Virgin Mary* 516.

[111] O'Carroll 296.

[112] Riley 56. Quote taken from *Commentarii in Evangelicam Historiam et in Acta Apostolorum*, tract. 41, 1604.

[113] Cross 846.

[114] Thomas A. O'Meara, O.P. *Mary in Protestant and Catholic Theology* (New York: Sheed and Ward, 1966) 121.

[115] Robert Payesko, *The Truth About Mary: A Scriptural Introduction to the Mother of Jesus for Bible-Believing Christians*, vol. 1 (Santa Barbara: Queenship Publishing, 1996) 54.

[116] Raymond Brown, et. al., ed., *Mary in the New Testament* (Mahwah: Paulist Press, 1978) 3.

[117] Brown 283.

[118] Brown 284.

[119] Brown 291–2.

[120] Brown 285; 287.

[121] Brown 288–99.

[122] David Bird, et.al., *Receiving the Vision: The Anglican-Roman Catholic Reality Today* (Collegeville: Liturgical Press, 1995) 157.

[123] Rahner, *Dictionary of Theology* 122.

[124] Rahner, *Dictionary of Theology* 58. See also Karl Rahner, "The Closure of Revelation," *The Content of the Faith*, ed. Karl Lehman, et. al. (New York: Crossroad, 1992): 401–2 for a discussion of what is and is not meant by revelation's being closed with the death of the last apostle. Rahner makes the important point that the Church's declaration of this closure is not a negative statement but a positive affirmation that "everything has been said in the Son of love, in whom God and the world have become one, forever without confusion, but forever undivided."

[125] Rahner, *Dictionary of Theology* 122.

[126] Rahner, "Truth and the Development of Dogma," *The Content of the Faith*, 408.

[127] Rahner, *Dictionary of Theology* 122.

[128] Rahner, *Dictionary of Theology* 122.

[129] *Catechism of the Catholic Church*, 2nd ed. (Washington: U.S. Catholic Conference, 1997) 47.

[130] Bauer 228.

[131] Hilda Graef, *Mary: A History of Doctrine and Devotion*, vol. 1 offers an excellent summary of the development of the doctrine of Mary's virginity *ante partum, in partu,* and *post partum.* No page references are listed here as they are too numerous and this history is traced throughout this resource. In addition, Luigi Gambero's *Mary and the Fathers of the Church* also offers much insight into how this doctrine of Mary's perpetual virginity presented itself in the thinking of the early Fathers.

[132] Judith A. Bauer, ed., *The Essential Mary Handbook* (Liguori, MO: Liguori Publications, 1999) 214; 201. In 1854, Pope Pius IX declared that the Blessed Virgin Mary was from the very first instant of her conception exempt from original sin and its effects. This does not mean that Mary was exempt from needing to be redeemed. Rather, in the words of Bl. Duns Scotus, she was given the grace of a preservative redemption according to the divine plan of God. While this doctrine is not explicitly revealed in scripture, it is considered to be implicit and an authentic development of doctrine. In 1950, Pope Pius XII declared that Mary, "Immaculate Mother of God ever Virgin, after finishing the course of her life on earth, was taken up in body and soul to heavenly glory." This privilege was given to Mary by means of God's divine power and according to His divine plan. This doctrine is also considered to be implicit in scripture. It is also contained in

sacred tradition from at least the 5th century and is likewise the result of an authentic development of doctrine.

[133] "*Dei Verbum*," *Documents of the Second Vatican Council*, ed. Austin Flannery, O.P. (Northport, NY: Costello, 1992) n. 10 755–6. "Sacred Tradition and sacred Scripture make up a single sacred deposit of the Word of God. . . . The task of giving an authentic interpretation of the Word of God, whether in its written form or in the form of Tradition, has been entrusted to the living teaching office of the Church. . . ." Anglican Catholics include themselves in this teaching office while recognizing the primacy of the successor of St. Peter.

[134] St. Thomas Aquinas, *Summa Theologica*, trans. Fathers of the English Dominican Province, vol. I (Westminster, MD: Christian Classics, 1981) Ia, q. I, art.10, ad. I 7.

[135] St. Thomas Aquinas Ia, q. I, art.10 7.

[136] *Catechism of the Catholic Church* 33.

[137] St. Augustine, *On Christian Doctrine*, trans. D. W. Robertson, Jr. (New York: Macmillan, 1958) 13.

[138] St. Augustine 16.

[139] St. Augustine 38–40. In Chapter VII of Book II, St. Augustine discusses the steps along the spiritual journey, from fear of the Lord to wisdom, that are required for the one who seeks to interpret scripture in a way that keeps the interpreter from turning away from the Truth "either in a desire to please men or for the sake of avoiding any kind of adversities to himself which arise in this life."

[140] St. Augustine 33.

CHAPTER 2

The 17th Century and the Golden Age of French Spirituality and Its Marian Son, St. Louis Marie Grignion de Montfort

Reformation and Post-Reformation Currents

Among Christians there is generally a belief that God always raises up Saints in response to the particular stresses and strains of the times to lead His people into the way of all truth. If ever there was such a time, it was certainly the post-Reformation era of the 17th century. In this chapter, we will focus our attention on the development of Marian thought in the Catholic Church in response to the reformers' complete skepticism about the place of any human cooperation in the work of Redemption. Even the brief space we can give to such a task in this writing reveals that the times were ripe for God's finally giving birth to St. Louis Marie Grignion de Montfort, in 1673, at Montfort-La-Cane in the country of France.[141]

In continuing our previous consideration of the reformers' views on Mary's role in Redemption, it is important to add that Luther and Calvin totally negated that long strain of thought, begun by St. Justin Martyr and St. Irenaeus, on the importance of the obedient yes of the Second Eve. In chronicling Luther's views in this regard, the noted historian of Marian thought, Hilda Graef, offers the following summary:

> Apart from her physical contribution, her co-operation in the divine motherhood is precisely nil. Luther does not object to the words of the *Regina caeli* "quem meruisti portare" (whom you have merited to bear), because we say the same of the Cross, which is only wood. This expression means no more than that she was suitable and foreordained to give birth to Christ, just as the wood of the Cross was suitable and foreordained to bear his body. According to Luther one must say this, "so that God's praise and honour might not be diminished by attributing too much to her. It is better to give too little to her than to the grace of God. Indeed, one can never give her too little. . . . The comparison of Mary with the wood of the Cross is characteristic of Luther, in whose theology human free will has no place. It deprives not only Mary of the honour due to her, but every human being of his dignity.[142]

As we noted in the previous chapter, Luther himself did use devotional language about Mary. He also allowed his followers to use such language about her and even allowed them to ask her for her intercession. However, he was insistent that she neither be implored nor considered to be our advocate, in any way, because the term advocate implies that she somehow actually contributes to the efficacy of prayer. He insisted on her lowliness to such an extreme that he even believed the Blessed Virgin to be a poor, despised little orphan. In a work of his entitled, *Anmerkungen zur Bibelübersetzung,* he even went so far as to equate the Catholic devotion of his day towards Mary with the cult of Baal denounced by the prophet.[143] Similarly, in a sermon preached by Luther in

1528 on the Wedding of Cana, he said that Christ expressed anger at his mother during that feast because he realized "that in time his mother would be given greater honour . . . than he himself, that is to say one would believe her to be a mediatress and an advocate between God and ourselves; in order to prevent this he addresses her very harshly not only here but also in other places in order to show that we ought not to be concerned with her but with him."[144]

While it hardly seems possible, John Calvin gave Mary an even lower place in the divine plan of Redemption. Since in his view everything depends solely on the will of God and all creaturely action and being have almost no importance, he rejected any practice of intercession to the Blessed Virgin. He even considered all prayer addressed to Mary to be against scripture, saying that "to ask her to obtain grace for us is no less than an execrable blasphemy because God has predestined the measure of grace for every man from all eternity."[145] While both Luther and Calvin never failed to recognize Mary as the Mother of God or perpetually virgin,[146] it was always with the view that she herself contributed absolutely nothing to help these mysteries of God's grace become realities in her life. In their reductionist view of the mystery of Redemption, Mary becomes a merely passive receptacle that God sovereignly invades and uses. While it is true that the human person is rendered more and more docile to God as the Blessed Trinity completely fills a human soul through the Divine Indwelling in the mystery we call grace, to say that Mary's perpetual willingness to receive and respond to the gift of grace was of no importance reduces not only Mary, but all human persons, to mere puppets on God's stage. Conversely, if the human person's giving God permission to fill us with His grace is of no importance in the divine plan, then how could the 'no' of Adam and Eve ever have been capable of wreaking such havoc?

Sadly, these reductionist views of the continental reformers also reached the British isles and dismantled not only the 'Lady altars' which graced both the smallest chapels and the largest cathedrals throughout England, but also the long standing honor which the Mother of God had been given for centuries in the English Church. By the sixteenth century, almost every parish church contained an image of Mary as the Mater Dolorosa. These images of Our Lady of Sorrows were typically used to flank the Rood across the chancel arch along with an image of the Beloved Disciple. Such images of the Blessed Virgin encouraged people to honor Mary's participation in her Son's Passion through her own sorrows and sufferings. Many churches also had images of Mary as the *Pietà*, or Our Lady of Pity, which served as a reminder that each person is called to identify himself or herself in some way with the sufferings of Christ. English Christians frequently invoked Mary as the supreme guide and companion along the way of the Cross that would finally unite them with her Son.[147]

While several Marian feasts were retained on the Anglican liturgical calendar by the English reformers, these feasts were stripped of any theological content. Article 22 of the Thirty-Nine Articles, first issued by the Church of England in 1563, forbade completely the invocation of the Blessed Virgin or any Saint. All Marian shrines in England were completely destroyed by the English reformers, including the most visited shrine in England, Our Lady of Walsingham, which was sacked in 1538. The statue of the Blessed Virgin from this shrine and hundreds of Marian statues from monasteries and churches throughout England were tragically taken to London and thrown into the fire for a massive burning.[148]

While the reformers claimed they were merely reacting to alleged abuses in both Marian and Christian piety, supposedly rampant in their day, a close review of the writings and actions of both the English and the continental reformers also reveals that they were deliberately bent on systematically destroying much of the accrued wisdom that had been handed on as part of sacred tradition from the time of the early Fathers. This is true not only as regards the Church's understanding of Mary but also as regards the Church's understanding of grace and free will, as well as the mystery of the interaction of these two in the divine plan of salvation and sanctification.

However, thankfully, the words of the reformers about Mary were not the only words God was allowing to be spoken during these horrific post-Reformation times. In the countries of Western Europe that were largely untouched by the Reformation, Italy and especially Spain, a great Marian revival began in the last years of the 16th century and the first years of the 17th century. In reflecting on the significance of this revival, noted Mariologist Fr. René Laurentin says that what was begun then has extended in so many ways even into our present day that it is accurate to use the term "Marian movement" when referring to this revival, because of its extent, breadth, and depth.[149] While there was understandably a negative impulse that fueled this Marian movement, namely the determination to react against the challenges raised by both Protestant and English reformers and to avenge the honor of the Virgin Mary, there was also a positive impetus. There began to be a genuine desire to know the Blessed Virgin better, to understand who she is in the divine plan, and to glorify God in her in many kinds of ways.[150]

The leaders of this Marian movement were the first great theologians of the Society of Jesus. We have already noted in the last chapter Alphonsus Salmeron, S.J., (d.1585), who played such a critical role in the Council of Trent and who clearly reiterated Mary's role in Redemption to be in line with the teaching of sacred tradition begun with St. Irenaeus. We must also note Francisco de Suarez, S.J., (d.1617), who put together the first systematic Mariology in 1590 and Chirino de Salazar, S.J., (d. 1646), who not only wrote the first great work on the Immaculate Conception in 1618, but is also credited with writing the first treatise precisely on the subject of Mary's part in Redemption.[151]

Suarez incorporated his Mariology in his treatise *De mysteriis Christii* and considered the Blessed Virgin in close relation with Christological truth.[152] Following Duns Scotus, he held that Mary herself was redeemed by Jesus Christ through a preservative

Redemption from the first moment of her conception. He argues that she received every grace that could be given to a pure creature and that the mysteries of her graces cannot be measured by laws. Because of the intense grace given to her initially, every single act of hers merited an increase of charity, grace, and glory because all her actions were deliberate and good. Thus, at the end of her life certainly, and most probably even from the moment of the Incarnation, she had obtained more grace than all the angels and saints combined.[153]

"The Blessed Virgin frequently merited more by her single acts than individual saints by all the acts of their life, . . . (nevertheless) . . . , it is certain that she merited nothing *de condigno* which is the proper privilege of Christ, but by meriting the Incarnation *de congruo* she merited a great good for us, and while she lived she could also merit many other good things."[154] Suarez also held that Mary had perfect knowledge of all things pertaining to divinity and the Trinity in particular. And, from the moment of the Incarnation, or at least from the moment of the birth of Christ, Mary also knew all that belonged to the mystery of Redemption. He held that she received many revelations and that at times she even saw clearly the divine essence.[155]

The perfection of her beatitude and beatific knowledge since her death and glorious Assumption likewise surpasses that of all the angels and saints. "Under Christ the Blessed Virgin is as it were the universal cause most intimately connected with Him; hence it belongs to her position to comprehend in the Word the whole universe and the state of all the blessed and the damned."[156] In specifically discussing her part in Redemption, Suarez says that just as Christ is our King because He has redeemed us, so the Virgin Mary is called the Mother of all men precisely because she has contributed in a special way to our Redemption. She has provided her own substance by her own free consent and has voluntarily offered him for us. In so doing, she has both desired (willed) and provided for our salvation in a unique manner.

While the terms Reparatrix and Mediatress are not used of her in the same way in which they are used of the divine Redeemer, Suarez was insistent that they do nonetheless apply to Mary when properly understood. We ask Christ actually to do things for us. We ask Mary to intercede and serve as a channel of grace for us in what her Son actually does.[157] "By entreating, by meriting *de congruo*, and by co-operating in her way in the Incarnation of Christ, she co-operated in some way in our salvation. . . . The Blessed Virgin co-operated in our salvation in three ways: first, by meriting the Incarnation *de congruo*; secondly, by praying and entreating, and meriting salvation for us *de congruo* while she was on earth; thirdly, by conceiving Christ, the Author of our salvation."[158]

This discussion of the Mariological understanding of Francis Suarez, who greatly influenced the writings of St. Louis de Montfort, raises the issue of what many Marian theologians of the 17th century and beyond, including St. Louis de Montfort, have meant by the concepts of both merit and meriting *de congruo* when speaking of the role of the Blessed Virgin in Redemption. These terms often tend to be either unfamiliar or misleading in contemporary theological conversations. Of all the explanations I have read, I have found the explanation of Fr. Reginald Garrigou-Lagrange in his noted work, *The Mother of the Saviour and our Interior Life*, to be most helpful. So, for the sake of our common understanding of the important concept of merit and the ways in which 17th century writers spoke of the Blessed Virgin meriting anything for us, let us now spend a moment considering Fr. Lagrange's explanation.

The term 'merit' in general means a right to a reward. Theologically speaking, the meritorious act confers a right to a reward even though the act itself does not produce the reward. And, the supernaturally meritorious act, which presupposes that the doer of the act is living in the state of grace and acts out of love for God, confers a right to a supernatural reward. It is important to note that merit must be distinguished from what is called 'satisfaction', whose purpose is to expiate the insult to God caused by sin's offense to the Divine Majesty and to "render God once more propitious."[159] Using the above definitions, we must always speak of Jesus Christ as the principal and perfect Mediator. It is in complete dependence on His merits and satisfaction, which are not only superabundant but also sufficient in themselves, that the Blessed Virgin exercises her subordinate mediation. We must also emphasize that Jesus in no way needed any complement on the part of Mary. This is why sacred tradition has often compared her to the neck in the Mystical Body of Christ that unites the Head to the members or to an aqueduct through which grace passes to us. However, Lagrange reminds us that we must also assert that Mary's mediation has nevertheless been willed by God.[160]

We can thus speak of three kinds of merit. The highest and most perfect would be that of the Incarnate Word, Jesus Christ. The merit of the divine Redeemer, being perfectly and fully worthy of a reward, is referred to as *perfecte de condigno*. This is because "the act of charity of the God-Man, since it is the act of a divine Person, is at least equal in value to the reward, even when evaluated in strict justice."[161] The second kind of merit results from the actions of a person living in the state of grace. Every person who is living "in the state of grace and who is endowed with the use of reason and free will, and who is yet a member of the Church militant, can merit an increase of charity and of eternal life with a merit commonly called *de condigno*."[162] The term *de condigno* may be translated literally as "worthiness" and thus means that a person is capable of doing acts that are truly worthy of a supernatural reward, in the sense that they are "proportionate to it since they proceed from habitual grace which is the germ or beginning of that eternal life which God has promised to those who keep His commandments"[163] (John 14: 21; 23).

While merit *de condigno* is not entitled to a reward in strict justice because of the human person who is the actor, we can only speak of the right to an entitlement to a reward in the distributive justice willed by God. This is pointed to in scripture through passages such as 2Tim. 4:8 which speaks of eternal life as a crown of justice; Rom. 2:6–7 which speaks of their being a retribution that will be made according to each one's work; and Hebrews 6:19 which speaks of the recompense for a labor which God could not pass over.[164] However, while a person in the state of grace can merit through distributive justice his or her own increase in charity in this life or the eternal reward of the Beatific Vision in the next life, he or she cannot merit the conversion of a sinner or another person's advance in charity. As we are taught in Acts 4:12, only Jesus Christ has been constituted to be head of the human race to regenerate all of us who are sinners and lead us to salvation. "And there is salvation in no one else, for there is no other name under heaven given among men by which we must be saved." Thus, while we can speak of merit *de condigno* for the just, even with regard to the Blessed Virgin Mary, we also say that this kind of merit is incommunicable.[165]

This brings us to the third kind of merit that is known as merit *de congruo proprie*, which means a merit of becomingness. "Merit *de congruo* is founded on charity or friendship with God rather than on justice: theologians say that it is founded on the rights of friendship, *in jure amicabili*. St. Thomas explains it thus: 'Since a man in the state of grace does God's will, it is in keeping with the proprieties (or rights) of friendship that God should do his will in saving another person (for his sake)—although it can happen that at times there will be an obstacle on the side of the other person (IaIIae,q.114,a.6).' In this way, a good Christian mother, for example, can, by her good works, her love of God and of her neighbor, merit the conversion of her son *de congruo proprie*. St. Monica obtained the conversion of St. Augustine by that kind of merit as well as by her prayers. . . ."[166]

It is this third kind of merit that the Blessed Virgin Mary offers to God for us. Her merit *de congruo proprie* is considered merit in the proper sense of the term since it is founded on the rights of friendship and presupposes the superabundant state of grace in which she consistently and constantly lived.[167] Fr.

Lagrange tells us that once we have properly understood what Suarez and others have meant by merit *de congruo*, it becomes evident that they are correct in asserting that the Blessed Virgin merited for us *de congruo proprie*, as her children, all that Jesus Christ merited for us *de condigno*.[168]

In closing this discussion of what Marian theologians have meant by the term merit in speaking of the Blessed Virgin's role in Redemption, it is important to note that this matter raises a further theological question which we must and will consider as we examine the writings of St. Louis, namely, the issue of causality.

As we return to our consideration of the theological currents of the 17th century Marian movement, it is important to note that many writers of this period[169] began to refer increasingly to the fact that Mary's divinely ordained part in the re-creation of humankind was proof of the fact that she had been immaculately conceived.[170] For example, John of Carthagena (d. 1617) in one of his homilies says that "since therefore the Virgin Mother of God was our Redemptrix in her way . . . it follows that she was entirely free from original sin. . . . It was necessary that the Virgin, Co-adjutrix and associate of Christ in the reparation of the human race, be purer than heaven."[171] Similarly, Frangipane (d. 1638) concludes in *Blasones de la Virgin Madre de Dios y Senora nuestra* that if indeed everything that Christ merited for us *de condigno* was merited for us *de congruo* by Mary, the title Co-redemptrix is correctly applied to the Blessed Virgin. And, such a title and responsibility necessarily requires innocence on her part. "How could she cleanse the world from sin, if she herself were subject to sin?"[172]

Among those who linked and defended both Mary's cooperation in the work of Redemption and her Immaculate Conception was the third Jesuit theologian mentioned above, Chirino de Salazar, S.J. In *Pro Immaculata Deiparae Virginis Conceptione Defensio* he states: "Christ Himself willed to perfect our Redemption by uniting His Mother to it as an auxiliatrix." "Our Redemption which was born, as it were, through Jesus and Mary, attained from Christ sufficiency, strength and constancy; and from Mary form and beauty."[173]

In response to those who objected that the Blessed Virgin could not be a Co-redemptrix because she herself required a pre-servative redemption, he responded: "There is nothing against her receiving the fruits of Redemption before others and after-wards joining her own merits with those of Christ to obtain the Redemption of the rest of men even from original sin."[174] Salazar also treated the problem of Mary's priesthood in his *Commentary on Proverbs*. "To offer Christ to and for us is the right solely of the Virgin and of no-one else."[175] Salazar held that Mary alone offers Him undoubtedly as something that belongs to her.[176] This theme of Mary's priestly offering of her Son also begins to be found in the writings of others of this period.[177]

Before ending our consideration of the general currents of the 17th century in preparation for focusing specifically on the contri-butions of the French School and its specific influence on St. Louis de Montfort, it is important to mention one significant neg-ative Catholic voice about Mary's role in Redemption during this period. In 1673, there appeared an anonymous booklet published under the title, *Monita salutaria Beatae Virginis Mariae ad cultores suos indiscretos*. Its author is generally considered to be Adam Widenfield (d. 1678), an eminent lawyer from Cologne and possi-bly a convert from Protestantism.[178] His stated purpose was to cor-rect what he considered to be exaggerated abuses in Marian piety in the Catholic Church so that Protestants would be more likely to return to the fold. He was also expressly opposed to the view of Mary as Co-redemptrix, which as we have shown above, had become quite common among Catholic authors in the 17th cen-tury.[179] Widenfield presents the Blessed Virgin as warning:

> It was Christ Who by His own merits appeased the wrath of God; He alone reconciles men with God; He alone has trodden the winepress, and no one else with Him. Let no one, therefore, attribute

these things to me; for if I was pleasing to God, it
was only in and through Jesus Christ my Redeemer
and Savior. Or was I perhaps crucified for you, or
were you perhaps baptized in my name? . . . Beware
of attributing to me in your exaggeration or
immoderate zeal anything which belongs to God
alone. Therefore, you shall not call me Salvatrix
or Co-redemptrix.[180]

While there were certainly hyperbolic expressions in the discussion of Mary as Co-redemptrix, such as the view that a particle
of the Blessed Virgin's "flesh and a few drops of her blood had been
preserved in Christ's body up to the time of the Passion when that
particle of flesh suffered, and those drops of blood were shed for
our salvation,"[181] it is important to note that "after an accurate
examination of the pamphlet, and duly weighing the circumstances, the Sacred Congregation of the Holy Office, in a solemn
session held on June 19, 1674, before the Holy Father, rightly and
deservedly inserted it in the Index of forbidden books."[182] On June
22, 1676, the Holy Office condemned the pamphlet without any
restrictions.[183] As expected, Widenfield's attack on Mary's cooperative role in the work of Redemption brought about even greater
efforts in the 17th century and beyond to defend and define what
had been taught since the days of the Fathers about the Blessed
Virgin Mary as the Second Eve.[184]

Cardinal Pierre de Bérulle's Contributions

While we cannot know for certain how aware St. Louis de Montfort was of the details of this specific thread in sacred tradition
that we have been tracing from the time of St. Justin Martyr and
St. Irenaeus, we can certainly postulate that much of what we
have reviewed thus far regarding the Virgin Mary's role in
Redemption formed, at least, the remote theological background
for the thought of Montfort. We can postulate this because the
copious footnotes found in the English translation of his col-

lected writings published by Montfort Publications in 1987 under the title, *God Alone: The Collected Works of St. Louis Marie de Montfort*, indicate quite frequently how particular ideas of Montfort resonate with those discussed by the Fathers and the theologians who followed in their wake. In addition, we do know that St. Louis de Montfort spent five years being educated by the Jesuits at the College of St. Thomas à Becket in Rennes, France and seven years preparing for ordination at the Seminary of Saint-Sulpice in Paris.[185] His education consisted of studying "the Fathers of the Church, the theologians of the Schools, [and] the pious works of his time," especially those of St. Francis de Sales and Cardinal Bérulle and his disciples. We know from his own notes that St. Bernard of Clairvaux was clearly one of his favorite authors.[186]

However, in order to understand adequately the writings of St. Louis in the context of his immediate theological and spiritual formation, we must now consider that specific train of thought which had the greatest influence on Montfort's writings. While this is often commonly referred to as merely the 17th century French School, perhaps it is most aptly called the Bérulle School of French spirituality in the 17th century.[187] For not only was St. Louis de Montfort directly formed during his seminary years by disciples of this school, but he is also usually considered to be the last of the great representatives of the Bérulle School of French Spirituality.[188] Thus, reflecting on the Marian thought of the Bérulle School will help us better understand the thought of Montfort himself. In considering this school, let us notice how its primary representatives both expressed and developed the line of thought on Mary's role in Redemption that we have traced from the early Fathers down through the centuries that followed. Additionally, while there is much that can be said about the writings of Bérulle and his various disciples, we will be giving particular emphasis to those aspects that seem to have influenced Montfort most profoundly. As the reader digests the later chapters of this book, it might be helpful to return to this section. Cardinal Pierre de Bérulle (1575–1629), from whom this school takes its name, is considered to be the first and founding representative of what we are referring to in this book as the 17th century Bérulle French School. A native of the French province of Champagne,[189] he was educated by the Jesuits, studied theology at the Sorbonne and greatly admired the mystical writings of St. Teresa of Jesus.[190] After his ordination in 1599, his desire grew for perfection and deeper integrity in his personal life. Seriously considering entering the Jesuits, he made a retreat under the direction of a Jesuit named Fr. Maggio in 1602. This retreat bore the lasting fruit of providing Bérulle with the thoroughly Christocentric orientation which came to characterize not only his thought but also the thought of his school's disciples. Specifically, he saw in the humiliation of the Incarnate Word "the model of annihilation of the human self and of that submission to God toward which the self aspires." He came to see that Jesus alone is the true fulfillment of our very beings as human persons.[191] In commenting on the significance of the influence of this Ignatian retreat on Bérulle, Raymond de Ville compares it to the role which Jesuit spiritual directors most probably had on St. Teresa of Jesus' intense devotion to the humanity of Jesus.[192] While Bérulle never became a Jesuit,[193] he was very instrumental in establishing many reformed Carmelite convents in France. He even saw his own mother enter the reformed Carmel of the Incarnation in Paris in 1605.[194]

After having experienced what Bérulle characterized as an authentic mystical grace in 1607, the divine Person of the Incarnate Word came to be at the heart of his thought, existence, teaching, and writings. This was so characteristic of him that Pope Urban VIII eventually named Bérulle, *the apostle of the Incarnate Word*.[195] Bérulle firmly believed and taught that the human person can find fulfillment only through union with God in adoration and love. And, it is Jesus alone who is, through the union of His two natures in His one divine Person, "by His very state" the perfect adorer.[196] Furthermore, Bérulle adored the divinized humanity of Jesus Christ. His contemplation of Jesus "gave rise in Bérulle to lengthy considerations of the 'states and mysteries' of the Incarnate Word." He maintained that the mysteries of the various states and stages of the Incarnate Word remain *eternally* a source of grace, a truth that we will hear echoed repeatedly in Montfort.

While we might speak of these mysteries as past—in terms of their initial or historical occurrence—they are in reality eternally present in the virtue they offer and will never pass away. Bérulle contended that the Christian life must thus consist of both adoring Jesus in His various states and mysteries and allowing ourselves to be conformed to the Incarnate Word in the various interior attitudes which characterize His states and mysteries. Only such adoration of Jesus in His various mysteries, expressed through our loving and obedient adherence to the various stages and interior attitudes of the life of Jesus, will enable us to undergo the radical self-denial and abnegation necessary for union with God.[197]

Of all the mysteries of the life of Christ that Bérulle considered to be important for contemplation and imitation, the Incarnation was consistently pointed out to be the most significant. He similarly considered the infancy of Jesus to be of critical significance. His reason for upholding the crucial place of both the event of the Incarnation and His infancy was that for Bérulle, "the state of infancy is the height of annihilation. It is the mystery of the Word, the Voice of God becoming mute (*infans*)."[198] It is in his desire to contemplate, adore, and imitate Jesus in this state of total Self-emptying that we find the source of Bérulle's deep love of both the Blessed Sacrament and the Blessed Virgin Mary. In a text of the best of Berulle's writings published under the title the *Grandeurs de Jésus* in 1623,[199] we encounter a prolonged meditation on the mystery of the Incarnation with special emphasis on the relationship of Jesus and Mary. The reader is led to contemplate not only the interior attitudes of Jesus but also the interior attitudes of Mary at His conception, birth, and during His infancy.[200] What follows is an excerpt from what is called the

"Second Part of the Discourse on the State and Grandeurs of Jesus" in which begins the "Life of Jesus," a section that exemplifies Bérulle's writings on the relationship of Jesus and Mary. It is important to note that what follows is only a small excerpt. The interested reader is urged to consult the entire discourse to appreciate fully the thought of Bérulle:

> When God held His first deliberations in the world after the creation of man and his sin, He spoke of Mary and set her in opposition to the serpent, the source of the curse of the universe. From then on God and the world have considered her the source of blessing for the world. . . .

> . . . Let us see what [the Son of God] is and what He does in His Blessed Mother. For she is the one who is the closest and the most united to Him by the state of this new mystery accomplished in her and through her. . . . after the divine Persons, there is no other person to whom the Son of God is more closely bound than to the Virgin.

> Moreover this bond imitates and adores the bond He has with the divine Persons. He is united to His Father through birth and nature, and He is united to the Virgin through nature and birth. He is joined to the Holy Spirit as to its origin since He is its source in eternity. He is united to the Virgin through production and the infusion of a Spirit in her spirit. . . . it will be for all eternity. . . . Yet He is joined to her in a state of dependence, since He is her Son and she is His Mother and since He is now living in her and living through her. . . . He is in this condition and shares in this blessed way with her for nine months without

reneging for a single moment. And after this He will offer her a share in His greatest works on earth and in souls. . . .

Since she is the first to share in Jesus, she is the first as well to share in the cross and humiliation of Jesus. . . . She knows the Father's plan to humble His Son and the Son's plan to humble Himself. She embraces these plans and agrees to be the humiliated Mother of the humiliated Son. Now this is the place and the time where she becomes aware of these truths and begins to accept the humiliation destined for her Son and for herself, for her Son's human filiation and for her divine Motherhood. For it is in Nazareth, in this birth of Jesus in her, in this moment that these things are accomplished. They are known to her, born in her and experienced by her according to the splendor of her knowledge, the strength of her love and the vitality of her sensitivity toward divine reality and the things of her Son and her God.[201]

Bérulle clearly puts himself squarely in the long line of sacred tradition that begins with Sts. Justin and Irenaeus by speaking of Mary's enmity with the serpent and God's deliberate choice to create and grace another woman after Eve and Adam's disobedience, a woman who would be capable of standing in opposition to Satan and sin. Similarly, he shows himself to be in league with that aspect of sacred tradition that speaks of Mary's essential cooperation in the Incarnation itself. By mentioning that the Blessed Virgin is given the role of sharing in the work her Son accomplishes in human souls, Bérulle also puts himself in line with those who have spoken of Mary's ongoing mediating function in the life of grace. However, where his unique emphasis lies, as well as that of the entire Bérulle School, is in his opening up a view of both Jesus' and Mary's interiority during not only the moment of the Incarnation but also during the nine months when Jesus was actually living in the womb of the Blessed Virgin.

Through his writings, we begin to catch a glimpse of the union of the two hearts of Jesus and Mary, which Bérulle says elsewhere we will only fully understand when we have been admitted into the life of heavenly glory. The glimpse given us by Bérulle helps us begin to understand that the Christ- conformation of the human person that is necessary for union with God took place first of all, as well as uniquely and most completely, in the Blessed Virgin herself. The difference between her Christ-conformation and our own is that we must allow ourselves to become conformed to Him so that we can be purified from the effects of original sin and finally be sanctified. While Baptism into Christ removes the guilt of sin, it is Catholic teaching that the effects of sin, known as concupiscence, remain.[202] Since Mary was redeemed by God by being miraculously preserved from both the guilt of original sin and its effects, she freely allowed herself to be conformed to Him, not out of necessity, but out of pure love for the God Who humbled Himself to take a human nature from her. The purest love ever given to God by any creature expressed itself in Mary's desire to share in her being all that God the Son undergoes and suffers in His humiliation.

While Bérulle does not specifically use the term co-redemption, nor the terms 'merit' or 'merit *de congruo*' that we have discussed earlier, his poignantly drawing our attention to Mary's loving choice to share in the suffering of her divine Son nevertheless seems to put Bérulle in line with that aspect of sacred tradition which sees co-redemptive merit in the suffering of Mary, lovingly united to that of her divine Son. And, what is most significant in this regard is the specific emphasis on Mary's intentionally joining herself to the redemptive Self-offering of her Son to the Father on our behalf from the very moment of the Incarnation itself. While those before Bérulle have emphasized Mary's co-passion in union with Jesus' suffering during the events leading to the crucifixion and at the moment of the crucifixion itself, Bérulle reminds us that the Incarnation itself is the prototype for all that would follow and flow from God's initial *kenosis* in the womb of Mary. The *kenosis* of God the Son in becoming flesh and undergoing the various states that we undergo from conception through natural death is, in its entirety, the redemptive Cross born for us. Furthermore, because of their freely chosen and inseparable union beginning at the Incarnation, Mary and Jesus became functionally as well as substantially one in the bearing of the Cross. Mary's yes to sharing in Jesus' ongoing humiliation from the moment of His Incarnation meant that her own suffering was lived *in union with* His and, in that sense, truly *co*-redemptive, while subordinate to that of the divine Redeemer.

While Bérulle does not use the term Co-redemptrix or speak specifically of Mary's cooperative role in Redemption as such in the above text, he does speak of such in another work, *Notre Dame dans l'Enfance de Jésus*, as "the happy companion of Jesus in His mysteries, in His labors, in His cross, in His life, in His death."[203] Knowing this, we would have to say that his acceptance of the tradition about her coredemptive role is at least implicit in all his writings. Furthermore, it is precisely Bérulle's particular attentiveness to the significance of the Incarnation as the foundational humiliation and Self-abnegation of God the Son, in the entire work of Redemption, that comes to full flower in the thought of St. Louis Marie de Montfort. We will also hear Montfort echo Bérulle's profound insight about Mary's divine maternity corresponding to, and even participating in, the Father's paternity of the Son.[204]

Contributions of the Other Bérullians

Our consideration of the Marian thought of the Bérulle French School leads us next to the writings of two of Bérulle's principle disciples, Jean-Jacques Olier (1608–1657) and St. John Eudes (1601–1680).[205]

A native of Paris, Olier was also educated by the Jesuits and studied theology at the Sorbonne.[206] After his ordination in 1633, he was introduced to the thought of Bérulle through the man who succeeded Bérulle as superior general of the Oratory begun by Bérulle upon his death in 1629, Charles de Condren. Olier's printed works consist largely of four small books published after his death and intended for the parishioners of the parish of Saint-Sulpice placed under his charge in 1642. He is not considered to be a great theologian but rather the "one who best popularized Bérulle's doctrine."[207] It is Olier who is credited with the popular phrase, *O Jesu vivens in Maria*, which so influenced St. Louis de Montfort during his priestly formation at the seminary of Saint-Sulpice, founded by Olier. It is this phrase which inspired the title I have given to this book, 'Jesus Redeeming in Mary,' replacing 'living' with 'redeeming'.

The original phrase, Jesus living in Mary, is taken from the following prayers written by Olier and recited daily by Montfort during his seminary days:

> O Jesus, living in Mary
> come and live in your
> servants,
> in your Spirit of holiness,
> in the fullness of your
> power,
> in the perfection of your
> ways,
> in the communion of
> your mysteries;
> dominate every hostile
> force,
> in your SPIRIT,
> for the glory of the
> FATHER.

JESUS, you who live in Mary,
    in the beauty of your virtues,
    in the fullness of your power,
    in the splendor of your divine,
       eternal riches,
give us some share in this holiness
    which belongs only to God;
Let us communicate with the zeal
    of this holiness for the Church;
finally, clothe us with yourself so totally
    that we may be nothing in ourselves,
    and so live only in
       and like your SPIRIT,
       for the glory of your FATHER.[208]

Olier's prayers give voice to that aspect of Bérulle's theology which holds that the various stages and mysteries of the Incarnate Word remain a source of grace for us, eternally. While we might speak of the Incarnation as past, in terms of its historical occurrence, in reality the mystery of Jesus living in Mary is eternally present, in God. Thus, Olier addresses Jesus eternally present in the mystery of His indwelling the Virgin's womb, asking for the grace that is perpetually offered us by the Blessed Trinity through this mystery.

In the few examples we have of Olier's more didactic writings on the Blessed Virgin, he says that she who had become the Mother of the Son is also the bride of the Father. "For she became, with Him, the source of the temporal generation of the Word, accomplishing together with Him (the Father) in the Incarnation what He accomplishes alone in eternity. That is the most wondrous activity and the most divine exaltation possible for a creature, to share with the eternal Father in His fecundity through the actual generation of His Son. The highest, the most sublime and most perfect power of the Most High is His fecundity. It is this He shares with the Blessed Virgin, in marrying her, in order to realize with her the temporal generation of the eternal Word. She becomes at the same time the temple of the Holy Spirit in the purest and most abundant fullness possible. Since she was destined to be the Mother of Jesus Christ, she received the fullness of grace."[209] We will see this idea of Mary as God's Spouse, which echoes Bérulle's emphasis on the correspondence between God's paternity and Mary's maternity, continued by St. Louis de Montfort. When we examine the full ramifications of this line of thinking in Montfort, we will endeavor to discern more carefully what exactly is meant, and not meant, by referring in any way to the Blessed Virgin as the Spouse of one or all the members of the Blessed Trinity. Olier also spoke of Mary as a figure of the Church, associated in the sacrifice of Calvary as the spouse of the new Adam.[210]

Another Bérullian, St. John Eudes, was from the Normandy region of France and also educated by Jesuits like the other key members of the Bérulle school. In his *Mémorial*, he describes the grace of these early years by saying that God gave him the special grace at 12 years old to consecrate his body to God through a vow of chastity. At 17, he entered the Confraternity of Our Lady; "there, Our Lord, through the mediation of his most holy Mother, granted me very great graces." At the age of 21, Bérulle received Eudes into the congregation of the Oratory in the house of Saint-Honore in Paris.[211] As might be expected, the influence of Bérulle on Eudes' thought and writings is enormous. He was considered by his peers to be among the greatest of preachers in the parish mission circuit popular in the Church of 17th century France. This ministry of parish missions, coupled with the ministry of spiritual direction, led Eudes to write many books. At 41, he decided to leave the Oratory and found a seminary and an order for diocesan priests known as the Society of Jesus and Mary.[212]

Bérulle's influence developed in Eudes the desire to live in constant loving intimacy with Jesus and Mary. His expression of the prayer he had learned at the Oratory was: "O Heart of Jesus living in and through Mary! O Heart of Mary living in and for

Jesus!" Where the Bérullian school spoke of the "interior of Mary" or the "interior of Jesus," John Eudes would use the word "Heart." He composed an Office in honor of the Heart of Mary, celebrated for the first time in public in 1648. He likewise composed an Office in honor of the Heart of Jesus, officially celebrated with approval in 1672.[213] While St. Margaret Mary Alacoque's apparitions, beginning in 1673, along with the preaching and devotions of the times popularized devotion to the Sacred Heart of Jesus, Pius X called Eudes the "Father, the Doctor, and the Apostle of liturgical devotions to the Sacred Hearts of Jesus and Mary" at the time of his beatification in 1909.[214]

What is most significant about this for our concerns is that St. John Eudes insisted on the unity of the Heart of Jesus and of Mary, often by using only one word and a single symbol-Heart-instead of Hearts.[215] The major work of writing that occupied his energy for many years is entitled, *The Admirable Heart of the Most Holy Mother of God*. In this work, Eudes develops the Bérullian idea of the perfect, loving union of Mary's interior state with that of Jesus by elaborately illustrating the specific ways in which Mary's heart is the perfect image of the adorable heart of God and of the God-Man.[216] Eudes constantly shows himself to be thoroughly committed to the Bérullian insistence on the primacy of Jesus in the midst of elaborating on the excellence of Mary. "Although the Heart of Jesus is distinct from that of Mary and surpasses it infinitely in excellence and holiness, yet God has closely united these two Hearts that it may be truly said that they are but one Heart since they are always animated by the same spirit and filled with the same sentiments."[217] Through the writings of Eudes, we come to see that what makes Mary's heart so admirable is that the mystery of the divine presence of the Redeemer in her has penetrated her heart, the very core of her being, so completely that she has been perfectly conformed to her divine Son. St. John Eudes profoundly sums up this view in speaking of Mary's uttering the words of the *Magnificat*:

For the corporeal heart of this divine Virgin, filled with a sensible and extraordinary joy, caused her holy mouth to chant this *Magnificat* with a fervor and extraordinary jubilation. Her spiritual heart, completely ravished and transported in God, caused ecstatic words to arise from her sacred lips: And my spirit is exalted in God my Savior. . . . Her divine heart, that is, her divine child, residing in her blessed womb and remaining in her heart, who is the soul of her soul, the spirit of her spirit, the heart of her heart, is the primary author of this Canticle.[218]

For St. John Eudes, Bérulle, Olier, and St. Louis de Montfort, it is this complete penetration of Mary by God in the Incarnation, and the consequent perfect conformation of Mary to Jesus Christ, that makes her worthy of not only our admiration and devotion but also our imitation, invocation, and even the entrustment of our very selves to her through an act and attitude of complete donation to the Blessed Virgin. In the words of St. John Eudes in *The Kingdom of Jesus* : "We must thank her for all the love, the glory, and the services which she has rendered to her Son Our Lord Jesus Christ, and referring all our being and our life to her, after God, put ourselves in dependence upon her, and beseech her to take charge of all that concerns us. We must beseech her to deign to make use of all our actions for honoring her Son, and to associate us with all the love and praises she has ever given Him in the past and will render to Him through all eternity."[219]

Controversial Language in the Bérulle French School

This brings us to a final category of thought and action, alluded to above, which characterizes and even fuels much of the thinking as regards Mary in the Bérulle French School. We might call this category that of consecration to Mary through a vow of holy servitude, also known as the "holy slavery of love." While St. Louis de Montfort had his own version of this vow, Bérulle's wording below is typical of the language used for such a vow by his disciples:

> To the perpetual honor of the Mother and the Son
> I wish to be in the state and quality of servitude
> with regard to her who has the state and quality of
> the Mother of my God . . . and I give myself to her
> in the quality of a slave. . . . I renounce the power
> and liberty I have of disposing of myself and my
> actions, and place myself entirely in her hands.[220]

It is important to note that for Bérulle and others in his school this vow of holy servitude to Mary was an extension of their profound desire to imitate the state of Jesus in the womb of Mary, where Mary has been given by God the Father maternal authority over God the Son. This desire was intensified by their belief that much grace is given to us by our conformation to the various states of the mysteries of Christ as discussed above in our look at Bérulle specifically.[221] As we shall see later, Montfort viewed a vow of servitude or consecration to Mary as the perfect way to imitate Jesus Christ in His own freely chosen dependence upon Mary. While there is much in the terms 'servitude' and 'slave' that may seem foreign and even offensive to our contemporary sensibilities, we must endeavor to understand the reality to which these terms point if we are to maximize the light that St. Louis de Montfort can shed on understanding Mary's role in Redemption.

In attempting to understand what the Bérullian School meant by the holy slavery of love, let us begin by acknowledging that this concept did not originate with Cardinal Bérulle and his successors and that their use of the words, slave or slavery, is not to be taken in any servile or pejorative sense. Its origin can be found in the New Testament use of the Greek word, *doulos*, which is often used by St. Paul and others who refer to themselves as the "*doulos* of Jesus

Christ" (cf. Rom. 1:1; Phil. 1:1; Tit. 1:1). In addition, St. Paul's words in Rom. 6:15–23 remind us that because of the gift of Jesus Christ we need no longer remain slaves of sin but—having been set free from sin—we must consider ourselves slaves of righteousness.

From these and other such instances, we can readily see that such use of the word, slave, in the Pauline epistles indicates a relationship of total dependence on God Who alone is the source of goodness and righteousness, including the total yielding of one's very person and possessions. Furthermore, it is clear, not only from the way Paul speaks but also from the way he acts, that he has freely chosen to give himself to Jesus Christ and the proclamation of the Gospel. He, along with many of the apostles of his day, ended up allowing their hands to be stretched out and taken where, left to their own preferences, they would rather not go (John 21:18). Paul surrendered himself even to the point of suffering imprisonment and finally death out of love for Jesus Christ to Whom he freely enslaved himself in total self-abandonment. If we can understand this desire for total self-abandonment and total surrender to the Beloved in responding to the call of Christian discipleship, then we can begin to grasp the reality intended by the term "slavery of love" in the language of both Bérulle and Montfort.

What is perhaps most confusing for many is the notion of extending the New Testament concept of being a slave of Jesus Christ to being a slave of the Blessed Virgin. When we look at the history of this idea and practice, we discover that such an idea, with its corresponding practice, was not original with Bérulle and Montfort. While some Marian scholars have said that the title 'slave of Mary' may be implicit in those early Fathers who referred to the Mother of God by the titles, "Queen" or "Lady," it has been discovered that a number of the Fathers themselves used the term "slave" in expressing their relationship to Mary. St. Ephraem is considered to be the first to speak of himself as a "slave of the Mother of God," however the text usually cited to prove this is now considered to be not entirely trustworthy.[222]

St. Ildephonsus of Toledo (d.669) definitely used this term in his work entitled, *De virginitate perpetua S. Mariae*. In addition, works by St. John Damascene, Euthymius of Constantinople, Blessed Marinus, the Abbot Odilon, St. Anselm of Canterbury, St. Bernard, and Adam of St. Victor have been found which speak of being slaves of the Mother of God.[223] Interestingly, the expression "slave of the Mother of God" is also found on official seals used in the fifth and sixth centuries in Africa; several popes dating from the 8th century on prided themselves on using this title in referring to their ministries.[224] The term was given official approval with the establishment and recognition of the religious order called the "Servites of Mary" in the 13th century. Thomas à Kempis also made extensive use of the term in his 15th century writings.[225]

When it comes to the particular expression of this slavery of love to the Blessed Virgin that appears in the Bérulle School, there is general consensus that Bérulle was greatly influenced by what was known as the Confraternity of the Holy Slavery, which originated in Spain in the 16th century under the leadership of Sister Agnes of St. Paul of the Franciscan Conceptionists at the convent of St. Ursula in Alcala de Henares. The rule of this confraternity required its members "to offer themselves to our Redeemer and His glorious Mother, becoming like living sacrifices, dedicating body and soul." Here, we recognize another Pauline reference: "Present your bodies as a living sacrifice, holy and acceptable to God" (Rom. 12:1). Such a consecration was urged to be made to both Jesus and Mary because of the spiritual current in 15th and 16th century Spain which recognized the unity between Jesus and His Mother.[226]

In 1608, another Franciscan, John of the Angels, rewrote and enlarged the statutes of this original Confraternity. Its popularity began to spread to the point where other similar confraternities were formed in Spain; even such notables as King Philip III of Spain and his wife, Queen Margaret, became members. Confraternities whose members practiced a consecration to Mary were approved by the papal office beginning in 1616. In 1631, Urban VIII recognized an offshoot of the Spanish confraternities that took root in Belgium soil. Similar ideas and practices also spread throughout Poland, Italy, and all of Catholic Europe.[227] Before this practice was further developed and refined by St. Louis de Montfort, it had been approved "by numerous popes and was being spread by many religious communities, including the Jesuits, Benedictines, Mercedarians, Trinitarians, Franciscans, Augustinians, Oratorians, Sulpicians, Theatines, and Dominicans. At times, some of the members of the various confraternities did go to an excess, insisting solely upon external signs of this devotion, and these abuses were condemned by Rome. Never, however, was the devotion itself condemned."[228] The abuses condemned by the papal office usually consisted of practices that enforced the wearing of what was called "little chains" as external signs of slavery to Mary.

This brings us back to our discussion of the specifically Bérullian expression of the Marian consecration movement made popular through the spread of the Spanish confraternities. Certainly one of the issues at stake in the Bérullian expression of consecration to Mary as her slave, as stated in the above formula, is the idea of giving oneself to Mary without specifically mentioning giving oneself also to Jesus. When Bérulle's formula of consecration to Mary was originally made public, there was consequently much debate and even attempts to censure his thinking and proposed practices in this regard. The concern was that giving oneself to Mary, alone, as a slave was to turn her into a goddess and to attribute to her attributes that belong to the Creator alone, since it is to God alone that we must become enslaved. In response to these criticisms, Bérulle responded in a treatise entitled, "Oblation to Jesus in a State of Servitude," that "to honor the oblation and gift of Himself that Christ gave to the Father, but also to honor the oblation of the Virgin to God at the moment of the Incarnation as well as the oblation she made a little later of this very same Son to God in His temple" was the sole aim of the consecration of himself and his Oratorians as a slave of the Blessed Virgin Mother of God.[229]

Bérulle was exonerated. With responses such as these to the criticisms leveled against him, it has long ago been concluded that Bérulle's specific line in the vast Marian consecration movement—itself an important strain within that larger Marian Movement to which we previously referred—not only retained but also beautifully expressed his own Christocentric view of reality. Furthermore, the vow of consecration to Mary is indicative of the Bérullian French School's insistence that Christology is never complete without Mariology.

For Bérulle and his disciples, the central Mariological principle is clearly the Blessed Virgin's Motherhood of Jesus. This is not only because of the event of the Incarnation itself but also because Bérulle viewed Mary's relationship with Jesus and Jesus' relationship with Mary as "emanating from the eternal inclination of the Father towards the Son, of the Son towards the Father."[230] Consequently, Bérulle believed that the servitude of love that existed in the Son toward the Father was expressed in the Son's loving servitude toward His Mother, with Mary's own soul participating in this same state of servitude from the moment of the Incarnation.[231] Thus, the reason for taking a vow of servitude to Mary and not just to Jesus is that "the varied states in which the soul in servitude to Mary finds itself correspond to the varied states of the soul of Mary herself."[232] In other words, in servitude to Mary the soul desiring perfection is greatly assisted in its own Christ-conformation because it actually comes to reflect the various states of Mary's own soul—states which arise from her incomparable union with the Son in His own relationship with the Father.

With the above in mind, it becomes easier to understand why it can be said that for the Bérulle French School consecration to Mary is none other than the intensification of our Baptismal covenant. Consecration to Mary is both the way to maximize by a formal act all that was intended at the time of our Baptism as well as the optimal means for becoming perfectly conformed to Jesus Christ.[233] It was this Bérullian belief that shaped so much of the thought of St. Louis de Montfort during his seminary days at

Saint Sulpice. And, more importantly, it was daily living into the practice of Marian consecration and experiencing its very real fruits in himself, over time, that fueled Montfort's contributions not only to the thought of Bérulle but also to that ongoing effort originating with Sts. Justin Martyr and Irenaeus that remains ours today—accurately articulating the divinely ordained role of the Blessed Virgin Mary in the work of Redemption.

NOTES

[141] St. Louis Marie de Montfort, *God Alone : The Collected Writings of St. Louis Marie de Montfort*, trans. team (Bay Shore, NY: Montfort Publications, 1987) xxii.

[142] Hilda Graef, *Mary: A History of Doctrine and Devotion*, vol. II (New York: Sheed and Ward, 1965) 9.

[143] Graef 10.

[144] Graef 11.

[145] Graef 12.

[146] Graef12–3.

[147] Eamon Duffy, *The Stripping of the Altars: Traditional Religion in England 1400–1580* (New Haven: Yale University Press, 1992) 256–65.

[148] Judith A. Bauer, ed., *The Essential Mary Handbook* (Liguori, MO: Liguori Publications, 1999) 250.

[149] René Laurentin, *A Short Treatise on the Blessed Virgin Mary*, trans. Charles Neuman, S.M. (Washington, NJ: AMI Press, 1991) 127.

[150] Laurentin 127–8.

[151] Laurentin 126.

[152] Graef 21.

[153] Graef 22.

[154] Graef 23.

[155] Graef 23.

[156] Graef 24.

[157] Graef 24.

[158] Lawrence J. Riley, S.T.D., "Historical Conspectus of the Doctrine," *Marian Studies* 2 (1951): 57.

[159] Reginald Garrigou-Lagrange, O.P., *The Mother of the Saviour and our Interior Life*, trans. Bernard J. Kelly, C.S.Sp. (Rockford, IL: Tan Books, 1993) 179.

160 Lagrange 177.

161 Lagrange 179.

162 Lagrange 179.

163 Lagrange 180.

164 Lagrange 180.

165 Lagrange 180.

166 Lagrange 180–1.

167 Lagrange 182. In his encyclical, *Ad Diem Illum*, Feb. 2, 1904, Pope St. Pius X tells us that since Mary surpasses all creatures in her holiness and union with Christ, and since she has been associated by Him with the work of salvation, she has merited for us *de congruo* all that Christ has merited for us *de condigno*. Thus she is the principal minister in the distribution of graces.

168 Lagrange 181.

169 This does not mean that this period was the first in which Mary's Immaculate Conception was spoken of. As mentioned earlier, I have chosen not to deal with the details of the development of this doctrine in this book both because of the limits of space and because it was not specifically defined as a dogma at the time of Montfort's writing. However, the truth which this dogma conveys, namely the sinlessness of the Blessed Virgin from the moment of her conception, did play an important part in the thinking of St. Louis de Montfort, as we shall yet see. In addition, its truth that Mary was conceived without original sin also offers us another rich vein in which we might pursue her comparison to the first Eve, who was created by God without original sin.

170 Riley 57.

171 Riley 57.

172 Riley 58.

173 Riley 68.

174 J.B. Carol, O.F.M., "Our Lady's Part in the Redemption according to Seventeenth-Century Writers," *Franciscan Studies* ns 3.1 (1943): 10.

175 Graef 43.

176 Graef 43.

177 Riley 65. In the *Mariale* of St. Lawrence of Brindisi (d. 1619), we even hear the following: "The spirit of Mary was a spiritual priest, as the cross was the altar and Christ the sacrifice; although the spirit of Christ was the principal priest, the spirit of Mary was there together with the spirit of Christ; indeed it was one spirit with Him as one soul in two bodies. Hence the spirit of Mary together with the spirit of Christ performed the priestly office at the altar of the cross and offered the sacrifice of the cross for the salvation of the world to the Eternal God. . . . For of her, as of God to

Whom she was most similar in spirit, we can truly say that she so loved the world as to give her only-begotten Son so that everyone who believes in Him will not perish, but will have eternal life."

[178] Carol 143.

[179] Carol 143–6.

[180] Riley 71–2.

[181] Carol 145. Carol says the above exaggeration can be found in Thomas Leroy, O.P., *Le culte de la B. Vierge Marie, défendu contre un donneur d'Avis anonyme par le R. P. F. Jérôme Henneguier* (St. Omer: 1674) 77.

[182] Carol 144.

[183] Carol 144.

[184] See Riley 72–4 and Carol 147–56 for a discussion of the various responses to Widenfield's *Monita*.

[185] George Rigault, *Saint Louis de Montfort His Life and Work*, trans. Montfort Fathers (Port Jefferson, NY: Montfort Fathers, 1947) 18–34.

[186] Rigault 25.

[187] Raymond Deville, *The French School of Spirituality*, trans. Agnes Cunningham, SSCM (Pittsburgh: Duquesne U Press,1994) 2; 9–10. In quoting and siding with Andre Ragez's view of the state of French spirituality in the 17th century as discussed in his *Dictionannaire de Spiritualité*, Deville makes the point that the term 17th century French School, which is often used in referring to the thought of Cardinal Bérulle and his principal disciples, is in reality a misnomer and misleading. In actuality, 17th century France was a time when many schools of spiritual thought flourished and not merely that developed by Bérulle and his followers. Not only did the ancient traditions of the Benedictines, Carthusians, Cistercians, Augustinians, Franciscans, Dominicans and others thrive during this century in France, but there are other distinctive schools which took shape. For example, the 17th century is often considered to be the golden age of Capuchin spirituality. In addition the Ignatian school "took shape in a manner all its own, with members of outstanding worth." The Salesian tradition grew rapidly and the works of the Carmelite reformers caught the minds and hearts of many. Thus, the more correct term to be used when referring specifically to that train of thought developed by Bérulle and his followers is the Bérulle School.

[188] Graef 57.

[189] F. L. Cross and E. A. Livingstone, ed., *The Oxford Dictionary of the Christian Church*, 2nd ed. (Oxford: Oxford U Press, 1985) 163.

[190] Graef 31.

[191] DeVille 32–4.

[192] DeVille 34.

[193] De Ville 39 -42. With the encouragement of St. Francis de Sales, Bérulle eventually launched the French version of the Oratory of St. Philip Neri in 1611. The aim of this movement was to renew "the state of perfection among the clergy . . . without separation from its ecclesiastical body." While Oratorians desire to lead a common life, they remain diocesan priests in every way.

[194] Cross163 and DeVille 34–6.

[195] DeVille 36–7.

[196] DeVille 37.

[197] DeVille 38.

[198] DeVille 38.

[199] Cross164.

[200] DeVille 38.

[201] William M. Thompson, ed., *Bérulle and the French School*, trans. Lowell M. Glendon, S.S. (Mahwah: Paulist Press, 1989)159 -71.

[202] O'Connor, Edward D., C.S.C., *The Catholic Vision* (Huntington, IN: OSV Publishing Div., 1992) 228–30.

[203] Riley 66.

[204] Thompson 133. In the first part of Bérulle's *Discourse on the State and Grandeurs of Jesus*, we encounter a further explanation of the Blessed Virgin's fruitfulness as a participation in the divine fruitfulness, specifically as regards her relationship with the Holy Spirit-another insight which Montfort continues. Bérulle states that the Holy Spirit "does not exercise His fertility within Himself but rather outside Himself, . . . not in eternity but in the fullness of time. For He impregnates the blessed womb of the most holy Virgin with His fecundity. He produces a God-Man and gives a new birth to the eternal Word within human nature. He produces nothing within Himself, but happily and blessedly He produces outside Himself this divine mystery of the Incarnation. . . ."

[205] Cross 998; 479.

[206] Cross 998.

[207] DeVille 76–7.

[208] DeVille 93.

[209] Thompson 271.

[210] Riley 66.

[211] DeVille 105–7.

[212] DeVille 112–4.

[213] DeVille 114–5.

[214] William G. Bilton, Ph.D., "St. John Eudes Apostle of the Sacred Hearts of Jesus and Mary," *Queen of All Hearts* Mar.- Apr. 1997:13.

[215] DeVille 116.

[216] See DeVille 129 -33 for a detailed excerpt from *The Admirable Heart of the Most Holy Mother of God*.

[217] Bilton 14.

[218] Thompson 54.

[219] Bilton 15.

[220] Graef 34.

[221] Graef 33.

[222] Patrick J. Gaffney, S.M.M. "The Holy Slavery of Love," *Mariology*, ed. Juniper B. Carol, vol. 3 (Milwaukee: Bruce Publishing Co., 1961)144.

[223] Gaffney144–5. See the footnotes on these pages of Gaffney's article for references to the specific works in which this title is found.

[224] Gaffney 145.

[225] Gaffney 146.

[226] René Laurentin, *The Meaning of Consecration Today*, trans. Kenneth D. Whitehead (San Francisco: Ignatius Press, 1992) 49.

[227] Gaffney 146–9.

[228] Gaffney 149.

[229] Laurentin 50.

[230] Thompson 48.

[231] Thompson 48–9. Thompson notes that in this belief Bérulle follows the lead of Dionysius the Areopagite. "There is a Christological and Mariological hierarchy . . . and the latter precedes the former, at least temporally."

[232] Thompson 49.

[233] Laurentin 51.

CHAPTER 3

Seeking and Being Sought
by Eternal Wisdom through Mary

Montfort's Passionate Love for Jesus Christ

Having discussed the broader theological and Mariological currents which formed both the mind and the heart of St. Louis Marie de Montfort, it is now time to focus specifically on the writings of this Saint with our specific purpose in mind. Namely, we will be searching the Marian writings of Montfort to see what aid he can offer in our task of understanding the Marian thread of sacred tradition that we have traced from Sts. Justin and Irenaeus to Montfort. We will be paying particular attention as to how Montfort's insights make more explicit all that is implicit in the patristic teaching that the Blessed Virgin Mary is the Second Eve.

Before delving into the content of his Marian writings, it is important to situate St. Louis Marie's insights about the Blessed Virgin within the larger context of his overall theological orientation and personal spirituality. As we examine these, we will discover that, true to the Bérullian French School which formed him at the seminary of St. Sulpice, he is entirely focused on Jesus Christ from beginning to end.

Perhaps the best way of getting in touch with the Christological zeal that not only characterized the personal spirituality of this canonized saint but also fueled his Marian thought is to recall an episode from the earliest days of his priestly formation, which in many ways epitomizes Montfort. This formative event not only typifies the ministry of one who has been called "the people's preacher" and "the apostle of the peasants of the West"[234] but also speaks volumes about his passionate love for Jesus Christ and the depth of his desire to be united with Him through imitating His interior dispositions. This event is significant because the more one studies Montfort, the more one sees that it is his very desire to be united with Christ, in all aspects of His life, that the Holy Spirit used to enable him to grasp the importance of the woman through whom the Son became incarnate. The following emblematic event took place on a highway in the Brittany of his day as he walked from his family home in Montfort-la-Cane, known today as Montfort-sur-Mer, to Paris in order to begin his seminary education at St. Sulpice in 1693

When it had become time for Montfort to begin his studies for the priesthood, a lady of the parish of St. Sulpice in Paris known as Mlle de Montigny, an acquaintance of the Grignions for business purposes, generously offered to pay for Louis Marie's board at the seminary. While Louis Marie's parents were people of modest means, his father had furnished this 20-year-old seminarian with one fine suit on his back, a second in a valise, and ten crowns. His father and brother set him on the road to Paris, accompanying him as far as "Cesson bridge," and left him to travel the rest of the way to Paris alone. As soon as they left him, he gave his new coat to the first beggar he met, his crowns and extra suit to the next, and exchanged clothes with the third. Upon donning the beggar's rags, he knelt down on the ground and made a vow to God never to possess anything and to be completely dependent upon Divine Providence. As he continued on his journey, he begged his bread and his night's lodging. While the dogs barked at him and the people of the towns he passed through ridiculed him, this young saint in-the-making considered himself deliriously happy. He had now become one of the poor of Jesus and had begun to know the immense joy of being one with Christ in His own poverty.[235]

There is considerable irony in this paradigmatic event of Montfort's life. When he arrived in Paris, it is recorded that he looked like a tramp. He was wearing patched breeches, a ragged jacket, and a shapeless hat upon his head. He carried a stick in his hand and a knapsack on his back; he smelled like the stable that had provided his lodging the night before. It is also recorded that Mlle de Montigny was horrified! She was expecting the son of a country gentleman who had been properly educated by the Jesuits.[236]

In 1684, Louis Marie had been sent by his parents to Rennes to attend the Jesuit College of St. Thomas á Becket, a very successful school with approximately 3,000 students in attendance. The program at St. Thomas went from first year up to the beginning of theology, including the study of Latin and Greek. The records show that in his eight years with the Jesuits Montfort studied classical humanities, philosophy, and even theology. He had even apparently received various awards at the end of his last year of training with the Jesuits at Rennes.[237] While the young Louis Marie did not bear an outer resemblance to the ideal Jesuit pupil that Mlle Montigny and others might have imagined, especially considering both the school's and Montfort's successful academic reputation, the irony is that his official entry into apostolic life cannot help but remind one of the seemingly foolish love for Jesus Christ exhibited in a series of similar events in the life of St. Ignatius of Loyola.[238]

Even though Montfort is most definitely counted today among the disciples of the Bérullian French school, we cannot help but see in Louis Marie's desire to imitate Jesus Christ in His poverty and total dependence upon His Father a foundational current in Ignatian spirituality, specifically as regards the spirituality of *The Spiritual Exercises*.[239] While a desire for union with Christ especially through imitation of Him in His various interior states of poverty is indeed key in the thought of Bérulle and his disciples, we would be remiss if we failed to note the great possibility of this desire's having been originally planted in Montfort by the Jesuits, who greatly influenced his life at the College of St. Thomas á Becket in Rennes, long before he had ever arrived at St. Sulpice. This possibility seems all the more likely when we remember that the event narrated above preceded Louis Marie's spiritual and theological formation in the thought of Bérulle, Olier, and Eudes. As we have already seen, Bérulle as well as many of his other disciples were also educated or influenced by Jesuits.

We do know for certain that one of the early Ignatian influences on Montfort was a priest known at St. Thomas College as Father Descartes, S.J. Not only was he an intellectual, a psychologist, and a mystic of sorts, but he was also the nephew of the great French philosopher, René Descartes. Fr. Descartes wrote a little treatise entitled, *The Palace of Divine Love*, and served as Montfort's spiritual director. It was said by one of Montfort's Jesuit biographers, Father Picot de Clorivière, S.J.,[240] that Fr. Descartes had "the grace of guiding souls to the utmost perfection."[241] The other significant source who undoubtedly also passed on to Montfort the ideals of Ignatian spirituality during his formation at the school of St. Thomas was Father Gilbert, S.J., a notable professor of rhetoric who "aspired to apostleship and martyrdom."[242]

Regardless of the extent to which the Jesuits at St. Thomas influenced Montfort, it is, nonetheless, in this ironic and paradigmatic event of his journey toward priesthood that we begin to catch a glimpse of his passion for union with the One he called Divine Wisdom or Eternal Wisdom Incarnate. It is also very important to note that many aspects of this seemingly foolish behavior in the eyes of polite society never left Montfort and characterized his apostolic ministry from beginning to end. In fact, the most enduring historical image of Montfort that remains with us is not very different from that offered by the event recounted above. His biographers generally describe him as a physically indefatigable vagabond preacher who carried a large rosary and an enormous stick surmounted by the cross as he journeyed on foot through town and countryside, totally dependent upon Divine Providence for food and lodging.

His powerful voice and ability to withstand insult, misunderstanding, and persecution out of love for the Cross of Christ enabled him to preach tirelessly and resolutely the tender love of Jesus and Mary to the common people of his day until his death on April 28, 1716 at the age of 43.[243] His zeal for preaching the Good News of the Incarnation of God in Jesus Christ was undoubtedly a God-given antidote for the theological pessimism that often characterized the common people of 17th and 18th century France whose faith had been ravaged by the errors of Jansenism.[244] While the span of his priestly ministry covered not quite sixteen years from his ordination on June 5, 1700, his missionary activity took him into almost two hundred parishes, travelling on foot.[245]

It is significant to note that while Montfort's continual practices of interior and exterior poverty enabled him to identify with the poor of Jesus who populated the towns and cities of France, his lifestyle was considered so extreme that it created distance between him and the superiors at St. Sulpice, both during and after his seminary days. Considering the poverty of his lifestyle to be severe, his ecclesiastical superiors often openly criticized him and failed to support his endeavors. They were ostensibly concerned that Montfort's penitential life style disconcerted many and thus could not serve as a realistic example to others.

In the midst of this criticism, itself an indication of the extent to which Montfort's life actually became an imitation of Christ, it is interesting to note that "the Jesuits never repudiated him, even at a time when the French clergy showed him hostility and persecution. [The Jesuits] welcomed him to their houses, supported him by their advice, helped him in his missions. His manners, his methods were very different from theirs; it would have seemed to them a strange and impossible thing to enroll him among their number. But they venerated his sanctity; they recognized in his teaching the Gospel itself, freed from all worldly and political alloy—eternal Catholicism, with all the wealth of its dogma, all the armory of its practice and its discipline."[246]

While I do not intend in the above discussion to overempha-
size the influence of Ignatian spirituality upon Montfort, it is
essential for our purposes to highlight the immense impact that
Montfort's desire to imitate Christ had upon his Mariological
writings. And, in this light at least, it is interesting to note the
importance of the *imitatio Christi* to the Jesuits who were his first
spiritual guides, as well as the enduring support of the Jesuits for
Montfort and his ministry. When we actually explore what Montfort tells us about the importance of our imitating Christ in His
dependence upon and submission to Mary, we will turn for theological support to one of the great contemporary sons of St.
Ignatius, Karl Rahner, S.J., whose theology of the redemptive
necessity of the *imitatio Christi* has been shaped by his experience
of *The Spiritual Exercises*. For, in the final analysis, it is Montfort's
intensely passionate desire to seek Jesus by imitating His own
relationship with the very woman through whom He sought us
that provides the fuel for all Montfort tells us about the Blessed
Virgin Mary.

Montfort's Christological Treatise
as Foundational for his Mariology

Montfort's ardent desire to seek and be found by Christ expressed
itself most specifically in a treatise whose primary focus was
Christological. While Montfort is probably best known to the
world for his two Mariological treatises, *The Secret of Mary* and
True Devotion to the Blessed Virgin, it has rightly been said that *The
Love of Eternal Wisdom* is "Montfort's principal book. It alone
presents a conspectus of his spirituality and in it we see the true
setting of his devotion to Mary and his devotion to the Cross."[247]
The Love of Eternal Wisdom was most probably written during the
years 1703 and 1704; it is thought to represent a series of confer-
ences given by Montfort at the seminary of the Holy Ghost
Fathers in Paris. Since it had been his hope that several of the
seminarians there would join him in his missionary work, it is

believed that he compiled this work to make a contribution towards their spiritual formation.[248]

Scholars who have looked closely at the original manuscript of *The Love of Eternal Wisdom* point out that it is unclear what the young Louis Marie meant by using the genitive case in his title, *L'Amour de la Sagesse Éternelle*. Did he intend this to have a subjective or an objective meaning? Did he intend this work to convey his understanding of the love offered by Eternal Wisdom to humanity or was he more concerned about developing in his readers a love for the divine Person of Eternal Wisdom?[249] A careful reading of the work easily demonstrates that a case can be made for Montfort's intending both meanings in his choice of the genitive case in the title. What seems most significant is what Montfort says at the end of the first chapter about his intention in writing this work:

> Starting with His very origin, we shall consider Wisdom in eternity, dwelling in His Father's bosom and object of His Father's love. Next we shall see Him in time, shining forth in the creation of the universe. Then we shall consider Him in the deep abasement of His Incarnation and His mortal life; and then we shall see Him glorious and triumphant in heaven. Finally we shall propose the means to acquire and keep Him. I leave to philosophers their useless philosophical arguments and to scientists the secrets of their worldly wisdom. Let us now speak to chosen souls seeking perfection of (*de*) True wisdom, Eternal Wisdom, Wisdom uncreated and incarnate.[250]

In this passage, Montfort gives us an outline of his reasons for seeking and acquiring union with Eternal Wisdom as well as his ardent desire for such union. In addition, the above excerpt clearly demonstrates that when Montfort used the term "Eternal

Wisdom" he meant specifically the Second Person of the Blessed Trinity.

After describing Wisdom's eternal excellence, goodness, and mercy in *The Love of Eternal Wisdom*, Montfort concludes by saying: "To possess Him we must seek ardently; in other words, we must be ready to give up everything, to suffer everything, in order to obtain possession of Him. Only a few find Him because only a few look for Him in a manner worthy of Him. . . . (W)e cannot but love Him and search for Him with all our strength."[251] Montfort goes on to elucidate Eternal Wisdom's great love for human persons and His earnest desire to give Himself to humankind by enduring the abasement of the Incarnation, as mentioned previously in the passage above:

> Finally, in order to draw closer to men and give them a more convincing proof of His love, Eternal Wisdom went so far as to become man, even to become a little child, to embrace poverty and to die upon a cross for them . . . and . . . in order fully to satisfy His love He instituted the sacrament of the Holy Eucharist and went to the extreme of changing and overturning nature itself. . . . He hides Himself under the appearance of a small piece of bread—man's ordinary nourishment—so that when received He might enter the heart of man and there take His delight. . . . Those who ardently love act in this way. 'O Eternal Wisdom,' says a saint, 'O God who is truly lavish with Himself in His desire to be with man!' "[252]

In these poignant words of chapter 6, we begin to hear the refrain of a theme that provides the Christological foundation for Montfort's sublime understanding of the Blessed Virgin Mary. Namely, it is none other than God the Son Who emptied Himself to become human in Jesus Christ. Here we also discover the biblical base for much of Montfort's Christological reflection, as well as much of his Mariological reflection. "Have this mind among yourselves, which is yours in Christ Jesus, who, though He was in the form of God, did not count equality with God a thing to be grasped, but emptied Himself, taking the form of a servant, being born in the likeness of men. And being found in human form He humbled Himself and became obedient unto death. . . ." (Phil. 2:5–11).

We have already noted previously the way in which the Bérullian French School as a whole emphasized the Self-emptying love of the Second Person of the Blessed Trinity. What is especially important to note about Montfort is his specific connection of the initial Self-emptying of Eternal Wisdom in His Incarnation with His death on the cross and His perpetual Self-offering to human persons in the Eucharist. These three are but different moments along the single unending continuum of Eternal Wisdom's *kenotic* love for humankind. Furthermore, as we shall see later, Montfort echoes Bérulle's view that all moments on this single continuum are already anticipated as well as humbly and obediently embraced by the Eternal Word in the sacred moment of His Incarnation in the womb of the Blessed Virgin, thus making the act of the Incarnation itself redemptive.

In Montfort's highlighting this redemptive continuum, we begin to see that his thought is squarely in line with St. Irenaeus and those after him who believe that we cannot separate the redemptive benefits to humankind accomplished by Jesus Christ in His sacrificial death on the cross from the Self-sacrifice of his having become flesh in the first place, through the Virgin Mary, the Second Eve. Furthermore, Montfort's connection of these three sacred moments helps us see that the Eucharist not only proclaims the death of Jesus until He comes again, as St. Paul tells us in 1Cor. 11:26, but also perpetuates God the Son's Incarnation among us and for us. Montfort's connection of these three aspects of God's Self-emptying act of love for human persons in Jesus Christ also provides his foundation for the premise that the

Blessed Virgin is indispensably involved in all that the Incarnation anticipates and thereby includes.

It is in the chapter that focuses specifically on the mystery of the Incarnation of Eternal Wisdom that we see what St. Louis Marie says in this Christological writing about the unique dignity of the Blessed Virgin Mary:

> At last, when the time appointed for the redemption of mankind had come, Eternal Wisdom built Himself a house worthy to be His dwelling place. He created the most holy Virgin, forming her in the womb of St. Anne with even greater delight than He had derived from creating the universe. It is impossible on the one hand to put into words the gifts with which the Blessed Trinity endowed this most fair creature, or on the other hand to describe the faithful care with which she corresponded to the graces of the Creator.
>
> The torrential outpouring of God's infinite goodness which had been rudely stemmed by the sins of men since the beginning of the world, was now released precipitately and in full flood into the heart of Mary. Eternal Wisdom gave to her all the graces which Adam and all his descendents would have received so liberally from Him had they remained in their original state of justice. The fullness of God, says a saint, was poured into Mary, insofar as a mere creature is capable of receiving it. O Mary, masterpiece of the Most High, miracle of Eternal Wisdom, prodigy of the Almighty, abyss of grace!
>
> I join all the saints in the belief that only the God who created you knows the height, the breadth and the depth of the grace He has conferred on you.[253]

After speaking of Mary's uniquely graced creation, Montfort goes on to describe her cooperation with the many graces poured upon her, a cooperation which prepared her for her unique participation in the Incarnation:

> During the first fourteen years of her life the most holy Virgin Mary grew so marvelously in the grace and wisdom of God and responded so faithfully to His love that the angels and even God Himself were filled with rapturous admiration for her. Her humility, deep as an abyss, delighted Him. Her purity so other-worldly drew Him down to her. He found her lively faith and her ceaseless entreaties of love so irresistible that He was lovingly conquered by her appeals of love. "So great was the love of Mary," explains St. Augustine, "that it conquered the omnipotent God"— *O quantus amor illius qui vincit omnipotentem.*

> Wondrous to relate, this divine Wisdom chose to leave the bosom of the Father and enter the womb of a virgin and there repose amid the lilies of her purity. Desiring to give Himself to her by becoming man in her, He sent the archangel Gabriel to greet her on His behalf and to declare to her that she had won His heart and that He would become man within her if she gave her consent. The archangel fulfilled his mission and assured her that she would still remain a virgin while becoming a mother. Notwithstanding her desire to be lowly, Mary wholeheartedly gave the angel that priceless consent which the Blessed Trinity, all the angels and the whole world awaited for so many centuries. Humbling herself before her Creator she said, "Behold the handmaid of the

Lord! Let it be done to me according to your word."

Notice that at the very moment Mary consented to become the Mother of God, several
miraculous events took place. The Holy Spirit
formed from the most pure blood of Mary's heart a
little body which He fashioned into a perfect living being: God created the most perfect soul that
ever could be created. Eternal Wisdom, the Son of
God, drew the body and soul into union with His
Person.[254]

Let us particularly note in the above passage that Montfort
emphasizes Eternal Wisdom's choice to create Mary in such a way
that the Holy Spirit could fashion God's own "body" from Mary.
Indeed, His most sacred Blood by which we are redeemed is
"formed from the most pure blood of Mary's heart." It is none
other than her flesh and blood that provide the incarnational
substance for the Holy Face of the invisible God (Col.1:15).
Here, Montfort concurs with the Fathers in claiming that Mary is
no mere passive vessel or conduit through whom God the Son
merely passes on His way to earth in the Incarnation.

Furthermore, Montfort tells us that the Blessed Virgin was
created such that she would be worthy for God actually to live in
her. She had to be the most magnificent being ever created by
God. She may be compared to a most sacred temple. She both
provides His incarnational substance and has become Eternal
Wisdom's "dwelling-place." In order to make her worthy to be
this sacred dwelling place, the Trinity poured into her the very
fullness of God, i.e., uncreated grace, to the greatest extent that
a creature can receive this. However, as great as this outpouring
of grace was on the Trinity's part, it is essential to note that
Mary's consent was required in response to this gift of God's own
inner life. Without this consent, she could not have become

God's holy of holies; nor could she have provided Eternal Wisdom with His body. As recorded in Luke 1:28, Montfort tells us
that Mary freely chose to cooperate perfectly and corresponded to
the request God put before her through the angel in the Annunciation. Montfort also affirms that Mary had chosen to live her
life in such a way that she always remained "full of grace"
throughout her life, i.e., in all moments prior to the moment of
the Annunciation itself. Because of her willing and perfect cooperation with the magnificent grace given her throughout her life,
the King desired the beauty of her charity and humility for Himself, *et homo factus est.*

This is a key insight for our particular quest. While all that
Mary is in herself was God's gift to her from the beginning, she
still had to choose to correspond to the profound graces given her
on a daily basis in order for God's desires for her to be fulfilled.
While Mary was profoundly and uniquely graced by God, such
grace did not in any way degrade or lessen the importance of her
free will. She was as free to choose to live in union with God and
the divine Will as were Adam and Eve.

By saying that Mary was as free as Adam and Eve to choose
faithful obedience to God, we mean that her freedom was not in
any way enslaved like ours by the wounding of original sin commonly called concupiscence, i.e., by the lust of the eyes, the lust
of the flesh, and the lust for holding first place.[255] When we truly
understand the importance of God's ensuring that Mary really had
such freedom, we can see the necessity of the preservative
Redemption given to her as the Second Eve in the grace of the
Immaculate Conception with a whole new light. In other words,
God saw to it that neither the unforgiven guilt nor the unruly
effects of original sin on the human appetites would in any way
hinder Mary in being truly free to choose for or against God. As
Catholic teaching affirms, this unique grace was made possible
only in anticipation of the salvation made possible by Jesus Christ.
In giving this grace to Mary, God really and truly signified a fresh
start for the human race. Since she is truly the new Eve both cre-

ated and redeemed by God, the Blessed Virgin Mary's *fiat* was capable of having a truly "recapitulating" or "re-heading" significance for the entire human race, in union with and in subordination to the divine *Fiat* of Jesus Christ. Furthermore, we can even say that it is precisely because God had uniquely graced Mary to be Eve's equal in the real freedom to choose for God—and against Satan—that Mary's *fiat* was such a "priceless consent."

Furthermore, since God Himself had set Mary's freedom free from original sin's disordering effects, as well as giving her a share in His own inner life that enabled her to love and trust Him, Mary was all the more capable of giving an authentic and full human consent. If His grace had reduced the significance or need for her human consent in any way, then the very humanity God the Son assumed from her would not have been a real humanity and Redemption could not have happened. Because grace made Mary so *fully* and perfectly human, her consent mattered all the more for the entire human race. Her full and perfect humanity made it possible for God the Son to receive a *fully* human nature from her, by the Power of the Holy Spirit.[256]

By viewing Mary's consent in this light, we can see that the presence of grace in the human person actually perfects human freedom and renders our choices for or against God all the more efficacious and consequential—as in the parallel cases of both Eve and Mary. Just as Adam and Eve's perfectly free choice against God was capable of bringing with it the profound consequences of sin as enumerated in Gen. 3:16–24, so was Mary's perfectly free choice for God capable of bringing with it the profound consequence of the Incarnation of God the Son. Whatever else can be said about Mary's role in Redemption, the role of her free consent is certainly the foundational building block.

In addition, a proper understanding of the dynamic of grace and human freedom as it exists perfectly in Mary is a reminder that the Reformation notion of *sola gratia* must be complemented by the Catholic understanding that the human recipient must willingly receive and correspond to grace—a human cooperation that is itself under the influence of grace but a willing surrender nonetheless. Furthermore, to the degree that such correspondence occurs, God's gift of grace becomes part of the human person in the sense that grace truly purifies and sanctifies the human person, over time. For ourselves, who are not given the grace of a preservative Redemption in an immaculate conception, this means that our continuous surrender and correspondence to grace through our own *fiats* will gradually cleanse us from the effects of original sin, over time, setting us free to trust and love God as heroically as Mary—which is what it means to be *fully* human.

Fr. Garrigou-Lagrange speaks well of this paradoxical mystery of freedom and grace as it applies to the Blessed Virgin's *fiat* in *The Mother of the Saviour and our Interior Life* :

> It may be objected that a divine decree such as that of the Incarnation could not depend on the consent of a creature who was free not to give it. To this, theology answers that God has efficaciously willed and infallibly foreseen everything that will happen in the course of time. Therefore, He willed efficaciously and foresaw infallibly Mary's consent to the realization of the mystery of the Incarnation. From all eternity God, Who works with strength and gentleness, decided to give Mary the efficacious grace which would move her to consent freely and meritoriously. Just as He makes the trees to bear their blossoms, so He makes our wills to produce their free acts; and far from doing them any violence He is the author of their freedom, for that too is a reality, a form of being. The 'how' of all this is the secret of God Omnipotent. Just as Mary conceived the Saviour by the operation of the Holy Ghost without losing her virginity, so she uttered her *fiat* infallibly

under the motion of efficacious grace without prejudice to her complete liberty—rather did her will, under the divine motion, flower spontaneously into the free consent she gave in the name of all mankind.[257]

There is more that can be gleaned from Montfort's view of Mary in the passage from *The Love of Eternal Wisdom* quoted above. Montfort also begins to give us a glimpse of how Mary, while undoubtedly a creature and merely a human person, has been indeed set apart by God from the beginning for a unique role among all her peers when "the time appointed for the redemption of mankind had come." Because this woman whom Montfort calls the "masterpiece of the Most High" is the first and only human person created and perfectly graced by God since Adam and Eve's fall, God has placed her above all the prophets and saints of the Old Testament. She is even above Abraham whom St. Paul tells us is the father of us all because God Himself made Abraham the "father of many nations" (Rom. 4:16–17).

While the Blessed Virgin's total reliance upon God's promises makes her a true daughter of Abraham, whose faith was "reckoned to him as righteousness" (Rom. 4:22), we must also claim that God has intervened in history in an entirely *new* way in the person of Mary by giving her this "full flood" of His own goodness. And, because this particular woman so perfectly receives and corresponds to this intervention on God's part, God freely chooses to incarnate His own Person through, with, and in her for the rest of us, by the Power of the Holy Spirit. "Do not imagine," Montfort writes elsewhere, "there is more joy in dwelling in Abraham's bosom than in Mary's, for it is in her that our Lord placed His throne."[258] Certainly, this profound realization, coupled with all that we have seen above, enables us to begin speaking of Mary as the instrumental cause[259] of the redeeming Self-Gift of God, for us and to us, in the Incarnation.

Montfort's Orthodox Christology

It is key to note in the passage quoted above from *The Love of Eternal Wisdom* that Montfort clearly presumes an orthodox Chalcedonian Christology as the basis for his Marian thought. "The Holy Spirit formed from the most pure blood of Mary's heart a little body which He fashioned into a perfect living being: God created the most perfect soul that ever could be created. Eternal Wisdom, the Son of God, drew the body and soul into union with His Person. . . . Eternal Wisdom became incarnate. God became man without ceasing to be God."[260] It is none other than the presuppositions of Chalcedonian Christology that give Montfort's Mariological treatises their great ring of truth. He clearly understands and emphasizes the contrasting difference between the uncreated Son, Incarnate Wisdom, and the mere human being and creature, the Blessed Virgin Mary, even with all her magnificence.

In other words, Montfort helps distinguish the fact that in Mary we discover not only a human nature but also a human person, i.e., a human being, a human personal subject. As a human being, Mary must receive the fullness of grace necessary for her own redemption and perfection entirely from the Trinity, who is by nature totally other from her. Montfort is clear that there is an infinite contrast between the human being, Mary, and the Lord Jesus Christ, Eternal Wisdom Incarnate. For He alone *is* divine whom we "confess one and the same Son, our Lord Jesus Christ, the same perfect in divinity and perfect in humanity, the same truly God and truly man composed of rational soul and body, the same one in being *(homoousios)* with the Father as to the divinity and one in being with us as to the humanity, like unto us in all things but sin. The same was begotten from the Father before the ages as to the divinity and in the latter days for us and for our salvation was born as to His humanity from Mary the Virgin Mother of God."[261]

In contemporary language, the Chalcedonian definition means that the divine Son is the only personal subject who experiences all the acts of the Incarnation.[262] The divine Son, also called the

Word or *Logos*, "lives by choice within the human material conditions of incarnated life."[263] Both the deity and the humanity subsist "perfectly intact, but not in any parallel association, rather in a dynamic interpenetration and mutuality that effected new conditions and possibilities by virtue of that intimate union."[264]

As we mentioned in our introduction, St. Cyril of Alexandria was a great defender of orthodox Christology. He insisted that "the Word of God, deity in all its fullness, united with a human existence. The Word did not unite with a man but with a humanity."[265] Concretely, this means that in Jesus Christ, we do not have a human person (Jesus, the Jewish rabbi from Nazareth) alongside a divine Person (the Eternal Word of God). St. Cyril instructed us to think of the humanity of our Lord and Savior Jesus Christ as the Incarnate Word's way of being, a manner of expressing His divine Identity in and through the material circumstances of bodily life.[266] The Personal Subject of the Incarnate Son is divine and can never be reduced to mere humanity or bodily life, yet He elected to express Himself through a real humanity and in a bodily manner. "As a result even the bodily life became a direct vehicle of the revelation of the divine."[267] Sadly, this primary and essential aspect of Catholic Christological Truth is often misunderstood, diluted, or even completely neglected.

However, Montfort constantly shows himself to be in full agreement with St. Cyril's definitive teaching that the Incarnate Son is *homoousios* with the Father from all eternity and that He remains so in the Incarnation. Because His divine nature cannot be added to or subtracted from in the Incarnation, both Cyril and Montfort see "the eternal God directly experiencing suffering and death insofar as like other men He too is brought under the terms of the human lifeform."[268] This dynamic interchange of properties without changing the distinct realities of either the divine or human nature is experienced by one personal subject who *is* God. This profound mystery is exactly the eternal Truth affirmed by both Montfort and Cyril in saying that Mary is the Mother of God and not simply the Mother of her Son's human nature.[269]

As splendid as Mary is as the Mother of God, Montfort always attributes this to her having received "the torrential outpouring of God's infinite goodness which had been rudely stemmed by the sins of men since the beginning of the world."[270] This means that the sinlessness of Mary's human soul was due to the profound grace of a creature's being given a preservative Redemption at the moment of her conception, as we have already discussed. In sharp contrast, St. Thomas tells us that the sinlessness of Christ's human nature was a result of His human soul's having been hypostatically united to the Second Person of the Blessed Trinity, the Eternal Word of God, from the first moment of His conception in the womb of Mary.[271]

This proper contrasting difference between Jesus Christ, the Incarnate Son Who *is* co-eternal and consubstantial with the Father, and the Blessed Virgin Mary, the created human being who receives both being and a preservative redemption from God, is key in our quest to understand much of what Montfort tells us. For, as magnificent as Mary herself and her role in Redemption might be, we must be constantly vigilant about maintaining the infinite difference between Jesus Christ and Mary. Paradoxically, it is only when we truly maintain this difference between the Lord Jesus Christ and the Blessed Virgin Mary that we can truly appreciate the splendid and magnificent nature of Mary's divinely ordained role in Redemption. Furthermore, it is this very real difference between Jesus Christ and Mary that allows the true splendor of what God has done in the Blessed Virgin to be revealed, manifesting God's proper glory in both Jesus Christ and Mary.[272]

Montfort's Consideration of the Suffering of Christ

Before leaving our consideration of *The Love of Eternal Wisdom*, there is yet one last Christological theme that is worthy of our attention because of its foundational significance in understanding St. Louis Marie's view of the Blessed Virgin. It is his understanding of the redemptive suffering of the Lord Jesus Christ. Montfort tells us that "among all the motives impelling us to love Jesus Christ, the Wisdom Incarnate, the strongest, in my opinion, is the suffering He chose to endure to prove His love for us. . . . This dear friend of our souls suffered in every way exteriorly and inwardly, in body and soul. . . . His most holy soul was grievously tormented because every sin committed by man was an outrage committed against His Father whom He loved infinitely; because sin was the cause of the damnation of so many souls who would be lost despite His passion and death; and because He had compassion not only for all men in general but for each one in particular, as He knew them all individually. All these torments were much increased by the length of time they lasted, that is, from the first instance of His conception to the moment of His death, because all the sufferings He was to endure were, in the timeless view of His wisdom, always distinctly present to His mind. . . . According to the Fathers of the Church, . . . Jesus Christ, Eternal Wisdom, could have remained in His heavenly glory, infinitely distant from our misfortunes. But He chose on our account to come down upon earth, take the nature of man and be crucified. Even when He had become man He could have imparted to His body the same joy, the same immortality, the same blessedness which He now enjoys. But He did not choose this because He wanted to be free to suffer."[273]

We see here a further elaboration of something we noted above, namely, the inseparable connection between the Incarnation and the redemptive suffering of Jesus Christ in Montfort's thought. He tells us that from the very first instance of His conception Jesus Christ began suffering the outrage caused by human sin in His most holy soul, as a direct consequence of the Incarnation itself. What exactly does Montfort mean by this, especially in light of the contemporary approach to Jesus Christ's evolving human consciousness? The answer lies in Montfort's believing with Bérulle that the *interior states* of the human soul of the Incarnate Son were in a state of servitude to the divine Person of the

Word, even from the very first moment of the Incarnation as a consequence of the Hypostatic Union. It was this belief that undergirded the Bérulle French School's attention to the inner dispositions of the soul of Jesus Christ as discussed in chapter 2 above. In holding with St. Cyril that the humanity of Christ was the supreme revelation of divinity and could not be either bypassed or surpassed, Bérulle and his disciples emphasized that "Jesus' humanity is one of poverty, of subsisting not in itself but in the Word, of *dénuement* or self-emptying."[274]

With this in mind, it seems clear that the above mentioned passage from *The Love of Eternal Wisdom* is another expression of Montfort's Chalcedonian Christology—wherein the human and divine natures of Jesus Christ subsist in the divine Person of the Word. Montfort seems to be in full line with St. Cyril in making this Bérullian-type claim about the *interior state* of the human soul of Christ. Theologically speaking, he is able to make this claim because the "Person of the *Logos* is the sole personal subject of all the conditions of His existence, divine or human. The *Logos* is, needless to say, the sole personal subject of all His own acts as eternal Lord (the creation, the inspiration of the ancient prophets, and so on), but after the Incarnation, the same one is also the personal subject directing all His actions performed within this time and this space, embodied acts which form the context of the human life of Christ in Palestine."[275]

Therefore, it does seem theologically possible for us to say, with Montfort, that because a human soul was from the moment of conception hypostatically united to the Eternal Word, Jesus Christ was always fully present in His divine interiority to the redemptive consequences of the Incarnation, manifested in the very Self-emptying He was undergoing by virtue of His descent to become God-with-us. Thus, we should have little problem humbly and adoringly declaring with Montfort that this "excess of love You have shown us in (the actual moment of) suffering and dying"[276] is but the full outward manifestation of that divine

Love which suffered the consequences of sin for us from the moment of becoming flesh for our salvation.[277]

Montfort develops this theme by telling us that "Incarnate Wisdom loved the Cross from His infancy. At His coming into the world, while in His Mother's womb, He received it from His eternal Father. He placed it deep in His heart, there to dominate His life saying, 'My God and my Father, I chose this cross when I was in your bosom. I choose it now in the womb of my Mother. I love it with all my strength and I place it deep in my heart to be my spouse and my mistress.' . . . He espoused the cross at His Incarnation with indescribable love. He sought it out and carried it with the utmost joy, throughout His whole life, which became but one continuous cross. . . . At last His wishes were fully satisfied. Bearing a stigmata of shame He was attached to the cross, indissolubly joined to it and died joyfully upon it as if in the arms of a dear friend and upon a couch of honor and triumph."[278]

Montfort's elaboration on the Eternal Word's embrace of redemptive suffering in the *interior states* of His human soul, from the first moment of the Incarnation through His Death, is very significant for our understanding of Mary's role in Redemption. This is because the consequence of Mary's own consent at the Annunciation becomes clearer. Regardless of the extent to which the Blessed Virgin herself was personally aware of the full ramifications of her *fiat*, Montfort reminds us that the redemptive intent of the Incarnation—as indicated by the Eternal Word's suffering for sin from the moment of the Incarnation because of the Hypostatic Union—was fully present in the divine Mind of God the Son. Because of Mary's free act of loving consent offered to God in the obedience of faith, she *ipso facto* opened herself to participating in the full realm of meaning that only the divine intention could and would provide for her actions, in time and eternity.

Therefore, we can add another insight to our earlier consideration about the mystery of human freedom and grace as this operates in Mary. Only the divine can determine and actuate the full meaning of even the most perfect surrender of human freedom to God. However, we must also affirm once again the other side of this mystery. God freely chooses to wait upon, and in that sense depend upon, the creature, Mary, to give this free consent for the divine intention and meaning in Redemption to be fulfilled. Montfort helps us begin to see not only the humility of Mary in her total obedience of faith but also the adorable humility of God the Son. He not only undergoes the *kenosis* of uniting a human nature to Himself to redeem us but also unites the intent of Mary with all her creaturely limitations to His divine intent.

If one is searching for a defining moment in Mary's own life which can be pointed to as revealing that "here" we see her to be coredemptrix, or mediatrix, or auxilliatrix, or whatever term one chooses to use to describe her redemptive role, Montfort reminds us that it is God the Son Himself, who determines and provides the content, as it were, for all Mary's defining moments. He is always Mary's Creator and she is always content to be merely the creature. By considering the intentions of the Eternal Word at the moment of His "being found in human form," we can see more clearly that the moment of Mary's *fiat* is precisely where her self-conscious choice to unite herself with all that this Word is and intends to accomplish by His Incarnation, in her flesh, is exactly the moment she chooses to allow God to involve her in the work of Redemption itself.

At the moment of her *fiat*, she was saying yes to allowing God alone to determine and work out the details of all that her obedient consent would contribute and make possible. She didn't need to know the details. She trusted God completely in the obedience of faith. Such trust and obedience were exactly the *fully* human elements that God needed from her for Redemption to begin. And, yes, she would have to repeat this *fiat* again and again as she lived into the fullness of God's meaning, a meaning that asked for her *fiat* at least seven times according to sacred tradition,[279] in order to correspond to Simeon's prophecy that "a sword shall pierce through your own soul also" (Luke 2:35).

NOTES

[234] George Rigault, *Saint Louis de Montfort His Life and Work*, trans. Montfort Fathers (Port Jefferson, NY: Montfort Fathers, 1947) 19.

[235] Rigault 23.

[236] Rigault 23.

[237] Raymond Deville, *The French School of Spirituality*, trans. Agnes Cunningham, SSCM (Pittsburgh: Duquesne U Press, 1994) 190.

[238] *St. Ignatius' Own Story as Told to Luis González de Cámara*, trans. William J. Young, S.J. (Chicago: Loyola U Press, 1980)10–26. In the initial stages of his conversion, St. Ignatius sets out upon a journey in which he intends "to go to Jerusalem . . . undertaking all the disciplines and abstinences which a generous soul on fire with the love of God is wont to desire. . . . Thus, as the pilgrim mounted his mule, another of his brothers wished to accompany him as far as Onate. . . . Before reaching Montserrat he arrived at a large town where he bought the clothing he had made up his mind to wear when he went to Jerusalem. It was some sacking of a very loose weave and a rough prickly surface, and he at once gave orders for a long garment reaching to his feet to be made of it. He bought a pilgrim's staff and a small gourd and attached it all to the mule's saddle. He continued his way to Montserrat, thinking as usual of the great deed he was going to do for the love of God. . . . When he arrived at Montserrat . . . he arranged with the confessor to have the mule taken away. . . . On the eve, then, of our Lady's Annunciation, March 24th, at night, in the year of 1522, he went as secretly as possible to a poor man, and removing his fine clothes gave them to him and put on his desired attire. . . . At daybreak he left, and . . . came to a small town called Manresa. . . . Every day he begged alms in Manresa. He ate no meat, drank no wine, although both were offered him. . . . Because he had been quite delicate about caring for his hair . . . he made up his mind to neglect it and to let it grow wild, without combing or cutting it or covering it either day or night. For the same reason he allowed the nails of this hands and feet to grow. . . . (A)t the beginning of the year 1523 he left for Barcelona to take ship, and although several offered to accompany him, he preferred to travel by himself, since his whole purpose was to have God alone for refuge. . . ."

[239] David L. Fleming, S.J., *The Spiritual Exercises of St. Ignatius: A Literal Translation and A Contemporary Reading* (St. Louis, MO: The Institute of Jesuit Sources, 1978) 64–102. During what is referred to as the Second Week of making the Spiritual Exercises, the exercitant is counseled to ask

for the grace not to be deaf to the call of our Lord Jesus Christ but to be ready and diligent to fulfill His Most Holy Will. After meditating and praying over various events in the life of Christ in order "to know Jesus intimately, to love Him more intensely, and so to follow Him more closely," the exercitant is finally directed to meditate prayerfully on what is called by St. Ignatius the "Three Manners of Humility." The third and most perfect humility to be sought in imitation of Christ and for the praise and glory of the Divine Majesty is spoken of as follows by Fleming in his literal translation of *The Spiritual Exercises* : "to imitate and be more actually like Christ our Lord, I want and choose poverty with Christ poor rather than riches, opprobrium with Christ replete with it rather than honors; and to desire to be rated as worthless and a fool for Christ, Who first was held as such, rather than wise or prudent in this world."

[240] Rigault 22.

[241] Rigault 19.

[242] Rigault 20.

[243] Rigault 32–3 and *God Alone: The Collected Writings of St. Louis Marie de Montfort*, trans. team (Bay Shore, NY: Montfort Publications, 1987) xxii–iv.

[244] Karl Rahner and Herbert Vorgrimler, *Dictionary of Theology* 2nd ed. (New York: Crossroad, 1981) 249. Rahner and Vorgrimler define Jansenism as an erroneous tendency in doctrine and piety that was named after C. Jansen, Bishop of Ypres (d.1638). Although the faulty doctrine of grace that was at the heart of this error was condemned by the Church in 1653, it affected large parts of France, Belgium, Holland, Italy, and Germany in the 17th and 18th century. The heretical aspects of the Jansenist view of grace were as follows: "grace was due to Adam by right, the virtues of the pagans are only vices, mankind is enslaved to concupiscence and even the justified remain subject to it at least interiorly; sin is possible even without interior freedom of choice; Jesus died for the elect only and the mass of men are damned."

[245] Patrick J. Gaffney and Richard J. Payne., eds., *Jesus Living in Mary: Handbook of the Spirituality of St. Louis Marie de Montfort* (Bay Shore, NY: Montfort Publications,1994) 759.

[246] Rigault 20.

[247] St. Louis Marie de Montfort, "The Love of Eternal Wisdom," *God Alone: The Collected Writings of St. Louis Marie de Montfort*, trans. team (Bay Shore, NY: Montfort Publications, 1987) 47. While Montfort's authorship of LEW is sometimes contested, this thesis has not been proven.

[248] Montfort, "The Love of Eternal Wisdom" 47.

[249] Gaffney, et. al. 634.

[250] Montfort, "The Love of Eternal Wisdom" 54.

[251] Montfort, "The Love of Eternal Wisdom" 67.

[252] Montfort, "The Love of Eternal Wisdom" 68–9.

[253] Montfort, "The Love of Eternal Wisdom" 79.

[254] Montfort, "The Love of Eternal Wisdom" 79–80.

[255] See 1John 2:16 and St. Augustine, *Confessions*, trans. F.J. Sheed (Indianapolis: Hackett Publishing, 1992) 44.

[256] Bovey-Crowley, Father Mateo, *Refuting the Attack on Mary* , 2nd ed. (San Diego: Catholic Answers, 1999) 49. "Father Mateo" was the pen name of a Catholic priest who was an emeritus professor of New Testament Greek at a prominent university. He spent nearly fifty years of his priesthood promoting the faith, especially among young people. He hosted the "Ask Father" forum on the Catholic Information Network.

[257] Reginald Garrigou-Lagrange, O.P. *The Mother of the Saviour and our Interior Life*, trans. Bernard J. Kelly, C.S.Sp. (Rockford, IL: Tan Books, 1993) 156–9. Fr. Lagrange agrees with the Fathers in their view that Mary's consent to be the Mother of the Redeemer has made her the New Eve. As scripture records, Mary was made fully aware that He was to be the Savior or Messiah in the angel's announcement to her that her Son was to be called "Jesus." She would not have been ignorant of the Messianic prophesies, especially those of Isaiah which foretold the redemptive sufferings of the promised Savior. Thus, her yes committed and involved her in the Redemption *ipso facto*. While some have objected that we could speak of the parents of the BVM as being equally associated with the Redeemer in the work of Redemption, the difference is that Mary alone received the light from God through the message of the angel to give a knowing consent to being the Mother of the Savior. Because of this light, she knowingly involved herself in the work of Redemption through her consent. On the other hand, scripture does not record her parents, Sts. Anne and Joaquim, having been given the light to see that their child would be the Mother of the Messiah or the Son of the Most High.

[258] St. Louis Marie de Montfort, "True Devotion to Mary," *God Alone: The Collected Writings of St. Louis Marie de Montfort*, trans. team (Bay Shore, NY: Montfort Publications, 1987) 352. Montfort attributes this quote to Abbot Guerric. According to the footnote given for this quote in *God Alone*, the original quote can be found in Guerricus, *Serm. in Assumpt.*, No. 4.

[259] St. Thomas Aquinas, *Summa Contra Gentiles Book Three: Providence Part II*, trans. Vernon J. Bourke (London: Univ. of Notre Dame Press, 1975)

226. "Again, that divine help is provided man so that he may act well is to be understood in this way: it performs our works in us, as the primary cause performs the operations of secondary causes, and as a principal agent performs the action of an instrument. . . . Now the first cause causes the operation of the secondary cause according to the measure of the latter. So, God also causes our works in us in accord with our measure, which means that we act voluntarily and not as forced. Therefore, no one is forced to right action by the divine help."

[260] Montfort, "The Love of Eternal Wisdom" 80.

[261] Josef Neuner, S.J., and Jacques Dupuis, S.J., ed., *The Christian Faith in the Doctrinal Documents of the Catholic Church* (New York: Alba House, 1998) 203 (DS 301).

[262] John Anthony McGuckin, "A Synopsis of St. Cyril's Christological Doctrine," *St. Cyril of Alexandria: On the Unity of the Person of Christ*, trans. and intro. John Anthony McGuckin (Crestwood, NY: St. Vladimir's Press, 1995) 45.

[263] McGuckin 38.

[264] McGuckin 38.

[265] McGuckin 39.

[266] McGuckin 39.

[267] McGuckin 39.

[268] McGuckin 44.

[269] Neuner 199–200 (DS 272).

[270] Montfort, "The Love of Eternal Wisdom" 79.

[271] St. Thomas Aquinas, *Summa Theologica*, trans. Fathers of the English Dominican Province, vol. IV (Westminster, MD: Christian Classics, 1981) III, Q.7, art. 13, 2068–69. In this article St. Thomas tells us that the habitual grace in the soul of Christ is caused by union of the human nature with the divine Person of the Son.

[272] By way of personal explanation, it is precisely because my study of Mariology has convinced me that this vast ontological difference between the divine Person of the Son and the human person of Mary cannot be over emphasized in understanding all that the Catholic Faith teaches about Mary that I have purposefully chosen in this book to return to the more traditional custom of capitalizing pronouns and certain nouns that refer to God and His Mysteries in contrast to those that speak merely of Mary or ourselves. Because we ourselves are incarnate creatures, it is my belief that such a contrast in grammar constantly before our eyes serves to remind us of this infinite difference between the divine Personal Subject of Christ and the human personal subject of Mary.

[273] Montfort, "The Love of Eternal Wisdom" 91–3.

[274] William M. Thompson, ed., *Bérulle and the French School*, trans. Lowell M. Glendon, S.S. (Mahwah: Paulist Press, 1989) 36.

[275] McGuckin 40–1.

[276] Montfort, "The Love of Eternal Wisdom" 94.

[277] McGuckin 41. McGuckin adds weight to this conclusion by saying that "in the twentieth century new problems have arisen over (Cyril's) understanding of what (Jesus Christ's being fully human) might mean, for today . . . we tend to see the whole issue of subjectivity and personhood in terms drawn from the analytical psychology of the nineteenth and twentieth centuries. Accordingly, we approach the notion and the problem insofar as it impinges on the doctrine of the Incarnation, in terms of what would be called 'psychic consciousness.' Cyril, however, would refuse to reduce the notion of person to those psychic experiences. For him, personhood (either in the case of Jesus, or in the case of humans in general) was not a product of a material based consciousness but, on the contrary, consciousness was the effect of a divinely created personhood. . . . For Cyril, then, there was only one personal subject, and one personal reality in Christ, and that was the divine *Logos*. . . . Christ was at once divine and human—inseparably so. Cyril regarded this 'at once' as a synchronized enjoyment of two life forms, neither of which prevented the terms of the other, but both of which were enhanced by the intimate experience of the other."

[278] Montfort, "The Love of Eternal Wisdom" 96.

[279] Judith A. Bauer, ed., *The Essential Mary Handbook* (Liguori, MO: Liguori Publications, 1999) 237. "Devotion to the Sorrows of Mary began as a popular movement in the fourteenth century and was expressed in prayers, meditations, poems, and hymns. The number and subject of the Sorrows of Our Lady varied but what we think of as the traditional list is one promoted by the Servite Order to commemorate Mary's participation in the sufferings of Jesus the Savior: (1) Simeon's prophecy; (2) the flight into Egypt; (3) the loss of Jesus (in the temple); (4) the meeting of Jesus on the road to Calvary; (5) the Crucifixion; (6) the taking down from the cross; and (7) the burial of Jesus. . . . The feast of Our Lady of Sorrows was fixed by Pope Pius X as the day after the Exaltation of the Holy Cross, that is, on September 15."

CHAPTER 4

Mary as Daughter of the Father, Mother of the Son, and Spouse of the Holy Spirit

Initial Considerations

Since we will now be turning to Montfort's treatises focused specifically on Mary, let us say a few words about the texts we are using. *True Devotion to the Blessed Virgin* will be the primary work we will consider because it is St. Louis Marie's Mariological masterpiece. In chapter 2 of this work, Montfort tells us that he has taken up his pen "to write down what I have been teaching with success both publicly and in private in my missions for many years."[280] While there is nothing in the work that indicates a definitive date for the manuscript, Montfort scholars estimate the date to be 1712. Because Montfort seems to have such a command of his subject and the work is so well organized, it is believed that he composed it after long meditation and that it represents a work of his maturity.[281] While the original manuscript was buried for safety during the French Revolution along with other books and documents, no one has ever questioned its authenticity since it was found on April 29, 1842—127 years after the death of St. Louis Marie.

We will also periodically refer to *The Secret of Mary*, which presents in the form of a spiritual letter many of the same themes developed in *True Devotion*. While the date of this letter is uncertain, it is also considered to be a work of Montfort's maturity. Even though the initial manuscript has never been found, the authorized copy dating from the first half of the 18th century leaves little doubt that St. Louis Marie was its author because of both style and content. It has long been accepted by the Montfortian religious communities as being their founder's authentic work.[282]

In addition to these two treatises, the reader will notice that a few other miscellaneous manuscripts of Montfort are also referenced. These, along with the two works mentioned above, have been translated into English and are contained in *God Alone: The Collected Writings of St. Louis Marie de Montfort*, published by Montfort Publications in 1987. While there is indeed much interesting material in the saint's letters, sermons, and miscellaneous manuscripts, *True Devotion* remains most pertinent for our concerns because it provides us with the best theological exposition of Montfort's Marian thought.

While some may say that *True Devotion to Mary* is not a theological treatise in the strict sense because it was written to support the Montfortian consecration to Jesus through Mary, Montfort clearly bases his recommendation for such consecration upon sacred tradition and Catholic doctrine. He even states in *True Devotion* that the devotion he recommends with regards to Mary "could not be condemned without overthrowing the foundations of Christianity."[283] It is precisely these underlying Christian foundations, as reflected in his obvious allusions to the scriptures, the thought of the Fathers, and the principles of orthodox Christology and Trinitarian theology, that make his spiritual doctrine such a rich ground for theological reflection on Mary and her role in Redemption.

Furthermore, it is very significant to note what John Paul II says about Montfort in one of the final paragraphs of his important encyclical letter on Mary's maternal mediation, *Redemptoris Mater*. In recommending that the Marian Year which began on Pentecost, June 7, 1987, be used to promote a new and more careful reading of what Vatican II said about the Blessed Virgin Mary in the mystery of Christ and the Church, he specifically draws our attention to considering "authentic 'Marian spirituality' seen in the light of Tradition. . . . In this regard, I would like to recall, among the many witnesses and teachers of this spirituality, the figure of Saint Louis Marie Grignion de Montfort, who proposes consecration to Christ through the hands of Mary, as an effective means for Christians to live faithfully their baptismal commitments."[284]

A Trinitarian Prelude

We hear Montfort align himself with the orthodox understanding of the Trinity in the West in a short manuscript entitled, *Methods for Saying the Rosary*. He recommends during his fourth method that the initial "Our Father" should be offered in honor of the unity of the one, living and true God; the first "Hail Mary" should be offered to honor the eternal Father who conceives his Son in contemplating Himself; the second "Hail Mary" should be offered in honor of the Eternal Word, equal to His Father and who with Him produces the Holy Spirit by their mutual love; and the third "Hail Mary" should be offered in honor of the Holy Spirit who proceeds from the Father and the Son by the way of love. The "Our Father" which immediately follows should be offered in honor of the immense charity of God.[285]

It is in this same treatise on methods for saying the Rosary that we encounter a summary of what St. Louis Marie has to say about the Blessed Virgin both in relationship to the Blessed Trinity and correspondingly to us in a prayer which he recommends being said at the end of the Rosary in his third method for saying the Rosary:

> Hail Mary, well-beloved daughter of the eternal Father, admirable Mother of the Son, most faithful spouse of the Holy Spirit, glorious temple of the Blessed Trinity. Hail, sovereign Queen, to

whom everyone is subject in heaven and on earth. Hail, sure Refuge of sinners, our Lady of mercy, who has never repelled anyone. Sinner as I am, I cast myself at your feet and beg you to obtain from Jesus, your dear Son, contrition and pardon for all my sins and the gift of divine wisdom. I consecrate myself to you with all that I have. I choose you today as my Mother and Mistress; treat me then as the weakest of your children and the most submissive of your servants. . . .[286]

It is the meaning of these words for Montfort that we will now explore from a theological viewpoint based on his expansion of these themes in *True Devotion to the Blessed Virgin*. Understanding what Montfort says about the relationship of the Blessed Virgin Mary to each of the Persons of the Blessed Trinity will make it very clear that, at least from God's point of view, Mary has played and continues to play a pivotal role in Redemption.

On Seeing the Blessed Virgin Mary More Clearly

In his introductory chapter to *True Devotion to the Blessed Virgin*, St. Louis Marie tells us that there is much about Mary that has by the Blessed Trinity's choice remained hidden and unknown up until now. She is the "supreme masterpiece of Almighty God and He has reserved the knowledge and possession of her for Himself."[287] Not only is there much about Mary that has remained hidden by God's choice, but as we heard in *The Love of Eternal Wisdom*, Mary's response to the fullness of God's own life poured into her was perfect humility. Her humility was so genuine that she wanted no praise to be heaped on her because her singular focus was giving loving service to God in response to the profound gifts she had received. Montfort elaborates on Mary's humility in *True Devotion*:

So great was her humility that she desired nothing more upon earth than to remain unknown to herself and to others, and to be known only to God. In answer to her prayers to remain hidden, poor and lowly, God was pleased to conceal her from nearly every other human creature in her conception, her birth, her life, her mysteries, her resurrection and assumption. Her own parents did not really know her; and the angels would often ask one another, 'Who can she possibly be?' for God had hidden her from them, or if He did reveal anything to them, it was nothing compared to what He withheld.[288]

Montfort's emphasis on Mary's hiddeness during her earthly life as a consequence of her own humility is reminiscent of what the Savior tells a woman in the crowd who wants to praise Mary because of the wonders God had worked in her by making her the Mother of Jesus. "Blessed rather are those who hear the word of God and keep it" (Luke 11:28). Jesus tells the woman in the crowd that Mary is to be praised because she has responded perfectly to God's call with humility and obedience as evidenced in the moment of her *fiat*. "She lived it sincerely, unstintingly, fulfilling its every consequence, but never amid fanfare, rather in the hidden and silent sacrifice of each day."[289]

Montfort goes on to tell us there is another set of reasons why so little was seen and understood about the Blessed Virgin during her lifetime:

Mary scarcely appeared in the first coming of Jesus Christ so that men, as yet insufficiently instructed and enlightened concerning the Person of her Son, might not wander from the truth by becoming too strongly attached to her. This would have apparently have happened if she had been known,

on account of the wondrous charms with which
the Almighty had endowed even her outward
appearance. So true is this that St. Denis the Areopagite tells us in his writings that when he saw
her he would have taken her for a goddess, because
of her incomparable beauty, had not his well-
grounded faith taught him otherwise.[290]

Thus, Montfort also tells us that during Mary's lifetime, "God
the Father willed that she should perform no miracle, . . . at least
no public one, although He had given her the power to do so."
And, furthermore, "God the Son willed that she should speak
very little although He had imparted His wisdom to her." And,
finally, even in the writing of the scriptures "God the Holy Spirit
willed that His apostles and evangelists should say very little
about her and then only as much as was necessary to make Jesus
known."[291]

St. Louis Marie testifies that for many centuries this humble
beauty of Mary's hiddeness has remained a reality in the Christian community, long after her assumption and departure from this
earth. "The saints have said wonderful things of Mary, the holy
City of God, and as they themselves admit, they were never more
eloquent and more pleased than when they spoke of her. And yet
they maintain that the height of her merits rising up to the
throne of the Godhead cannot be perceived."[292] "De Maria
numquam satis: We have still not praised, exalted, honored, loved
and served Mary adequately." Using the words of St. Paul, Montfort goes on to tell us that the Church must admit that "'eye has
not seen, nor has ear heard, nor has the heart of man understood'
the beauty, the grandeur, the excellence of Mary, who is indeed a
miracle of miracles of grace, nature and glory." [293]

With this understanding in mind, Montfort announces that
while "Mary has been unknown up till now," it is his special joy
to be able to share with us the gift that has been given to him,
namely, seeing Mary more clearly. Why has he been given this

gift of seeing more about her than was given to ages past and why is he so intent on passing this gift on to us? It is the sincere sense of this Saint that it is finally time that more be made known about Mary, precisely so that more might be made known about Jesus Christ.[294] While it was expedient for her to remain hidden up until now for the sake of revealing who Jesus Christ was in his first coming, "in the second coming of Jesus Christ, Mary must be known and openly revealed by the Holy Spirit so that Jesus may be known, loved and served through her. The reasons which moved the Holy Spirit to hide His spouse during her life and to reveal but very little of her since the first preaching of the gospel exist no longer. . . . As she was the way by which Jesus first came to us, she will again be the way by which He will come to us the second time though not in the same manner."[295]

With these and similar statements, we might say that Montfort crystallizes this vast Marian movement mentioned in chapter 2 and in which he plays such a pivotal role by proclaiming that we are in a new stage of salvation history. And, this new stage is precisely a time when the Holy Spirit will make clearer to us everything that has already been revealed implicitly in scripture and sacred tradition about the Blessed Virgin. It is essential that we note Montfort's assertion that the reason we are coming to understand more about Mary is not for the sake of our approaching the Blessed Virgin Mary as an end in herself. Montfort explains that Mary's coming out of hiding, as it were, is because if "the knowledge and kingdom of Jesus Christ must come into the world, it can only be as a necessary consequence of the knowledge and reign of Mary. She who first gave Him to the world will establish His kingdom in the world."[296]

This means, in our current quest to understand more about the Blessed Virgin Mary's role in Redemption, we must never forget her personal desire to remain the hand-maiden of the Lord and to lead us to the divine Fruit of her womb. However, we must also hear St. Louis Marie's clear insistence that if Mary is not known and understood as she should be, Jesus Christ will not be fully known and the grace of Redemption will not be fully received. Because "Mary has been unknown up till now . . . Jesus Christ is not known as He should be."[297] "It was through the Blessed Virgin Mary that Jesus Christ came into the world, and it is also through her that He must reign in the world."[298] Let us assert that Montfort's counsel applies not merely to our personal or saving knowledge of Jesus Christ. It applies to the Church's theological understanding as well.

The Blessed Virgin Mary as Daughter of the Father

In the Introduction of *True Devotion*, Mary is referred to as "the magnificence of the Almighty where He hid His only Son, as in His own bosom, and with Him everything that is most excellent and precious."[299] With these relatively few words, Montfort begins to offer us an important insight. He compares the Blessed Virgin's way of relating to the Son with the Father's way of relating to this same Son. He tells us that the Father's hiding of the Son in the bosom of the Blessed Virgin in the Incarnation is like the Father's hiding of the Son in His own bosom in the mystery of the Father's begetting the Son. What is the deeper meaning of this comparison that Montfort offers for our reflection?

The Gospel of John affirms that the Word of God, the only Son, is in the bosom of the Father (John 1:18) and that the Word was God and with God (the Father) from the beginning (John 1:1). In 325 AD, the First Council of Nicaea expands on this apostolic witness to the Son's having been generated by the Father through the following dogmatic definition: "We believe in one God, the Father almighty, maker of all things, visible and invisible. And in one Lord Jesus Christ, the Son of God, the only-begotten generated from the Father, that is, from the being of the Father, God from God,. . . begotten, not made, one in being (*homoousios*) with the Father."[300] To this dogmatic understanding of the origins of the Son, Montfort is now adding that in the mystery of the Incarnation the only-begotten Son is not only eternally generated in the bosom of the Father but He has also become hidden in the bosom of His mother. It is in the bosom of Mary, where, in the language of the Council of Nicaea, He becomes flesh and is made man.[301] In the mystery of the Incarnation, Jesus Christ's filial link with the divine Father and the human mother become intimately united and inseparable throughout time and eternity. Jesus Christ is now "always and everywhere the fruit and Son of Mary"[302] as well as the only-begotten Son of the Father.

This comparison between the bosom of the Father and the bosom of the mother, as well as the inseparable and eternal link between the two, provide rich food for thought. While no one has ever seen the Father, except the only-begotten Son who has made Him known and perfectly reveals Him (John 1:18; 6:46; 14:9), Montfort's comparison seems to be telling us that there is something about the way the Blessed Virgin relates to the Son in the Incarnation that reflects and participates in something about the way the Father eternally generates the Son in His divine Bosom. In making Mary His own "magnificence," the Father has created, not begotten or generated, a beloved human daughter who in some manner also "magnifies the Lord" (Luke 2:46). While she is merely human in nature and therefore not begotten of the Father as is the Son, i.e., she is not *homoousios* with the Father, there is still something about the creature, Mary, that causes something about the Father Himself to be magnified, enlarged, or held in greater esteem.

Montfort tells us that the Father has given to His daughter "everything that is most excellent and precious" to Himself, along with the gift of the Son. As the magnifier of the Lord God, we might think of Mary in the Incarnation as a magnification or enlargement of some aspect of the Father Himself, some aspect that is even involved in His own generation of the Son. The question seems to be, what aspect? What is this most excellent and precious gift of the Father given to her, along with the Son? What is it that Mary magnifies and in so doing helps us see, as if under a magnifying glass, about the Father, in the very act of her being the Mother of the Son?

Montfort answers this question in paragraph 17 of *True Devotion*. "God the Father imparted to Mary His fruitfulness as far as a mere creature was capable of receiving it, to enable her to bring forth His Son and all the members of His mystical body."[303] We see from this succinct statement that it is the fruitfulness of the Father that is His most magnificent gift to her. It is none other than the very fruitfulness of God that Mary magnifies and helps us see!

In other words, the Father has made His beloved daughter, Mary, both an instrument and a magnifier of His own Being in the very act of bringing forth the Incarnate Son, who is the Redeemer. At the same time, the Father made her His instrument and magnifier in the act of bringing forth the members of His mystical body, which is the work of Redemption. As we heard Montfort state in *The Love of Eternal Wisdom*, the moment of the Incarnation and the work of Redemption cannot be separated from each other; they are forever conjoined. Because the Blessed Virgin is involved in the Incarnation of the Son, she is necessarily involved in the birth of all the members of the mystical body of Christ. And, all the fruitfulness that we not only see in the Blessed Virgin, but also receive through her, is nothing less than the result of her having first received a share in the Father's own Being. This is profound!

Montfort enables us to say that, by divine design, the Blessed Virgin's fundamental role in Redemption is that of serving as the instrumental cause through, with, and in whom the Father manifests and brings to fulfillment His own fruitfulness in the Incarnation of the Son, the divine Redeemer. And, as a consequence of that fundamental choice, the Father has also made Mary the instrumental cause for all persons to be restored to God through the work of Redemption. It is only through her that both Jesus Christ, the Second Adam, and the members of His mystical body are given birth. Because she was created and chosen as the instrumental cause for bringing to full flower the divine fruitfulness, Mary perfectly images or magnifies the divine fruitfulness by her very participation in it, insofar as a human person can. With this realization, Montfort opens up for us the heart of what is meant theologically by the very concept of mediation.

When we use the term 'instrumental cause' in regard to Mary, it is important to assert with Montfort in paragraphs 14 through 16 of *True Devotion* that we can never claim that the Father had any absolute need of Mary in either the Incarnation of the Son or the bringing forth of His mystical body. On the other hand, we must never hesitate to affirm with Montfort that since God Himself has chosen to need her for Redemption, so do we:

> With the whole Church I acknowledge that Mary, being a mere creature fashioned by the hands of God is, compared to His infinite majesty, less than an atom, or rather is simply nothing, since He alone can say, "I am He who is." Consequently, this great Lord, who is ever independent and self-sufficient, never had and does not now have any absolute need of the Blessed Virgin for the accomplishment of His will and the manifestation of His glory. To do all things He has only to will them.

> However, I declare that, considering things as they are, because God has decided to begin and accomplish His greatest works through the Blessed Virgin ever since He created her, we can safely believe that He will not change His plan in the time to come, for He is God and therefore does not change in His thoughts or His way of acting.

> God the Father gave His only Son to the world only through Mary. Whatever desires the patriarchs may have cherished, whatever entreaties the

prophets and saints of the Old Law may have made
for 4,000 years to obtain that treasure, it was Mary
alone who merited it and found grace before God
by the power of her prayers and the perfection of
her virtues. "The world being unworthy," said St.
Augustine, "to receive the Son of God directly
from the hands of the Father, He gave His Son to
Mary for the world to receive Him from her.[304]

The Motherhood of Mary as the Image of Divine Fruitfulness

With this essential perspective in mind, we must nonetheless be
aware of the fact that in the act of the Incarnation, which manifests not only the divine Son to us but also makes present the glory
of the Blessed Trinity in time and space,[305] the Father has chosen
to involve not only a human person as an instrument of divine
fruitfulness but also specifically a person who is a woman, a person
whose specific function in the conception of the Son can be none
other than that of mother. A further question seems to arise from
this realization. Is there something revelatory about the Father's
own fruitfulness in the *mothering* of the only-begotten Son in the
bosom of the Blessed Virgin and in the *mothering* of all who are to
be adopted sons and daughters of the Father through the Son?

In other words, is the Father, in His very choice of Mary to
serve as the instrumental cause of His own fruitfulness in the
mothering of the Son and the mothering of us, trying to reveal to
us something about the inner-Trinitarian life of God? Does Mary
as daughter of the Father indeed serve as a magnifier of some
aspect of the Father Himself to us? Even though she is not
homoousios with the Father and not strictly speaking the Revealer
of the Father as is the Son, does she still reveal to us something
essential about God's Being and consequently about all of us who
are created and being re-created in the image of God? And, what
does such a revelation tell us about her role in Redemption?

Once again, St. Louis Marie's own thinking seems to shed some light on our questions. In chapter 1 of *True Devotion*, Montfort tells us that "just as in the natural and bodily generation there is a father and a mother, so in the supernatural and spiritual generation there is a Father who is God and a mother who is Mary." He believes this so strongly that he goes on to say that those "who hate, despise, or ignore the Blessed Virgin, do not have God for their Father though they arrogantly claim they have, because they do not have Mary for their mother."[306]

With this simple yet profound logic, he invokes a fundamental principle in Catholic theology, namely, the lower order of creation reflects both the spiritual and supernatural and thus reveals to us something, albeit in an analogous manner, about the supernatural realm and ultimately about God, the Creator of all that exists. St Thomas speaks of this in the *Summa Theologica*. While univocal predication between the natural realm and the supernatural realm is impossible, we can speak of perfections which we see in the natural realm of creatures as names or attributes of the Creator in an analogous sense, that is according to proportion.[307]

The theological term often used to refer to this analogous correspondence between the creation and the Creator of all being is termed 'analogy of being'. By this we mean that "the objective relation between God and the world and the affirmation of this relation in cognition are not two states of affairs or factors which can be separated or interpreted separately. On the contrary, they radically constitute the fundamental structure or texture of what analogy in the ultimate resort is." Furthermore, we can say that this analogous correspondence between the world and God "shows itself as the event of the absolute *identity-in-difference* of finite and infinite, conditioned and unconditioned, world and God. . . . All that is finite, because and inasmuch as it is the event of the participation of being, is one in difference with the infinite. The language or utterance of this event is analogy, the nature of which is therefore only manifested if its fundamental structure is thought out to the end in this way."[308]

With the 'analogy of being' in mind, let us base our considerations about Mary as the reflection of the Father's fruitfulness upon there being this *identity-in-difference* between created reality and God.[309] It seems, therefore, that with St. Louis Marie's aid we might begin to speak about the Blessed Virgin Mary—in the very mystery of her being Mother of God the Son Incarnate—reflecting for us, analogously, something about the mothering aspect of God's own fruitfulness, both in regard to the Incarnation of the Son and the spiritual regeneration of all who become adopted sons and daughters through the Son.[310] In other words, perhaps one way to understand the Blessed Virgin and her crucial role in Redemption is to see her *analogously* as reflecting the mothering aspect of divine fruitfulness to us. This does not mean that Mary herself is divine. Rather, it does mean that as a created person she has been chosen to reflect and participate in the inner-Trinitarian Life, in an entirely unique and unrepeatable manner, precisely as Mother of the Incarnate Son as well as of the Redemption He brings.

In this light, it is instructive to note that in the scriptures themselves the Incarnate Son specifically invites the crowds who listened to His sermon on the mount to pray to God by saying "Our Father" and not " Our Mother" (Matt. 6:9). On the other hand, the Savior did call upon the beloved disciple in John 19:26–27, along with all whom this disciple represents when this passage is read in the spiritual sense as discussed earlier in chapter 1, to behold Mary as our mother. "When Jesus saw His mother, and the disciple whom He loved standing near, He said to His mother, 'Woman, behold, your son!' Then he said to the disciple, 'Behold your mother!'"

St. Thomas Aquinas reminds us that God is most properly named by God's own Self-revelation in Ex. 3:13–14, "I AM WHO I AM." While the divinely revealed Name is perhaps best translated into English without being gender specific because the Being of God transcends the specifics of gender as we know them in the creation,[311] scripture testifies that in the maleness of the only-begotten Son of the Father, incarnate from the Virgin Mary, the Fatherly face of the Trinitarian God is revealed to us in human form. In John 14:9, we even hear the Incarnate Son, not daughter, say: "He who has seen me has seen the Father." With the aid of Montfort and the reminder that the revelation of the Trinity is made present in time and space and finds its highest manifestation in the Incarnation and subsequent story of Jesus Christ, it seems highly likely that Mary, though a mere human person, reflects in some way the Mothering face of God, and even of the Father, to us.

Not only does this discussion point to the unique and sublime dignity of the Mother of God herself but it also affirms that there is, analogously, both a mothering *and* a fathering aspect to the inner-Trinitarian Life of Love and Fruitfulness—in Whose image men and women are created and upon which rests the very foundation of both the human family and human community. In other words, there is an eternal giving and receiving of Love and Being among the Persons of the Trinity Themselves that is revealed to us in the Incarnation, analogously, as *both* mothering *and* fathering. Jesus Christ, the Incarnate Son, *is the Revealer* of the Fathering Face of this aspect of the inner-Trinitarian Life. The Blessed Virgin Mary, by virtue of the mystery of the Divine Maternity by which she uniquely participates in that divine Fruitfulness that incarnates the Son, *is a magnifier* of the Mothering Face of this same inner-Trinitarian Life. The ramifications for this realization are enormous for creatures whose very purpose and fulfillment are found only in imaging faithfully the God Who created them.[312]

This conclusion that the Blessed Virgin Mary magnifies the mothering aspect of the inner-Trinitarian Life seems to be all the more underscored by the fact that Mary is both virgin and mother. Because of her virginal Motherhood of God the Son, we cannot say that Mary reflects God's fruitfulness in merely the same way we might speak about human parenting in the natural order.[313] While Mary is indeed a fully human mother, there is something of an entirely different order that also goes on in Mary at the moment of the Incarnation. Because she is virgin and mother, there is simply no other explanation for Mary's virginal motherhood than the supernatural. Not only does this mean that she is totally dependent upon God for the Fruit that her mothering produces. It also makes it all the more likely that her virginal Motherhood manifests something profound to us about God's own fruitfulness because she herself participates in it. For in her virginal Motherhood of the Son, we have to note that she mysteriously resembles the Father who begets the Son on His own, i.e., virginally, analogously speaking. In the words of Fr. René Laurentin, "the Father gave birth eternally, alone, virginally, to a unique Son who was necessarily unique. As the image of the Father, the generation of Mary is unique, virginal, with authority and interiority, with their temporal and corporal modalities."[314]

The consequences of this discussion about St. Louis Marie's insight into Mary's unique relationship with the Father in the mystery of the Divine Maternity are endless for understanding Mary's role in Redemption. By the Father's *Fiat*, the Blessed Virgin shares in the Father's own generation of all that the Person of the Son has now become in time and eternity—the Incarnate, only-begotten Son of the Father. Because the mystery of the Incarnation involves no less than the Second Person of the Blessed Trinity, Mary's mothering of the Son is a perpetual Reality in God, extending far beyond the historic moment in which the Incarnation first occurred into eternity itself. "Moreover, Jesus is still as much as ever the fruit of Mary, as heaven and earth repeat thousands of times a day, 'Blessed is the fruit of thy womb, Jesus.'"[315] "Jesus is always and everywhere the fruit and Son of Mary and Mary is everywhere the genuine tree that bears that Fruit of life, the true Mother who bears that Son."[316]

The Blessed Virgin Mary as Mother of the Son

With the above in mind, let us now take a further look at what St. Louis Marie helps us see about the Blessed Virgin's mothering of the Incarnate Son of God. The following paragraphs from Chapter 1 of *True Devotion* are crucial:

> God the Son came down into her virginal womb as a new Adam into His earthly paradise, to take His delight there and produce hidden wonders of grace.
>
> God-made-man found freedom in imprisoning Himself in her womb. He displayed power in allowing Himself to be borne by this young maiden. He found His glory and that of His Father in hiding His splendors from all creatures here below and revealing them only to Mary. He glorified His independence and His majesty in depending upon this lovable virgin in His conception, His birth, His presentation in the temple, and in the thirty years of His hidden life. Even at His death she had to be present so that He might be united with her in one sacrifice and be immolated with her consent to the eternal Father, just as formerly Isaac was offered in sacrifice by Abraham when he accepted the will of God. It was Mary who nursed Him, fed Him, cared for Him, reared Him, and sacrificed Him for us.
>
> The Holy Spirit could not leave such wonderful and inconceivable dependence of God unmentioned in the Gospel, though He concealed almost all the wonderful things that Wisdom Incarnate did during His hidden life in order to bring home to us its infinite value and glory. Jesus gave more glory to God His Father by submitting to His Mother for thirty years than He would have given

Him had He converted the whole world by working the greatest miracles. . ..

If we examine closely the remainder of the life
of Jesus Christ, we see that He chose to begin His
miracles through Mary. It was by her word that He
sanctified St. John the Baptist in the womb of His
mother, St. Elizabeth; no sooner had Mary spoken
than John was sanctified. This was His first and
greatest miracle of grace. At the wedding of Cana
He changed water into wine at her humble prayer,
and this was His first miracle in the order of
nature. He began and continued His miracles
through Mary and He will continue them until the
end of time.[317]

Clearly, for Montfort, the key to understanding the relationship of Jesus Christ to the Blessed Virgin is to be found in the
meaning of His submission to her and even His dependence upon
her for the accomplishment of His mission as God the Son Incarnate. At first glance, our natural human response to such submission and dependence of the divine Son upon Mary is like that of
Mary herself. With Mary, we wonder how this might be (Luke
1:29). Why would the Second Person of the Blessed Trinity Who
is one in Being with the Father choose to humble Himself by
accepting such a posture of dependence upon a mere human
being? Furthermore, how could such submission to Mary possibly
bring glory to God? In addition, what can we say about the
redemptive significance of this submission and dependence upon
Mary by God the Son?

It is in answer to these questions that the thought of St. Irenaeus helps reveal the deeper meaning of what Montfort is saying
about Mary's role in Redemption. Conversely, Montfort's insights
about the Son's freely chosen dependence upon Mary advance St.
Irenaeus' theology of recapitulation yet another step.

For this to be seen, let us consider once again the Genesis account of the fall of Adam and Eve, paying special emphasis to Genesis 3:15. It is here that God says to the serpent, that is to Satan, who took the form of the serpent, "I will put enmity between you and the woman, and between your seed and her seed; he shall bruise your head, and you shall bruise his heel." The Catholic Faith has frequently referred to this verse from Genesis as the *Protoevangelium* ("first gospel") because it is the first announcement to humankind of the good news that God will not have His ultimate design for creation thwarted.[318]

When Gen. 3:15 is understood according to its spiritual sense as we discussed in chapter 1 of this book, i.e., "within the whole plan of Revelation,"[319] it is clear that God is herein promising that the tragic consequences of Adam and Eve's disobedience and seduction by Satan will be reversed by an enmity that God Himself will place between Satan and another woman coupled with her offspring. Catholic tradition has long understood this promised woman of Genesis 3:15 to refer to the Blessed Virgin Mary.[320] We hear this reference to Mary affirmed by the fathers of the Second Vatican Council in *"Lumen Gentium"* : "The earliest documents, as they are read in the Church and are understood in the light of a further and full revelation, bring the figure of a woman, Mother of the Redeemer, into a gradually clearer light. Considered in this light, she is already prophetically foreshadowed in the promise of victory over the serpent which was given to our first parents after their fall into sin (Gen. 3:15)."[321]

Returning to our concerns, this very salvific victory, dependent upon the enmity that God will put between Mary and Satan, is central to understanding why the Son freely humbles Himself to be dependent upon her. In the Person of the Son, God Himself effects yet one more "recirculation" in the mystery of Redemption. The divine Son undoes the seduction of woman by Satan precisely by allowing Himself to be seduced, as it were, by the inestimable charms of another woman, the Blessed Virgin Mary. He gives Himself completely into her hands and humbly allows this woman, Mary, to become His own Mother to reverse the effects of Satan against the other woman whom God had originally chosen to be the "mother of all the living," the first Eve (Gen. 3:20). By submitting Himself to Mary and entrusting Himself to her so totally that He even takes His own most sacred body from her,[322] the Word through Whom all is created, including the first Adam and Eve, makes "another woman" (Gen. 3:15) God's own helpmate in crushing Satan.

This means that in addition to preserving Mary from original sin to ensure her freedom from the effects of Satan's having seduced the human race, the divine Son elevates this particular human woman to a level of unfathomable union with Him by humbling Himself to establish His own Motherhood in her. Through this perpetual union with the divine Son occasioned by His own submission to and dependence upon her precisely as Mother, Mary joins the divine Redeemer perpetually as a partner in His enmity against Satan. "So closely are they united that one is wholly in the other. Jesus is all in Mary and Mary is all in Jesus. Or rather, it is no longer she who lives, but Jesus alone who lives in her."[323] "God has established only one enmity—but it is an irreconcilable one which will last and even go on increasing to the end of time. That enmity is between Mary, His worthy Mother, and the devil. . . . Thus the most fearful enemy that God has set up against the devil is Mary, His holy Mother."[324]

With this in mind, it is possible to understand why Montfort says that in this very act of submission to Mary the Son renders the highest obedience to the Father. By becoming forever dependent upon a human woman, as Mother, God the Son puts the greatest enmity between the human race and Satan, even reversing Satan's curse. By raising up the woman, Mary, definitively and perpetually to the supernatural order through His dependence upon her as Mother, the Son thwarts and reverses the work of the devil who mocked the Father's plans at the beginning by seducing the first woman and "mother of all the living" to turn against God.

Thus, with the aid of Montfort's insights, we can say that the great work of Redemption began with the Son's submission of Himself into the womb of the Blessed Virgin and ended with His being entrusted into her arms beneath the Cross, with the climax of the union of Mother and Son occurring at the moment of His death and final Self-oblation to the Father. "It was Mary who . . . sacrificed Him for us."[325] By nothing less than divine choice, the Redeemer has chosen to associate Himself entirely with Mary in His work of Redemption—even to the point of designing Redemption in such a way that He freely submits to and becomes dependent upon her to reverse the seduction of Eve by Satan.

As St. Louis de Montfort says in the paragraphs quoted above, Mary had to be present with Him at His death as well as at His Incarnation. The Son waited upon and required her consent at the foot of the cross just as much as He did at His holy Incarnation. It is her free consent coupled with His free choice to submit to her that makes Mary the Second Eve and the associate of the Redeemer from beginning to end. Just as there never was a time when the Father was without the Son, we have to say that there never was a time when the Second Adam was without the Second Eve. "Lord, you are always with Mary and Mary is always with you."[326]

The Further Significance of Humility

We would be highly negligent if we failed to mention the impact on Mary of God the Son's free submission to and dependence upon her. In discussing the fear that Protestant Christians sometimes have about God the Son's choice to depend upon Mary and involve her in His work of Redemption, it is paramount that we hear what Montfort tells us in *The Secret of Mary*. In regard to Mary herself, "it is no longer Mary who lives but Jesus Christ Himself, God alone, who lives in her. Her transformation into God far surpasses that experienced by St. Paul (Gal. 2:20) and other saints, more than heaven surpasses the earth. . . . Mary is the wonderful echo of God. . . . When we say 'Mary,' she re-echoes 'God.'"[327]

In other words, Mary is perfect humility and her humility surpasses that of all the saints. Mary, more than any creature ever created, understands the vast difference between herself and her Creator and Redeemer. She has no illusions about how much she owes to the Divine Majesty and what God has done for, with, and in her. The Blessed Virgin's own response to God the Son's submission to her at the Incarnation resounds through the words of her Magnificat. "My soul magnifies the Lord and my spirit rejoices in God, my Savior . . . for He who is mighty has done great things for me and holy is His Name" (Luke 1:46b-49).

Montfort even instructs us that the enmity that God has established between Satan and Mary is even intensified by Mary's perfect humility. "Satan fears her, not only more than angels and men, but in a certain sense more than God Himself. This does not mean that the anger, hatred, and power of God are not infinitely greater than the Blessed Virgin's, since her attributes are limited. It simply means that Satan, being so proud, suffers infinitely more in being vanquished and punished by a lowly and humble servant of God, for her humility humiliates him more than the power of God. Thus, the most fearful Satan, being so proud, suffers infinitely more in being vanquished and punished by a lowly and humble servant of God. . . . What Lucifer lost by pride Mary won by humility."[328]

In our further consideration on the significance of humility, we must mention that Montfort speaks of the *eternal* submissiveness of Jesus Christ to Mary. Because Jesus is forever the fruit of Mary's womb as mentioned previously in this chapter, God the Son has forever chosen to be submissive to Mary precisely as Mother. This means His posture of humility in regard to her goes on for all eternity because the mystery of the Incarnation is not just a moment in historical time. Rather, the Incarnation is a Reality that exists in God for all eternity. Central to this mystery is the very fact that in the Resurrection the divine Son's humanity has been raised up, including His most sacred body, into the very Life of the Blessed Trinity. Consequently, in the very Life of the Trinity, Jesus Christ's relationship of dependence upon Mary, specifically as Mother, also exists for all eternity.

In the following passage we begin to hear how the Son's eternal dependence upon Mary as Mother plays a role in the distribution of grace, a topic which will be taken up in detail in our next chapter:

> . . . (O)ur Lord remains in heaven just as much the Son of Mary as He was on earth. Consequently, He has retained the submissiveness and obedience of the most perfect of all children towards the best of all mothers.
>
> We must take care, however, not to consider this dependence as an abasement or imperfection in Jesus Christ. For Mary, infinitely inferior to her Son, who is God, does not command Him in the same way as an earthly mother would command her child who is beneath her. Since she is completely transformed in God by that grace and glory which transforms all the saints in Him, she does not ask or wish to do anything which is contrary to the eternal and unchangeable will of God. . . . (T)he authority which God was pleased to give her is so great that she seems to have the same power as God. Her prayers and requests are so powerful with Him that He accepts them as commands in the sense that He never resists His dear mother's prayer because it is always humble and conformed to His Will.[329]

The above passage mentions another aspect of the Son's eternal dependence on the Blessed Virgin in the distribution of grace, namely, Mary's own perfection in glory. What was begun in this life with regards to her relationship to her Son has been perfected in the next. Karl Rahner echoes Montfort quite profoundly in his book, *Mary Mother of the Lord*:

> So if we now ask what importance as mediatrix the blessed Virgin must have, now that she lives in heaven, adoring the eternal love of the triune God, her life and her heart now perfectly fulfilled, we must reply, that it is impossible to envisage the office of mediatrix that belongs to her, except as being of the same order as her importance was in the divine plan for the history of the earth and mankind and redemption. For, even for her, eternity is the outcome of life here on earth before death. The importance she had in the earthly history of redemption has become valid and irrevocable, precisely because she has entered death into her ultimate eternal glory and perfection. Now none has had a profounder, more comprehensive function, or one more decisive for the whole divine plan, than the blessed Virgin mother of our Lord Jesus Christ. . . . And what once happened on our behalf through her in that unsurpassable, unique way, must in a true sense have become eternal.[330]

We must add one final thought to this section in light of what we previously discussed about the redemptive significance of the Son's initial submissiveness to and dependence upon Mary. The eternal submissiveness of the Incarnate Son to the prayers and intercessions of the Blessed Virgin on our behalf is yet another aspect of God's ensuring the total defeat of Satan and the final victory of His plan of Redemption. By eternally depending upon His Mother to be "mother to us in the order of grace,"[331] that very grace by which the Redeemer restores us from the wounding caused by original sin, God the Son is putting further enmity between Mary and Satan as promised in Genesis 3:15. Giving Mary such a profound share in His power for all eternity is the Son's way of finally crushing the head of the serpent that seduced our first mother and poisoned the life we receive from her. As Montfort tells us:

> Mary is the great mold of God, fashioned by the Holy Spirit to give human nature to a Man who is God by the hypostatic union, and to fashion through grace men who are like God. No godly feature is missing from this mold. Everyone who casts himself into it and allows himself to be molded will acquire every feature of Jesus Christ, true God, with little pain or effort, as befits his weak human condition. He will take on a faithful likeness to Jesus with no possibility of distortion, for the devil has never had and never will have any access to Mary, the holy and immaculate Virgin, in whom there is not the least suspicion of a stain of sin.[332]

And, last but not least, because Mary herself is also a daughter of our first parents, her perfect transformation in God and eternal access to her Son on our behalf, precisely as one of us, assures us that our predicament as human persons is daily united to Him. "Since God is everywhere, He can be found everywhere, even in hell. But there is no place where God can be more present to His creature and more sympathetic to human weakness than in Mary. It was indeed for this very purpose that He came down from heaven. Everywhere else He is the Bread of the strong and the Bread of angels, but living in Mary He is the Bread of children."[333]

The Blessed Virgin Mary as Spouse of the Holy Spirit

While the Blessed Virgin's relationship to the Father and the Son are shrouded in mystery, which the mind unaided by grace cannot even begin to comprehend, it is perhaps in trying to grasp the Blessed Virgin's relationship to the Holy Spirit that we most experience the limits of human reason. For it seems that here we encounter a mystery in God whose details may never be entirely revealed on this side of the Beatific Vision. That mystery has to do with the nature of the intimate union between the Holy Spirit and the Blessed Virgin Mary, a union so profound that it could bring about nothing less than the Incarnation of God the Son, Eternal Wisdom.

In speaking of this mystery at the beginning of *True Devotion*, St. Louis Marie describes Mary as "the sealed fountain and the faithful spouse of the Holy Spirit where only He may enter."[334] Montfort reiterates this image again at the close of this same treatise. Here he expands his earlier reference to the Sg. 4:12 by telling us that it is difficult for us to have the freedom, the ability, and the light to enter the exalted and holy place of Mary because it is not guarded by a cherub, like the first earthly paradise, but by the Holy Spirit Himself who has become the absolute Master of the holy place of Mary. "Referring to her, He (the Holy Spirit) says: 'You are an enclosed garden, my sister, my bride, an enclosed garden and a sealed fountain.' Mary is enclosed. Mary is sealed. The unfortunate children of Adam and Eve, driven from the earthly paradise, can enter this new paradise only by a special grace of the Holy Spirit. . . ."[335]

St. Louis de Montfort is by no means the first to use bridal imagery in referring to the Blessed Virgin and her relationship to God. The spousal connotations in the Annunciation narrative are quite clear in the angel's announcement that Mary will conceive a child in her womb because the Holy Spirit will come upon her and the power of the Most High will overshadow her (Luke 1:31–34). Mary's own admission of having no human husband makes the biblical text even more suggestive of the spousal love relationship between God and the Blessed Virgin Mary.

Although some trace the beginnings of the idea of the Blessed Virgin as the spouse of God to the Fathers as early as Origen, St. Athanasius, and St. Cyril of Alexandria, most look to St. Ephraem in the fourth century as the first who uses the term definitively. However, he did not call Mary spouse of the Holy Spirit but rather the spouse of Christ. This latter term has often been considered misleading and problematic in referring to the relationship of the divine Son to Mary, unless it is taken in a purely spiritual sense wherein Mary represents the pre-eminent example of the spousal relationship between every soul in grace with its Savior. While other Fathers continued to speak of Mary as either the spouse of Christ, or simply as "God-wed," or even spouse of the Father, Aurelius Clemens Prudentius begins to speak of Mary as spouse of the Holy Spirit as early as the fourth century in his theological poetry.[336]

Fr. René Laurentin has recommended staying away from the word, spouse, with regards to Mary's relationship to the Holy Spirit. His reason is that this word can connote Mary's having been, literally, fecundated by the Holy Spirit. He sees this to be problematic for two reasons. First, this false connotation is reminiscent of pagan myths that frequently held that pagan gods had sexual relations with human beings. Secondly, we must be diligent in differentiating between models of human paternity and divine paternity when speaking of the Incarnation of God the Son since the Incarnation is not a procreation but a new creation.[337] Thus, it is not surprising to see that while the fathers of the Second Vatican Council concurred with Montfort in calling Mary the beloved daughter of the Father and Mother of the Son of God, they did not call her spouse of the Holy Spirit. Instead they referred to her as the "temple of the Holy Spirit."[338]

While Fr. Laurentin's concerns certainly point to the fact that one must be clear about what is not intended by referring to the Blessed Virgin as spouse of the Holy Spirit, it seems important to investigate exactly what St. Louis Marie intended by his consistent use of the word, spouse, when referring specifically to her relationship with the Holy Spirit. Certainly, a first glance reveals that spouse connotes much more of an inter-personal relationship between Mary and the divine Person of the Holy Spirit than does temple, which connotes an inanimate object such as a tabernacle or building. Likewise, Montfort's choice of a marital term that conveys a genuine inter-personal relationship of mutual love resulting in fruitfulness between Mary and the Holy Spirit seems consistent with a significant truth that Montfort has already helped us see, namely, the importance of Mary's free and active consent in becoming the Mother of God. "God the Holy Spirit formed Jesus Christ in Mary but only after having asked her consent through one of the chief ministers of His court."[339] Likewise, the use of this inter-personal term, "spouse of the Holy Spirit," puts Mary's relationship with the Third Person of the Blessed Trinity on the same level as her relationship with the Father and the Son, since daughter and mother clearly convey the dynamics of inter-personal relationships.

It is important to add that Montfort does not intend to insinuate that the Holy Spirit fecundates Mary as a human spouse potentially would. St. Louis Marie clearly assumes and upholds the Church's teaching on Mary's perpetual virginity as well as the virginal conception of the Incarnate Son. Not only does he constantly refer to her with such terms as the "Virgin Mother of God,"[340] but her perpetual virginity is exactly the mystery that he is alluding to by his clear reference above to Sg. 4:12, saying that, "Mary is sealed."[341] Thus, we can state without hesitation that in calling Mary the "spouse of the Holy Spirit" Montfort intends for the reader to understand that Mary is filled with the Holy Spirit. The term "spouse of the Holy Spirit" is obviously being used by Montfort in an analogous sense. Because of the obvious reverence that Montfort holds for the virginity of Mary, coupled with his orthodox Christology as previously mentioned, he would never intend fecundation by anyone, including God Himself.[342]

With this in mind, let us now return to *True Devotion* where we encounter the deeper meaning St. Louis Marie is pointing to by describing the Blessed Virgin's relationship to the Holy Spirit specifically as spouse. "God the Holy Spirit, who does not produce any divine Person, became fruitful through Mary whom He espoused. It was with her, in her and of her that He produced His masterpiece, God-made-man, and that He produces every day until the end of the world the members of the body of this adorable Head."[343] St. Louis is quick to add that this does not mean that Mary confers on the Holy Spirit a fruitfulness which He does not already possess. "Being God, He has the ability to produce just like the Father and the Son, although He does not use this power and so does not produce another divine Person. But it does mean that the Holy Spirit chose to make use of our Blessed Lady, although He had no absolute need of her, in order to become actively fruitful in producing Jesus Christ and His members in her and by her."[344]

These short phrases of Montfort are heavily laden with profound theological significance. There is clear reference to Mary's contribution in the Holy Spirit's Incarnation of the Second Person of the Blessed Trinity, a mystery which Montfort says is similar to the generation of the Son by the Father and the Holy Spirit by the Father and the Son. In comparing the Incarnation of the Son by the Holy Spirit freely united to the Blessed Virgin with the procession of Persons within the Trinity, Montfort further develops his initial insight that the Father gave the Blessed Virgin a share in His own fruitfulness. Now, we hear that this share in the Father's own fruitfulness is nothing less than the gift of an unprecedented and unique union with the Holy Spirit! Montfort even goes so far as to say that the Holy Spirit's generative action within the Trinity is not accomplished in union with another divine Person but rather with the human person, Mary, not by necessity but by choice. It is no wonder that St. Louis Marie concludes these profound phrases about Mary's relationship to the Holy Spirit with the reminder that we are now talking about "a mystery of grace unknown even to many of the most learned and spiritual of Christians."[345]

Certainly one way to make theological sense out of what Montfort is trying to tell us is to use the familiar principle of Trinitarian theology which holds that the economic Trinity truly reflects the immanent Trinity, i.e., the Trinity that we encounter in the created order and brings about our salvation truly reflects the Trinity that exists in God's own Self. [346] With this in mind, if what we encounter about the Persons of the Blessed Trinity in Their dealings with us truly tells us something about the inner-Trinitarian life, we can theologically support Montfort's claim that the Holy Spirit's free choice to be coupled or united with the Blessed Virgin Mary in bringing about His most significant masterpiece, God Incarnate, really reveals something about the relationship of the Blessed Virgin to the Holy Spirit in God's immanent mystery. To this consideration, let us add Montfort's previous reminder that the Son has become Incarnate through, with, and in Mary not just for a season, but for all eternity. This helps us see why Montfort can say that the intimate union between the Holy Spirit and Mary must be spoken of as occurring not only at the moment of the Incarnation but also lasting throughout time and eternity. It is a consequence of the divine choice to raise the Blessed Virgin into *being* the Mother of God perpetually *in* the mystery of the inner-Trinitarian Life of the Godhead. "Mary, in union with the Holy Spirit, still conceives Him and brings Him forth daily."[347]

In other words, it seems that St. Louis Marie is trying to tell us that the Blessed Virgin Mary is forever united (wed) to the inner-Trinitarian life of God in such a manner that she is the eternally chosen means through whom God the Holy Spirit is fruitful. Recalling what we have previously said about the importance of orthodox Christology in doing Mariology, let us remember that there is an infinite difference between the bridal union of Mary and the Holy Spirit and the hypostatic union of the divine and human natures in the one divine Personal Subject of the Incarnate Son. For as great as her union with the Holy Spirit and the entire Trinity is, the personal subject of Mary remains "a mere creature fashioned by the hands of God." She is, "compared to His infinite majesty, less than an atom, or rather, simply nothing, since He alone can say, 'I am He who is.'"[348]

What Montfort is trying to help us see about Mary's relationship with the Holy Spirit sounds much like the language often used to describe the unitive life, i.e., the final stage in the mystical ascent as spoken of by the great Christian Saints and mystics, such as St. John of the Cross and St. Teresa of Jesus. Harvey Egan, S.J., eloquently describes the unitive stage of the spiritual life in his anthology of Christian mysticism:

> The mystic becomes as closely united to God through God's love as God is united to his own being by nature. Mystically married to God, the mystic becomes "God by participation." Nonetheless, this union remains differentiated, that is, God and the mystic become one while remaining distinctly two. The mystic's person does not dissolve into God. In fact, the more deeply united to God the mystic becomes, the more the mystic's individuality is confirmed and enhanced.
>
> Mystical marriage bestows a conscious sharing in God's own life and power and almost complete self-forgetfulness. The mystic now seeks only God's will and honor and desires to serve God totally. . . .
>
> The mystic is united to a love that communicates itself to all persons and to all things. . . . Transformed by and into Love itself, the mystic becomes creative, totally self-giving, radically concerned about others—in short, spiritually fecund.[349]

This resemblance between what can rightly be said about the mature Christian mystic and much of what Montfort has given us to ponder about the Blessed Virgin is present because, as Montfort himself would say, Mary is the Mother of the Christian mystical life. It is that divine spiritual fecundity which comes to full flower and fruit through her unique bridal union with the Holy Spirit that produces Saints and mystics. "I do not believe that anyone can acquire intimate union with Our Lord and perfect fidelity to the Holy Spirit without a very close union with the most Blessed Virgin and an absolute dependence on her support. Mary alone found grace before God without the help of any other creature. All those who have since found grace before God have found it only through her."[350]

However, while the bridal mystical union which the great Saints share with God in some sense resembles the nature of that union which the Blessed Virgin Mary enjoys specifically with the Person of the Holy Spirit, we must also acknowledge with St. Louis de Montfort that we cannot fully comprehend the true nature of this union. It is certainly one of the mysteries in God that awaits the blessed to contemplate for all eternity in being given the 'light of glory'. "Moreover, we should repeat after the Holy Spirit, 'All the glory of the king's daughter is within,' meaning that all the external glory which heaven and earth vie with each other to give her is nothing compared to what she has received interiorly from her Creator, namely, a glory unknown to insignificant creatures like us, who cannot penetrate into the secrets of the king."[351]

Even a limited comparison of Mary's union with the Holy Spirit to the bridal mystical union of the Saints, in light of the fact that Mary's sharing in the divine fruitfulness through her union with the Holy Spirit is imparted to her specifically as Mother, helps us see that 'spouse of the Holy Spirit' is indeed a very apt analogous term for describing what is finally a profound mystery in God. The term points to her special dignity, specifically, both as a woman and "the woman," promised by the Blessed

Trinity in Genesis 3:15 in response to original sin. It is only through, with, and in "the woman," Mary, that the Holy Spirit both produces the Incarnate Redeemer and daily imparts the Redemption for the members of the mystical Body of Christ, as well as for the whole creation. While it can certainly be said that the Holy Spirit, and indeed the Blessed Trinity, indwell Mary as a tabernacle or a temple,[352] she is no mere inanimate container— as elegant as a tabernacle or a temple might be! Rather, Montfort helps us realize that the Holy Spirit has mysteriously chosen to be in a permanent *personal* relationship of loving and fruitful union with this real human woman as His "inseparable spouse."[353] For, "from the moment the substantial Love (Holy Spirit) of the Father and the Son espoused Mary to form Jesus, the Head of the elect, and Jesus in the elect, He has never disowned her, for she has always been faithful and fruitful."[354]

Montfort helps us see yet another aspect of the significance of Mary's fully and full human consent. Far from being a mere passive receptacle, with Mary's loving consent the Holy Spirit constantly produces His own fruit only through, with, and in her. "You are always my spouse, as faithful, pure, and fruitful as ever. May your faith give me believers; your purity, virgins; your fruitfulness, elect and *living* temples."[355] Certainly, her personal and intimate union with the Holy Spirit in His sanctifying mission gives us yet one more reason to speak of the Blessed Virgin Mary as a real participant in the work of Redemption, subordinate, but nevertheless *substantially* essential and thus, always alongside, the divine Redeemer.

NOTES

[280] St. Louis Marie de Montfort, "True Devotion to Mary", *God Alone: The Collected Writings of St. Louis Marie de Montfort* , trans. team (Bay Shore, NY: Montfort Publications, 1987) 323.

[281] Patrick Gaffney and Richard J. Payne, eds., *Jesus Living in Mary: Handbook of the Spirituality of St. Louis Marie de Montfort* (Bay Shore, NY:

Montfort Publications, 1994)1210–16. These pages offer many more facts with regard to the origin and other questions about the manuscript of *True Devotion to the Blessed Virgin* that may be of further interest to the reader.

[282] Gaffney 1113–16. These pages offer many more facts with regard to the origin and textual questions surrounding *The Secret of Mary* that may be of further interest to the reader.

[283] Montfort, "True Devotion" 341.

[284] John Paul II, *Redemptoris Mater* , Vatican trans. (Boston: Pauline Books, 1987) 68.

[285] St. Louis Marie de Montfort, "Methods for Saying the Rosary", *God Alone: The Collected Writings of St. Louis Marie de Montfort*, trans. team (Bay Shore, NY: Montfort Publications, 1987) 243.

[286] Montfort, "Methods for Saying the Rosary" 242–3.

[287] Montfort, "True Devotion" 292.

[288] Montfort, "True Devotion" 291.

[289] Faculty of Theology of the University of Navarre, *The Navarre Bible: Saint Luke's Gospel in the RSV and New Vulgate with a Commentary* 2nd ed. (Dublin: Four Courts Press, 1998)150–1.

[290] Montfort, "True Devotion" 303.

[291] Montfort, "True Devotion" 291–292. In St. Thomas Aquinas, *Summa Theologica*, trans. Fathers of the English Dominican Province, vol. IV (Westminster, MD: Christian Classics, 1948) IIIa, q.27, art. 5, ad.3 2162–3, we hear concurrence with Montfort's view about the hiddeness and gifts given the Blessed Virgin during her lifetime. St. Thomas tells us that "there is no doubt that the Blessed Virgin received in a high degree both the gift of wisdom and the grace of miracles and even of prophecy, just as Christ had them. But she did not so receive them, as to put them and such like graces to every use, as did Christ . . . in order that all might fix their attention on Christ."

[292] Montfort, "True Devotion" 292.

[293] Montfort, "True Devotion" 293.

[294] Montfort, "True Devotion" 293.

[295] Montfort, "True Devotion" 303.

[296] Montfort, "True Devotion" 293.

[297] Montfort, "True Devotion" 293.

[298] Montfort, "True Devotion" 291.

[299] Montfort, "True Devotion" 292.

[300] Josef Neuner, S.J. and Jacques Dupuis, S.J., ed., *The Christian Faith in the Doctrinal Documents of the Catholic Church* (New York: Alba House, 1998) 6 (DS125).

[301] Neuner 6 (DS125).

[302] Montfort, "True Devotion" 301.

[303] Montfort, "True Devotion" 294.

[304] Montfort, "True Devotion" 294.

[305] Pope John Paul II, "Celebrating the Trinity," *National Catholic Register* 16 April 2000: 5. During his weekly general audience of April 5, 2000, in St. Peter's Square, Pope John Paul II's reflections upon the mystery of the Trinity testify to the connection between the Incarnation and the entire Blessed Trinity. "The conception of Christ was seen by Luke in the light of the Trinity: it is the words of the angel that attest to this, words directed to Mary. . . . The words the angel proclaims are like a small Creed, which sheds light on the identity of Christ in relation to the other Persons of the Trinity. . . . Christ is the Son of the Most High God, the Great One, the Holy One, the King, the Eternal One, whose generation in the flesh is completed by the work of the Holy Spirit. . . . The Incarnation stands at the center of our faith. In it the glory of the Trinity and Their love for us are revealed. . . . In the Incarnation, we contemplate the Trinitarian love that unfolds itself in Jesus, a love that does not remain closed within a perfect circle of light and glory, but radiates into the flesh of men and women. . . ."

[306] Montfort, "True Devotion" 298.

[307] St. Thomas Aquinas, *Summa Theologica*, trans. Fathers of the English Dominican Province, vol. I (Westminster, MD: Christian Classics, 1981) Ia, q.3, art. 5 63–4.

[308] Jörg Splett and Lourencino Bruno Puntel, "Analogy of Being," *Sacramentum Mundi*, ed. Karl Rahner, S.J., et. al., vol. 1 (New York: Herder, 1968) 24–5. "An ever deeper experience of this fundamental structure of analogy, and reflection on it, may be regarded as the secret law and hidden stimulus of the development of Christian thought. It is only logical that in this process discourse about God changes and must change."

[309] Neuner 150 (DS 850). It is also important to note that this theological principle was confirmed by the Fourth Lateran Council in 1215 with the following words: "For between Creator and creature no similitude can be expressed without implying a greater dissimilitude."

[310] St. Thomas Aquinas Ia, q.1, art. 8 5. St. Thomas tells us that while theology cannot argue in proof of its principles, which are the Articles of Faith, from them it goes on to prove something else. Thus, what we are doing in this argument is accepting as an Article of Faith the fact that God the Son was born of the Blessed Virgin Mary and became man through her precisely as mother, by the Power of the Holy Spirit. Having accepted this truth as an Article of Faith, what else can we say?

[311] St. Thomas Aquinas Ia, q.13, art. 11 70–1. While St. Thomas translates the name of God using specifically the masculine gender, "HE WHO IS," most probably taken from the Vulgate, the Revised Standard Version of the Bible translates the name of God as "I AM WHO I AM," preferring not to be gender specific. This seems more correct if we take gender specific pronouns and nouns as themselves analogous when referring to the Infinite God as discussed above and as St. Thomas himself implies in Ia, q.13, art. 5. Thus, rather than involving God in our gender wars by pitting "HE WHO IS" against "SHE WHO IS," it seems that God can be most properly spoken of as "I AM WHO AM" or Being Itself. The gender neutral language of the Revised Standard Version and other contemporary English translations of the scriptures seems to be in line with the intent of this article by St. Thomas who says that the name which most properly speaks of God does not signify form, but simply existence itself. "Therefore, the less determinate the names are, and the more universal and absolute they are, the more properly they are applied to God. . . . and therefore it (the Name) denominates the *infinite ocean of substance*." However, this is not to say that the created realities of *both* man *and* woman do not image the One who created them since both male created beings and female created beings equally derive their very being from Being Itself (cf. Gen. 1:27, certainly one way of understanding this passage is to say that it takes *both* male *and* female to image God).

[312] *Catechism of the Catholic Church*, 2nd ed. (Washington DC: U.S. Catholic Conference Publications, 1997) n. 2357, 566. For example, this understanding of the revelation of both the mothering and the fathering aspects of the inner-Trinitarian Life, that Montfort helps us realize, lends enormous support to the enduring teaching of the Catholic Faith that "homosexual acts are intrinsically disordered. They are contrary to the natural law....They do not proceed from a genuine affective and sexual complementarity."

[313] *Catechism of the Catholic Church* n. 2205, 532. "The Christian family is a communion of persons, a sign and image of the communion of the Father and the Son in the Holy Spirit. In the procreation and education of children it reflects the Father's work of creation."

[314] René Laurentin, "The Mother of the Lord in the Trinity," course ms., International Marian Research Institute, part II, July 1999 39.

[315] Montfort, "True Devotion" 298–9.

[316] Montfort, "True Devotion" 301. This is also confirmed in *"Lumen Gentium," Documents of the Second Vatican Council* , ed. Austin Flannery,

O.P. (Northport, NY: Costello, 1992) 414. As the Mother of God, Mary is "united to him (the Son) by a close and indissoluble tie. . . ."

[317] Montfort, "True Devotion" 295.

[318] *Catechism of the Catholic Church* 104. Also, see Stefano M. Manelli, FFI, *All Generations Shall Call Me Blessed* , trans. Peter Damien Fehlner (New Bedford, MA: Academy of the Immaculate, 1995) 21. Quoting E. Testa, O.F.M., *La Sacra Bibbia, Genesi*, vol 1 (Rome and Turin: 1977) 310. Manelli points out that sacred tradition has often rendered the translation of this text in a way that says that "the woman" would tread upon the head of the serpent and not her offspring, i.e., "*she* shall crush your head." This was because "the feminine reading of some manuscripts of the old Latin (*ipsa*) later passed into the Vulgate, as attested by the better manuscripts of the Vulgate." However, modern scholarship has shown that "so ancient and respectable a tradition must give way to the masculine reading found in the Masoretic text, in the Samaritan, and also in the Syriac version." Nevertheless, as Manelli points out, sacred tradition has consistently held that "the historical datum of this fundamental text of Genesis opens our eyes to that stupendous drama whose conclusion is the promised salvation."

[319] *Catechism of the Catholic Church* 33.

[320] Michael O'Carroll, C.S.Sp., *Theotokos* (Collegeville: The Liturgical Press, 1982) 371. The Protestant Reformers rejected any Marian sense being attributed to the woman of Genesis 3:15. The Marian interpretation has been defended by Catholic tradition in spite of differences over the *ipsa* pronoun as discussed in the prior footnote. Pope Pius IX said that the woman in Gen.3:15 was a clear reference to Mary in the Bull, *Ineffabilis Deus*, issued to declare the dogma of the Immaculate Conception in 1854. In 1953, Pope Pius XII celebrated the 100th anniversary of Pius IX's declaration by concurring in *Fulgens Corona Gloriae* that the woman of Gen.3:15 is the BVM. Furthermore, Pius XII stated that this passage is the biblical evidence for the dogma of the Immaculate Conception.

[321] "Lumen Gentium" 415.

[322] Laurentin 35. "Mary conceived Christ from her own ovum. She formed him integrally. She is integrally his mother according to nature: from conception to birth."

[323] Montfort, "True Devotion" 368.

[324] Montfort, "True Devotion" 304.

[325] Montfort, "True Devotion" 245.

[326] Montfort, "True Devotion" 308.

[327] Montfort, "The Secret of Mary" 268.

[328] Montfort, "True Devotion" 304–5.

[329] Montfort, "True Devotion" 297.

[330] Karl Rahner, S.J., *Mary Mother of the Lord*, trans. W.J. O'Hara (New York: Herder, 1963) 99–100.

[331] *"Lumen Gentium"* 418. ". . . she is a mother to us in the order of grace."

[332] Montfort, "The Secret of Mary" 267.

[333] Montfort, "The Secret of Mary" 268.

[334] Montfort, "True Devotion" 292.

[335] Montfort, "True Devotion" 374.

[336] Michael O'Carroll, C.S.Sp., *Theotokos* (Collegeville: The Liturgical Press, 1982) 333–4; 386.

[337] René Laurentin, "Mary and the Trinity," International Marian Research Institute, Summer Coursework, Dayton, Ohio, 19–23 July 1998.

[338] *"Lumen Gentium"* 414.

[339] Montfort, "True Devotion" 294.

[340] Montfort, "True Devotion" 293.

[341] O'Carroll 327–8; 357–60. As regards a Marian interpretation of the Song of Songs, individual verses were applied to Mary from the early days of the Church. St. Ambrose is considered to be the first to do so. It is known that St. Jerome specifically interpreted Sg. 4:12 to speak of Mary's virginity. This was also done by St. Epiphanius, St. Isidore, and St. John of Damascus. As Father O'Carroll also aptly points out, "the perpetual virginity of Mary is strongly implied in the sacred text and, with the exception of Tertullian, has been held by important theologians from the beginning of Christianity. . . . Vatican II taught Mary's virginity as an uncontroverted truth in theology. . . . The Council texts refer over thirty times to Mary as Virgin, Virgin Mother, ever-Virgin." Fr. O'Carroll also states that the "late sixties and the seventies have seen a theological ferment within the Church, a desire to investigate with the maximum freedom truths long accepted. . . . In the flow of writing appear a large number of studies on the virginity of Mary." Thus, we would have to conclude that it is only in recent times that anyone would hear the term "spouse of the Holy Spirit" in a way that intends some type of divine fecundation. Due to the rising tide of secularization which has tended to reduce the sacred truths of the tradition to terms which the culture can easily comprehend and accept, it seems all the more urgent that theologians uphold the teaching on the perpetual virginity of Mary. For the theological significance of Mary's perpetual virginity for the Incarnation of the Son of God, see St. Thomas Aquinas, *Summa Theologica*, IIIa, q.28.

[342] Montfort, "Love of Eternal Wisdom" 79–80. It seems important to

reiterate several phrases from a previously quoted passage by Montfort in chapter 4 of this book which would indicate that Montfort clearly holds to the traditional teaching on the perpetual virginity of Mary. " He (Eternal Wisdom) created the most holy Virgin. . . . Her purity so other-worldly drew Him down to her. . . . Wondrous to relate, this divine Wisdom chose to leave the bosom of His Father and enter the womb of a virgin and there repose amid the lilies of her purity." Furthermore, it is also important to note that Montfort clearly holds to the chaste nature of Mary's relationship to St. Joseph as her earthly spouse. In *Love of Eternal Wisdom* 80, Montfort says: "He (Wisdom Incarnate) wished to be born of a married woman, though she was indeed a virgin, lest he should be reproached as one born out of wedlock." Also, on page 81, Montfort says: " Forty days after His birth He chose to offer Himself in the Temple, observing all that the Law of Moses prescribed for the redeeming of the first-born. Some time later the angel told St. Joseph, spouse of the Blessed Virgin, to take the infant Jesus and His Mother and flee into Egypt to escape the wrath of Herod."

[343] Montfort, "True Devotion" 295.

[344] Montfort, "True Devotion" 295–6.

[345] Montfort, "True Devotion" 296. Continuing the Marian thought of St. Louis de Montfort, St. Maximilian Kolbe (1894–1941) says: "The Third Person of the Blessed Trinity never took flesh; still, our human word 'spouse' is far too weak to express the reality of the relationship between the Immaculata and the Holy Spirit. We can affirm that she is, *in a certain sense, the 'incarnation'* of the Holy Spirit. It is the Holy Spirit that we love in her; and through her we love the Son." Further in this regard, Kolbe says: "Jesus Christ has two natures, divine and human, which are united in one single divine Person; such is the exact and precise formulation of the dogma. The Immaculata is united to the Holy Spirit so closely that we really cannot grasp this union. But we can at least say that the Holy Spirit and Mary are two persons who live in such intimate union that have but one sole life."

Commenting on the meaning of these two related statements by Kolbe, H.M. Manteau-Bonamy notes that the notion of union between Jesus and the Word that Nestorius wrongly posited about Jesus Christ (as discussed in our own introduction) can be used to illustrate the nature of the union between Mary and the Holy Spirit according to Kolbe. Thus, while it is inaccurate to say that "The Word became incarnate IN Jesus" because in reality Jesus IS the Incarnate Word, we can, so to speak, say that the Holy Spirit became incarnate IN Mary. The difference is that with regard to Jesus Christ, there are two natures united in one divine Person.

With regard to Mary and the Holy Spirit, there are two persons, one divine and the other human, as well as two natures. Kolbe expresses this by saying: "Mary's nature and person are totally distinct from the nature and Person of the Holy Spirit. Still their union is inexpressible, and so perfect that the Holy Spirit acts only by the Immaculata, His spouse. . . ." H.M. Manteau-Bonamy, O.P., *Immaculate Conception and the Holy Spirit: The Marian Teachings of St. Maximilian Kolbe*, trans. Richard Arnandez, F.S.C. (Libertyville, IL: Franciscan Marytown Press, 1977) 33–50.

[346] Karl Rahner, S.J., and Herbert Vorgrimler, *Dictionary of Theology* 2nd ed. (New York: Crossroad, 1981) 515.

[347] Montfort, "True Devotion" 333.

[348] Montfort, "True Devotion" 294.

[349] Harvey D. Egan, S.J., *An Anthology of Christian Mysticism* (Collegeville: The Liturgical Press, 1991) xviii-xix.

[350] Montfort, "True Devotion" 301.

[351] Montfort, "True Devotion" 293.

[352] Montfort, "True Devotion" 292. Montfort himself speaks of Mary here as the "sanctuary and resting-place of the Blessed Trinity where God dwells in greater and more divine splendor than anywhere else in the universe, not excluding His dwelling above the cherubim and seraphim." He also speaks of her similarly in *Love of Eternal Wisdom* 79: "Eternal Wisdom built Himself a house worthy to be His dwelling-place." In these two places where Montfort uses an inanimate object as a metaphor for Mary, he does not give her the title or name of "sanctuary or temple of the Holy Spirit" or "House of Eternal Wisdom." He uses these passive terms metaphorically and sticks to the relational terms of daughter, mother, and spouse when properly speaking of who Mary *is* in relationship to God.

[353] Montfort, "True Devotion" 299–300.

[354] Montfort, "True Devotion" 300.

[355] Montfort, "True Devotion" 299. Italics added for emphasis.

CHAPTER 5

Mary as Mother of the Redemption and Mother of Our Redemption

Remaining Questions

While our study of what St. Louis de Montfort says about the Blessed Virgin's relationship with each member of the Blessed Trinity has produced much fruit, there are two key questions we have yet to explore. These final questions will put into sharper focus much of what we have already learned:

> What can we say about the Blessed Virgin's role in what has traditionally been called the "acquisition" of the grace of Redemption?

> What can we say about her ongoing role in what has traditionally been called the "distribution" of the grace of Redemption?

This first question pertains to Mary's role in what is commonly called objective Redemption and the second to her role in what is known as subjective Redemption. Our pursuit of how Montfort answers these questions will lead us into the heart of his elaboration on the Bérulle French School's practice of explicit consecration to Jesus through Mary. "I am all yours and all I have is yours, O dear Jesus, through Mary, your holy Mother."[356]

However, before we can understand the additional light that Montfort is trying to shed for us in response to our two remaining questions, there are some Catholic understandings about the meaning and nature of Redemption that we must first clarify. Such clarity will help us continue to appreciate the manner in which the writings of St. Louis de Montfort both presume and build upon the foundations of sacred tradition.

Theological Clarifications about Redemption and Mediation

Perhaps the first and most obvious concern that we must address is the meaning of the very term "Redemption." How do we speak of what Redemption consists, in both the objective sense and in the subjective sense? What needed to be accomplished, objectively speaking, for Redemption to be "finished," as the Savior proclaims from the Cross (John 19:30)? And, congruently, what must take place for that which was finished at the Cross to be applied and made efficacious to a particular person, such that a particular person might be truly born of water and the Spirit and enter the kingdom of God (John 3:5)?

Citing Isa. 53:11–12, John 8:34–36, and Acts 3:14, as the biblical foundations for its discussion, the *Catechism of the Catholic Church* speaks of Redemption in general as the divine plan of salvation which was accomplished "through the putting to death of 'the righteous one, my Servant' . . . as the ransom that would free men from the slavery of sin."[357] The *Catechism* goes on to say that "Jesus, 'the Author of life,' by dying destroyed 'him who has the power of death, that is, the devil, and [delivered] all those who through fear of death were subject to lifelong bondage' (Heb. 2:14–15)."[358] And, finally and most importantly, "'if Christ has not been raised, then our preaching is in vain and your faith is in vain'(1Cor. 15:14). . . . The Paschal mystery has two aspects: by

His death, Christ liberates us from sin; by His Resurrection, He opens for us the way to a new life. This new life is above all justification that reinstates us in God's grace, 'so that as Christ was raised from the dead by the glory of the Father, we too might walk in newness of life'(Rom. 6:4). Justification consists in both victory over the death caused by sin and a new participation in grace. It brings about filial adoption so that men become Christ's brethren. . . . We are brethren not by nature, but by the gift of grace, because that adoptive filiation gains us a real share in the life of the only Son, which was fully revealed in the Resurrection."[359]

Using what the *Catechism* tells us, we might summarize the key elements of Redemption as follows:

> (1) Humankind's freedom from the slavery of bondage to sin and death; (2) through destruction of the power of the devil; (3) accomplished by the righteous Servant who is both true God, "the Author of life," and a true human, who could really be put to death as a ransom for all; (4) whose death and Resurrection have truly opened up the way for human persons to walk in newness of life by reinstating them in God's grace, which is none other than a real share in the very life of God.

In their *Dictionary of Theology*, Karl Rahner and Herbert Vorgrimler add to these key elements by specifically distinguishing between objective and subjective Redemption. Objective Redemption refers to the real historical event "in which God's forgiving desire for redemption freely offered to mankind is now rendered eschatologically irrevocable in the historical reality of Jesus Christ, in which and from which alone man can freely accept the forgiveness offered to him."[360] On the other hand, subjective Redemption is "justification and sanctification" or the "free acceptance of this atonement by the individual human being," which is also God's doing.[361] Thus, we might say that objective Redemption is God's saving "event and its consequence"[362] freely offered to humankind while subjective Redemption is the free acceptance of God's saving event and its consequence by a particular human person.

As we have seen already, St. Irenaeus and many since him have imputed to the Blessed Virgin some kind of real cooperation with the Savior in the work of Redemption, even in the objective event of Redemption itself. Thus, as we consider the meaning of objective Redemption, it is important to ask how we might speak theologically of anyone, besides Jesus Christ, contributing anything to the event of Redemption and its consequence, as defined by the four key elements of Redemption identified above. In terms of our overall question, we must seriously ask if we can really attribute to Mary a moral or possibly even a physical instrumental causality in the work of Redemption? In what way can we even dare to speak of the Blessed Virgin, a mere human person, as having contributed anything to the acquisition of the graces of Redemption, alongside the divine Mediator, Jesus Christ? If she does have a role, is it necessary that we acknowledge her mediation of grace to us? Isn't it enough to speak about all grace being given to us by Jesus Christ through the power of the Holy Spirit?

St. Thomas Aquinas provides us with the classic Catholic theological base line for answering these crucial questions in the *Summa* as follows:

> Properly speaking, the office of a mediator is to join together and unite those between whom he mediates: for extremes are united in the mean (*medio*). Now to unite men to God perfectively belongs to Christ, through Whom men are reconciled to God, according to 2 Cor. v. 19: *God was in Christ reconciling the world to Himself.* And, consequently, Christ alone is the perfect Mediator of God and men, inasmuch as, by His

death, He reconciled the human race to God. Hence the Apostle, after saying, *Mediator of God and man, the man Christ Jesus,* added: *Who gave Himself a redemption for all.*

However, nothing hinders certain others from being called mediators, in some respect, between God and man, forasmuch as they cooperate in uniting men to God, dispositively or ministerially.[363]

In commenting on the significance of St. Thomas' words for Marian mediation, Fr. Garrigou-Lagrange says that it is clear that the office of Mediator belongs fully only to Jesus Christ, Who alone could reconcile us with God. It is only the Lord Jesus Christ Who could offer the infinite sacrifice of the Cross that reconciled humankind to God because Jesus Christ *is* God. While it is as a human man that Jesus Christ is Mediator, He alone is the "Man in Whom humanity is united hypostatically to the Word and endowed with the fullness of grace, the grace of Headship, which overflows on men."[364]

However, when it comes to the Blessed Virgin, St. Thomas tells us that after Christ, there is no reason why there cannot be other secondary mediators between God and the human race who *cooperate with* the Mediator. "Such mediators dispose men for the action of the principal Mediator, or transmit it, but always in dependence upon His merits. . . . Since she (BVM) is a creature, she is, of course, altogether below God Incarnate. But at the same time she is raised far above men by the grace of the divine maternity, which is of the hypostatic order, and by the fullness of grace which she received from her Immaculate Conception." Thus, while the mediation of Mary is subordinated to that of Jesus Christ and dependent upon the merits of the principal Mediator, Mary's mediation "has however been willed by God as a kind of radiation of the Saviour's mediation, and of all radiations the most perfect."[365]

The fathers of the Second Vatican Council aptly substantiate Fr. Lagrange's conclusions through their own comments on the topic of Marian mediation in *"Lumen Gentium."* The mediation of Mary "in no way obscures or diminishes this unique mediation of Christ, but rather shows its power."[366] This is because "the unique mediation of the Redeemer does not exclude but rather gives rise to a manifold cooperation which is but a sharing in this one source."[367] The Blessed Virgin's salutary mediation and influence on all humankind *"originates not in any inner necessity but in the disposition of God."*[368] Thus, the "Church does not hesitate to profess this subordinate role of Mary, which it constantly experiences and recommends to the heartfelt attention of the faithful . . . so they may the more closely adhere to the Mediator and Redeemer."[369]

With this theological understanding in mind, we can say that while her mediation is by no means necessary—both in the sense of God's having to involve Mary and in the sense of God's strictly needing her contribution to make up for something lacking in the merits of the Incarnate Son—the Blessed Trinity, nevertheless, intentionally chose to include Mary in Their mediating work in the created order. By this we are affirming that the human encounter with God is *always* a "mediated experience rooted in the historical, and affirmed as real by the critical judgment that God is truly present and active here or there, in this event or that, in this person or that, in this object or that."[370]

Furthermore, let us add to the above affirmation what we gleaned from our study of the soteriological perspective of St. Irenaeus. Namely, that God included Mary in His redeeming work precisely because God's very way of redeeming is that of *reversal,* as pointed to by the biblical witness of Gen. 3:15. In other words, because a human woman was involved in the downfall of the human race, God purposefully chose to include another human woman in the re-creation and Redemption of humankind. In fact, as St. Louis de Montfort has helped us see, God's involvement of "another woman" in His redeeming work of *reversing* the effects of the sin of Eve and Adam manifests the glory of God and His infinite Love for creatures in a way that is absolutely perfect.

Just as Bl. Duns Scotus (1266–1308) argued that the singular gift of a preservative Redemption from original sin offered to Mary in her Immaculate Conception was evidence of God's having worked the most perfect Redemption possible,[371] we might claim that God's very involvement of Mary in the work of Redemption itself is further evidence still of God's working the most perfect Redemption possible. If Satan tempted and enslaved the human race through the weakness and instrumentality of a woman, how fitting and absolutely perfect that God would choose to restore the human race through the instrumental causality of a woman, whom He Himself makes strong by divine preservation from the effects of both the devil's seduction and Adam and Eve's acquiescence.

Fr. Lagrange offers additional help in how to speak about God's mediating work in the created order being accomplished at one and the same time by both the mediation of the One Mediator and the mediation of the Blessed Virgin. He does this by explaining the dynamics of causality. While we can rightly speak of the work of Redemption as proceeding entirely from God as the First Cause of grace, entirely from Jesus as principal and perfect Mediator, and entirely from Mary as subordinate mediatrix, "these three causes are not partial and co-ordinate—as are three men who drag the same load—but total and subordinated: the second acts under the influence of the first, and the third under the influence of the second. An example that may make the point clear is that of the fruit which proceeds entirely from God the Author of nature, entirely from the tree, and entirely from the branch on which it grows. It does not proceed in its different parts from different causes: neither is our Redemption the work in part of the Divinity, in part of the Humanity, and in part of Mary."[372]

Fr. Lagrange's illustration is not only helpful; it specifically answers many of the questions and fears often raised, especially by Protestant Christians, about Mary's mediation. As human persons who live and work in very competitive situations of our own making, we instinctively have a difficult time understanding how the Blessed Virgin's mediation can keep from either adding to or taking away from the mediation of Jesus Christ. Fr. Lagrange reminds us that we must look to the things that God has created to understand the spiritual realm. In line with our previously mentioned principle of the "analogy of being" in chapter 4, we see that the way the Creator works in the natural process of a tree bearing fruit is analogous to the way God has deemed that the fruit of the Redemption comes to us.

Further Clarifications about Subjective Redemption

Before returning to our consideration of what Montfort says about the Blessed Virgin, it is necessary to take a closer look at what the Catholic Faith means by subjective Redemption. In order to do this, we must determine exactly what sacred tradition has always understood by justification and sanctification. This is especially important since these concepts have sometimes been misconstrued or deleted entirely in the vocabulary of reform Protestants. Confusion in this realm has been and remains the source of even greater confusion with regard to misunderstanding of the role of Mary in Redemption.

Karl Rahner and Herbert Vorgrimler are again helpful to us. "Catholic doctrine holds that justification is the event in which God, by a free act of love, brings man . . . into that relationship with Him which a holy God demands of man and which God of overflowing grace is prepared to give him. He does so by giving man a share in the divine nature (2Pet. 1:4). This happens when God causes the Holy Spirit, His own Spirit, to dwell efficaciously in the depths of man's being as the spirit of adoption of sons (Rom. 8:15), of freedom (2Cor. 3:17) and of holiness (Rom 1:4), divinizing him, and gives him proof of this new creation . . . through the word of faith and the signs of the sacraments."[373]

It is important to underscore here that, according to Catholic doctrine, this justification offered humankind by God is not merely external or imputed to us in a purely juridical fashion, as many Protestants in the wake of the Reformation have mistakenly held. On the contrary, justification makes a human person truly just, even interiorly. When a person's sins are truly forgiven by the grace of Jesus Christ in the sacrament of Baptism, she or he "genuinely and radically passes from the state of sin to that of justification, even though man remains exposed to the attacks of sin, is not able to discover for certain what his condition is before God, continues to sin and in this three-fold respect remains a man fleeing from his own perdition to the grace of God."[374]

How does this interior change or transformation occur? How does a human person pass from the state of sin to that of justification? Once again, Rahner and Vorgrimler are helpful. "In the New Testament, God's gracious act for man is a justification which is not merely an eschatological promise or an external imputation but a present, abiding, interior, salvific possession bestowed in the event of *metanoia*, becoming a believer and being baptized. According to Scripture this is a new creation, a passage from death to life, a rebirth from above and above all the communication of the divine Pneuma, which is the true, regenerative being of God Himself (2Pet. 1:4). This abiding, interior, efficacious communication of the divine Spirit, with its effects, is known in Catholic theology as sanctifying grace."[375]

What is important to note here is that in order to be justified in the eyes of God, the Catholic tradition holds that one must possess that infused charity by which we love God supernaturally and our fellow men and women for God's sake, known as sanctifying grace. It is not enough to reduce justification to mere faith in Christ and exclude sanctifying grace. In the justification of a human person, *it is this very infusion of sanctifying grace that actually blots out sin by healing and transforming rather than merely covering sin with a mantle*, while supposedly awaiting some future action of the Savior on one's behalf after death.

"If it were otherwise," writes Lagrange, "God's uncreated love for the man whom He converts would be merely an idle affection, and not an effective and operative love. But God's uncreated love for us, as St. Thomas shows, is a love which, far from presupposing in us any *lovableness*, actually produces that lovableness within us. . . . Sanctifying grace . . . makes us truly the children of God because it makes us partakers of His nature. We cannot be sons of God by nature, as the Word is; but we are truly sons of God by grace and by adoption. And whereas a man who adopts a child brings about no interior change in him, but simply declares him his heir, God, when He loves us as adoptive sons, transforms us inwardly, giving us a share in His own intimate divine life."[376]

Rahner and Vorgrimler also point to the fact that the human person's initial justification is not the end. "In accordance with the doctrine of God's freedom with respect to grace, of the necessity of the correct disposition and of the growth of grace, sanctifying grace exists in varying measure in various justified individuals."[377] This means that after our initial justification and sanctification, we must continue to avail ourselves of sanctifying grace by means of the sacraments, prayer, and the daily conversion of our lives along the arduous path to holiness.

Rahner also tells us in this regard that there is a "development of man's capacity for an ever more total self-commitment by ever deeper personal acts. The impossibility of being able to commit oneself totally at every moment—the impossibility of a totally making-of-oneself in every moment what one wants to be—is, however, nothing more than what is called concupiscence in the strictly theological sense of the word. . . . Hence, growth in this possibility is nothing more than growth in overcoming concupiscence."[378] In the very real contexts of our lives, sanctifying grace cleanses us from sin and even transforms sin's residual effects in us until we can truly love God with our whole heart, which includes loving our neighbors as God has loved us, in preparation for seeing and loving God face to face in the Beatific Vision.

With this is mind, it is instructive to hear what the *Catechism of the Catholic Church* says about the way to obtain that increase of sanctifying grace needed to enable us to see God immediately in the Beatific Vision, that is to see God as He sees Himself and to love Him as He loves Himself:[379]

> Since the initiative belongs to God in the order of grace, *no one can merit the initial grace* of forgiveness and justification, at the beginning of conversion. Moved by the Holy Spirit and by charity, *we can then merit* for ourselves and for others the graces needed for our sanctification, for the increase of grace and charity, and for the attainment of eternal life. Even temporal goods like health and friendship can be merited in accordance with God's wisdom. These graces and goods are the object of Christian prayer. Prayer attends to the grace we need for meritorious actions.
>
> *The charity of Christ is the source in us of all our merits* before God. Grace, by uniting us to Christ in active love, ensures the supernatural quality of our acts and consequently their merit before God and before men. The saints have always had a lively awareness that their merits were pure grace.[380]

As regards the relationship between the merits of Jesus Christ and Mary's role in subjective Redemption, the following passage from *Ad Diem Illum*, an encyclical written by Pope St. Pius X on February 2, 1904, in honor of the fiftieth anniversary of the proclamation of the dogma of the Immaculate Conception is clarifying:

> From the community of will and suffering between Christ and Mary she merited to become the restorer (*reparatrix*) of the world that was lost, and the dispenser (*dispensatrix*) of all the benefits which Jesus won for us by His death and at the

price of His blood. We do not deny indeed that the distribution of these gifts belongs personally to Christ by a unique right. For they were won through His death alone and He alone has the power to be mediator between God and human beings. Nevertheless, on account of the union of sorrow and pain between mother and Son, of which we have spoken, it has been given to the august Virgin to be the most powerful mediator (*mediatrix*) and advocate (*conciliatrix*) for the whole world with her only-begotten Son. . . . Since she stands above all others in sanctity and in union with Christ, and was drawn by Christ into the work of our salvation, she merits for us by equity (*de congruo*), as it is said, what Christ merited by right (*de condigno*), and she is the primary minister in the distribution of the divine graces.[381]

The above assertions are strengthened by the long standing Catholic affirmation that "our way to God and God's way to us is not only a mediated, but also a communal way. Even when the divine-human encounter is most personal and individual, it is still communal, in that the encounter is made possible by the mediation of a community of faith."[382] In other words, the grace of Redemption, mediated in the first place by Jesus Christ, is secondarily mediated to us through the mystical body of the whole Christ in the community we call the Church.

The significance of this communal aspect of the mediation of grace cannot be overestimated—because it is nothing less than a reflection of the divine community of Persons in the one God. The Second General Council of Lyons declared in 1442 that the three distinct Persons are one God and not three gods, "for the three are one substance, one essence, one nature, one Godhead, one infinity, one eternity, and everything [in Them] is one where there is no opposition of relationship."[383] "On account of this unity the Father is wholly in the Son and wholly in the Holy Spirit; the Son wholly in the Father and wholly in the Holy Spirit; the Holy Spirit wholly in the Father and wholly in the Son. None precedes the other in eternity, none exceeds the other in greatness, nor excels the other in power. For it is from eternity and without beginning that the Son has taken His origin from the Father, and from eternity and without beginning that the Holy Spirit proceeds from the Father and the Son."[384]

This means that although the Persons are distinct in manifestation as Father, Son, and Holy Spirit—because there is a real distinction of Persons *in* the Trinity—God is a real community of Persons, as long as this community is not envisaged in spatial terms.[385] It is entirely correct to speak of this community of Persons as being everywhere doing one and the same thing in the created order because the Persons of the Trinity are a single, operative principle with regard to creatures.[386] Thus, we can rightfully say that the entire mediation of grace in the created order is communal because of the communal nature of the very Source of grace.[387] Furthermore, the divine Persons have extended in time and space the mediation of grace to us through the community of human persons who are made one with Them through grace—with the Blessed Virgin's being not merely this secondary community's preeminent member but in reality its very Mother, as Montfort will show us next.

Mary's Role in the Acquisition of the Graces of Redemption

With these theological foundations in place, it is now time to focus on our two remaining questions. And, in trying to discover what the writings of St. Louis de Montfort tell us about the Blessed Virgin Mary and her role in objective Redemption, we must return to the heart of what he tells us about Mary's importance in the Incarnation itself. For herein lies the key:

Because God gave her His Son, it is His Will that we should receive all gifts through her, and that no heavenly gift should come down upon earth without passing through her as through a channel.[388]

For God, having given her power over His only-begotten and natural Son, also gave her power over His adopted children, not only in what concerns their body-which would be of little account—but also in what concerns their soul.

Mary is the Queen of heaven and earth by grace as Jesus is king by nature and by conquest.[389]

The salvation of the world began through Mary and through her it must be accomplished.[390]

In these passages Montfort reminds us of the importance of our having an orthodox Trinitarian theology if we are to appreciate the depth of what he is saying. In this case, it is necessary for us to apply an important principle derived from the very mystery of the Blessed Trinity Itself for understanding Mary's role in Redemption. Namely, just as there is an order of procession that exists in God with regards to the mystery of the Persons of the Blessed Trinity, there is an order of procession in the mystery of Redemption. In the Blessed Trinity, the Son proceeds from the Father, and the Holy Spirit proceeds from the Father and the Son, "as from one principle and through one spiration." Thus, "when the holy Doctors and Fathers say that the Holy Spirit proceeds from the Father through the Son, this must be understood in the sense that, as the Father, so also the Son is what the Greeks call 'cause' and the Latins 'principle' of the subsistence of the Holy Spirit. And, since the Father has through generation given to the only-begotten Son everything that belongs to the Father, except being Father, the Son has also eternally from the Father, from whom He is eternally born, that the Holy Spirit proceeds from the Son."[391]

Correspondingly, in the work of Redemption, the Father has given the Son to the Blessed Virgin, such that the Incarnate Son now proceeds *through* the Blessed Virgin Mary by the Power of the Holy Spirit. Thus, the entire work of Redemption, including the graces that flow from it, proceed *through* her by grace and from the Incarnate Son by nature, "as through one spiration." Let us recall that we mentioned in chapter 1 that St. Irenaeus points to just such a fact in his own theology. Namely, he states that the Redemption proceeds from both the Incarnate Son and the Blessed Virgin, as from one single and total principle of salvation, as Eve was in fact associated with Adam, as one single and total principal of the Fall. Let us also remember what Fr. Lagrange helped us see about the inner dynamics of causality. His example about the three men dragging the same load taught us that proceeding as from one principle means that the Redemption does not proceed from partial and co-ordinate causes, but rather from causes that are total and subordinate, i.e., ordered, such that there is a hierarchical flow.

It is essential to note that Montfort is telling us that this order of procession in the work of objective Redemption is *not optional*. Neither is it a mere product of pious imaginations. Rather, this order was established by God the Father in the very act of choosing Mary as the one *through* whom His eternally begotten Son would be conceived for all eternity as incarnate, from the moment of her *fiat*, by the Power of the Holy Spirit. Precisely because the Incarnation of the Son proceeds through her by divine choice, all that comes to us as the consequence and fruit of His Incarnation *must* now proceed through her as well, by divine choice. And, as we saw in the preceding chapter, Montfort also states that the Father has made her the inseparable associate of the Holy Spirit. Consequently, the Father has given her the very same power and dominion over souls that belongs to the Incarnate Son by virtue of His divinity and infinite merits:

. . . Mary has received from God a far-reaching dominion over the souls of the elect. Otherwise she could not make her dwelling in them as God the Father has ordered her to do, and she could not conceive them, nourish them, and bring them forth to eternal life as their mother. She could not have them for her inheritance and her possession and form in their heart the roots of her virtues, nor be the inseparable associate of the Holy Spirit in all these works of grace. None of these things, I repeat, could she do unless she had received from the Almighty rights and authority over their souls.[392]

With Montfort's help, we see that the primary reason we may refer to Mary as mediatrix, or coredemptrix, or reparatrix, or any similar title speaking of her mediating role in Redemption is that the Father, Himself, made the choice to involve her in the entire work of Redemption, by choosing her to be the Mother through whom the divine Son became incarnate. This was one and the same deliberate choice on the part of the Father. While Mary's full consent and substantial self-oblation signaled by her *fiat* are certainly the necessary human contributions that enabled her to take her place in the mystery of Redemption, Montfort is clearly reminding us that the most important contribution was God's. It is nothing else than divine Choice and divine Power that are the real deciding factors. It is the Father, Himself, Who has chosen Mary to be the Mother, in the entire mystery of Redemption, from start to finish.

We also notice that St. Louis Marie goes so far as to say that all grace proceeds through Mary as through a channel. In the passage below, we hear Montfort declaring that this is true not only for the distribution of the graces of Redemption but also for the very acquisition of these graces, i.e., for all that we have said above about the meaning of objective Redemption. As we have said earlier, this is true because the whole mystery of Redemption is necessarily implied and even contained in the divine *Fiat* of the eternal Son when He condescends to be conceived as the Incarnate Redeemer, only, through, with and in the Virgin Mary:

> The Incarnation is the first mystery of Jesus Christ; it is the most hidden; and it is the most exalted and the least known.

> It was in this mystery that Jesus, in the womb of Mary and with her cooperation, chose all the elect. For this reason the saints called her womb the throne-room of God's mysteries.

> It was in this mystery that Jesus anticipated all subsequent mysteries of His life by His willing acceptance of them. Consequently, this mystery is a summary of all His mysteries since it contains the intention and the grace of them all.

> Lastly, this mystery is the seat of the mercy, the liberality, and the glory of God. It is the seat of His *mercy* for us, since we can approach and speak to Jesus through Mary. We need her intervention to see or speak to Him. . . .

> It is the seat of *liberality* for Mary, because while the new Adam dwelt in this truly earthly paradise God performed there so many hidden marvels beyond the understanding of men and angels. . . .

> It is the seat of *glory* for His Father, because it was in Mary that Jesus perfectly atoned to His Father on behalf of mankind. It was here that He perfectly restored the glory that sin had taken from

His Father. It was here again that our Lord, by the sacrifice of Himself and of His will, gave more glory to God than He would have given had He offered all the sacrifices of the Old Law. Finally, in Mary He gave His Father infinite glory, such as His Father had never received from man.[393]

In this segment from *True Devotion*, St. Louis Marie can be theologically interpreted as invoking and building upon a principle of St. Thomas Aquinas about the efficacy of each and every action of the Incarnate Word to accomplish the work of Redemption. "There is a twofold efficient agency—namely, the principal and the instrumental. Now the principal efficient cause of man's salvation is God. But since Christ's humanity is the *instrument of the Godhead* . . . , therefore all Christ's actions and sufferings operate instrumentally in virtue of His Godhead for the salvation of men."[394]

With this teaching of St. Thomas in mind, we might say that St. Louis de Montfort is applying the Christological principle of the *communicatio idiomatum* discussed in chapter 1 to help us see the significance of the moment of the Incarnation for the whole work of Jesus Christ in objective Redemption. First, let us remember that it really was, and is, the Second Person of the Blessed Trinity, God the Son, Himself, Who humbled Himself out of loving obedience to the Father and out of love for all that the Father had created from nothing, through the Son, by the Power of the Holy Spirit. Secondly, "stooping to our level in His Love and Self-revealing to us,"[395] in order "to bring again the corruptible to incorruption,"[396] God the Son both desired and freely chose to be conceived as incarnate and be, thereby, confined to the womb of the Blessed Virgin. It is precisely this freely chosen suffering of diminishment to be conceived as flesh, on the part of the eternal Son, that can be said to "operate instrumentally" for the Redemption of humankind. Thus, in building upon what St. Thomas has said, we can say that the Redemptive Power of God *is* fully manifest in the very moment of the Incarnation itself because in the very act of obedience and complete Self-abnegation that took place, at that moment, the eternal Son intended both His perfect obedience to His Father and His total Self-abnegation that occurred throughout His life, passion, death, resurrection, and ascension to the right hand of the Father, where He remains seated, forever, as the Incarnate Word.

In other words, in the very giving of His initial consent to become incarnate, the Eternal Word was not only consenting to His passion and death but also to being both Son of the Father and son of Mary, throughout eternity. This initial act of obedient Self-oblation was, itself, atoning and remains that way for all eternity precisely because it is God, Himself, Who undertakes this kenotic suffering of taking on a human nature on behalf of humankind in the Incarnation—a Self-abnegation that will necessarily bring with it the experience of suffering all the consequences of sin experienced by human beings, although He was God. And, because this act of obedient Self-oblation required to become incarnate will last throughout eternity—even on the other side of His passion and death where the Incarnate Son is seated at the right hand of the Father after His resurrection and ascension—this act of perfect obedience on behalf of humankind can be said to be not only of infinite merit but also of eternal duration. Clearly, in the very diminishment of the Incarnation, the Eternal Word has already perfectly sacrificed His Will to the Father, for all eternity, by becoming and remaining flesh forever, thereby reversing the sin of Adam's disobedience.

St. Thomas sheds additional light on the meritorious value of the Son's diminishment in the Incarnation made possible through Mary. "Christ's Passion in relation to His flesh is consistent with the infirmity which He took upon Himself, but in relation to the Godhead it draws infinite might from It, according to 1Cor. 1:25; *The weakness of God is stronger than men;* because Christ's weakness, inasmuch as He is God, has a might exceeding all human power. . . . But in so far as it is compared with the will of Christ's soul, it acts in a meritorious manner: considered as being within Christ's very flesh, it acts by way of satisfaction, inasmuch as we are liberated by it from the debt of punishment; while inasmuch as we are freed from the servitude of guilt, it acts by way of redemption: but in so far as we are reconciled with God it acts by way of sacrifice."[397]

Finally, with these weighty insights about the redemptive significance of the Incarnation of God the Son in mind, what else can we possibly add to our understanding about Mary's role in the acquisition of the graces of Redemption that we haven't already said? As St. Louis Marie himself would tell us, it is at last time to contemplate, prayerfully, not only the mysterious event of the Incarnation itself but also all its ramifications for salvation history and throughout all eternity, including, and even especially, the diminishment that it has meant and still means for the divine Son to take a human nature. Such prayerful contemplation will help us grasp the fact that from God's viewpoint the very work of Redemption itself is both implicit and explicit in the divine choice of the Blessed Virgin Mary to be the Mother of God. And, when we have grasped this, perhaps then we will really understand the significance of the Blessed Virgin's own *fiat* , which resulted in her substantial self-offering as the crucial link in the chain of causality upon which the entire Blessed Trinity freely chose to depend, in bringing about the event of Redemption itself. And when we have grasped this, in light of all we have seen, we will know for ourselves what Montfort has been trying to say to us about God the Son's choice to accomplish His work of objective Redemption *only* through, with, and in Mary. "'If you wish to understand the mother,' says a saint, 'then understand the Son. . . .' *Hic taceat omnis lingua:* Here let every tongue be silent."[398]

Mary's Role in the Distribution
of the Graces of Redemption

Having established that the work of objective Redemption happens only through, with, and in the Blessed Virgin, St. Louis de

Montfort now takes us into his considerable understanding of the importance of Mary in the work of subjective Redemption. His basic premise is that "being necessary to God by a necessity which is called 'hypothetical', (that is, because God so willed it), the Blessed Virgin is all the more necessary for men to attain their final end."[399] He agrees completely with a 16th century Jesuit theologian whom we have previously named, Francisco de Suarez, "a devout and erudite theologian," who "proved incontestably that devotion to Our Blessed Lady is necessary to attain salvation." Quoting St. John Damascene, Montfort also proclaims: "Devotion to you, O Blessed Virgin, is a means of salvation which God gives to those whom He wishes to save." And, Montfort states that many of the Fathers held that "lack of esteem and love for the Virgin Mary is an infallible sign of God's disapproval. On the other hand, to be entirely and genuinely devoted to her is a sure sign of God's approval."[400]

The reason that the Blessed Virgin is not optional for the course of each individual in receiving the grace of his or her salvation is that each of the Persons of the Blessed Trinity has given her the role of distributing *all*[401] the graces that flow from Them. As we saw in regards to the objective Redemption, her role in the subjective Redemption is inherent in the divine plan of salvation that God made manifest in the Incarnation:

> The plan adopted by the three Persons of the Blessed Trinity in the Incarnation, the first coming of Jesus Christ, is adhered to each day in an invisible manner throughout the Church and They will pursue it to the end of time until the last coming of Jesus.[402]

> Mary alone found grace before God without the help of any other creature. All those who have since found grace before God have found it only through her. . . . (T)he Almighty made her the

sole custodian of His treasures and the sole dis-
penser of His graces.[403]

Commenting on Mary's relationship to the Son and the Holy
Spirit specifically in the distribution of the graces of Redemption,
Montfort tells us:

> God the Son imparted to His mother all that
> He gained by His life and death, namely, His infi-
> nite merits and His eminent virtues. He made her
> the treasurer of all His Father had given Him as
> heritage. Through her He applies His merits to His
> members and through her He transmits His virtues
> and distributes His graces. She is His mystic chan-
> nel, His aqueduct, through which He causes His
> mercies to flow gently and abundantly.[404]

> God the Holy Spirit entrusted His wondrous
> gifts to Mary, His faithful spouse, and chose her as
> the dispenser of all He possesses, so that she dis-
> tributes all His gifts and graces to whom she wills,
> as much as she wills and when she wills. No heav-
> enly gift is given to men which does not pass
> through her virginal hands.[405]

Clearly, a point of great significance for St. Louis Marie in
understanding the role of Mary in subjective Redemption is the
fact that each Person of the Blessed Trinity continues to relate to
her in the same manner as in the Incarnation itself. She is forever
the Father's splendid daughter with whom He shares not only His
own fruitfulness but all that is "beautiful, resplendent, rare, and
precious, even His own Son. This immense treasury is none other
than Mary whom the saints call the 'treasury of the Lord.' From
her fullness all men are made rich."[406] Likewise, our Lord and Savior, Jesus Christ, "remains in heaven just as much the Son of Mary

as He was on earth. Consequently, He has retained the submissiveness and obedience of the most perfect of all children towards the best of all mothers."[407] Finally, the Holy Spirit has chosen to work His wonders only through Mary, His "inseparable spouse" as St. Louis Marie calls her, because "from the moment the substantial love of the Father and the Son espoused Mary to form Jesus, the Head of the elect, and Jesus in the elect, He has never disowned her, for she has always been faithful and fruitful."[408]

What exactly is Mary's perpetual contribution, as a human person, that makes it possible for the Persons of the Blessed Trinity to unite her so fully to Themselves and work so entirely and mightily through her? This contribution, as we have been profoundly helped to see by Montfort, remains perpetually, precisely, the full and willing surrender of the Blessed Virgin Mary's heart, mind, soul, and body—in perfect humility and loving conformity to the divine will. More than any of the other saints, the Blessed Virgin has been completely transformed by grace and "she does not ask or wish to do anything which is contrary to the eternal and unchangeable will of God. . . . (T)he authority which God was pleased to give her is so great that she seems to have the same power as God. Her prayers and requests are so powerful with Him that He accepts them as commands in the sense that He never resists His dear Mother's prayer because it is always humble and conformed to His will."[409]

Furthermore, Montfort tells us that it is precisely because of Mary's profound and perfect humility during her earthly life that God now wishes to reveal to us who Mary really *is* in the divine plan of salvation. "God wishes therefore to reveal Mary, His masterpiece, and make her more known in these latter times because she kept herself hidden and in her great humility considered herself lower than dust."[410] And, it is essential for us that God does make her known because "she is the sure means, the direct and immaculate way to Jesus and the perfect guide to Him. It is through her that souls who are to shine forth in sanctity, must find Him. He who finds Mary finds life, that is, Jesus Christ, who is the way, the truth and the life. But no one can find Mary who does not look for her. No one can look for her who does not know her, for no one seeks or desires something unknown. Mary then must be better known than ever for the deeper understanding and the greater glory of the Blessed Trinity."[411]

This takes us to another crucial point for Montfort. The *only* way to find Jesus is through Mary. The only way to have one's own soul formed in the image of Jesus is through Mary. The only way to be born again into the life of the kingdom of God is through Mary. The reason for this is that, once again, by divine *Fiat*, she was truly made our Mother when she was made the Mother of God the Son Incarnate. Here is the real reason why Mary is not an optional or mere pious link in the human journey toward union with God. She *is* eternally conceiving us in the order of grace, every bit as much as she *is* eternally conceiving God the Son as Incarnate. "God the Son wishes to form Himself, and in a manner of speaking, become incarnate every day in His members through His dear Mother."[412] To His Mother, Montfort says the divine Son has said: "To the good I shall be father and advocate, to the bad a just avenger, but to all I shall be a judge. But you, dear Mother, will have for your heritage and possession only the predestinate represented by Israel. As their loving mother, you will give them birth, feed them and rear them. As their queen, you will lead, govern and defend them."[413]

Now, what Montfort is saying here is serious business as regards our reception of sanctifying grace, healing, transformation, and entrance into eternal life. He is echoing the same powerful theme that we have encountered from him before. Namely, by the divine plan, there must be a mother in the supernatural sphere just as there is in the natural sphere. Having a mother in the spiritual sphere is no more optional than it is in the physical sphere. For, if "Jesus Christ, the head of mankind, is born of her, the predestinate, who are members of this head, must also as a necessary consequence be born of her. One and the same mother does not give birth to the head without the members nor to the members without the head, for these would be monsters in the order of nature. In the order of grace likewise the head and the members must be born of the same mother."[414]

By now, it is hopefully clear that when Montfort speaks of the necessity of having a mother in the spiritual or supernatural sphere, he is not speaking of someone who can merely offer us the spiritual equivalent of a hug, an encouraging word, or a feminine touch of some kind—as important as these may be. Rather, he is speaking of something far more significant and essential. He is speaking of one who confers life on us by serving as the instrumental cause, both substantially and ontologically (in the order of being), through whom we are born anew as redeemed and re-created human beings. He is telling us that dual parenting is as much God's design for bringing about life in the supernatural sphere as it is in the natural sphere. In the natural sphere, it is God's design for human life to occur both, and only, through the father's contribution of the sperm and the mother's contribution of the ovum. Both mother and father give of themselves to bring about life, as though from one single principle. Thus, there must be, and is, an analogous equivalent in the spiritual sphere because the lower reflects the higher, as we discussed in chapter 4.

This is testified to by the very fact that God the Son Incarnate, the Second Adam, now has a Father who is God and a Mother who is Mary for all eternity. The One who is the only way to the Father became incarnate to both delineate and mediate the way we must follow, if we desire eternal life. He shows us that our supernatural life of grace is co-authored and re-capitulated by both the Second Adam and the Second Eve—by both the Eternal Word of the Father through Whom all things are made and by the Virgin Mary who is our mother in the order of grace, because she is the Mother through whom human nature has been hypostatically united to the Word of Life Himself. She really *is* our Mother in the supernatural order because it *is* from her humanity that the very incarnate reality of the Mediator Himself has come into being, by the Power of the Holy Spirit. This is true for each and every one of us, regardless of the extent to which we are consciously aware of this truth.

Now, it is in this serious consideration of Mary as a true mother for us[415] as well as for the Incarnate Son that we at last find the answer to the fundamental question raised in this book's introduction. Is the Blessed Virgin Mary merely the first and best example of someone who responded to the universal call to holiness? Or, does everything we've seen so far about the Blessed Virgin's unique and perpetual relationship with each Person of the Blessed Trinity place her in a position superior to us in the hierarchical chain of re-created being, such that all eternal life really is mediated to us through and even with, and in, Mary as mother? Congruently, is she merely the greatest of the disciples and intercessors before the Lord on our behalf or is she really our Mother in the supernatural order from whom we must be "born anew" (John 3:3), if we desire the fullness of Redemption to be accomplished in us? What did the Savior really intend for all of us to understand when he told the beloved disciple in the moments before His death, "Behold, your mother!" (John 19:27)?

By this point, the reader has hopefully begun to hear the truth Montfort teaches us. In order to really hear Montfort, however, it is important to remember that he has been quite clear, all along, that Mary is merely a human person, which means she is a created being like the rest of us. However, Montfort has helped us see repeatedly that the Blessed Trinity has freely chosen to elevate this particular human being and woman into a perpetual union with Their very Selves, in a singular way, in the divine plan of salvation. It is because of her unique relationship with the Blessed Trinity that Montfort chooses the hierarchical order in the processions of the Trinity to help us hear the depth of what he is saying:

> (I)t is Mary's role to lead us safely to her Son, just as it is the role of Our Lord to lead us to the eternal Father.
> Our Lord is our Advocate and our Mediator of

Redemption with God the Father. . . . It is through Him that we have access to God the Father. We should never appear before God, our Father, unless we are supported by the merits of His Son. . . . But have we no need of a mediator with the Mediator Himself? Are we pure enough to be united directly to Christ without any help? Is Jesus not God, equal in every way to the Father? . . . If in His infinite love He became our security and our Mediator with the Father, whom He wished to appease in order to redeem us from our debts, should we on that account show Him less respect and have less regard for the majesty and holiness of His Person?[416]

Montfort answers our questions still further by speaking specifically of how Mary's inseparable relationship with the Holy Spirit effects us:

If we desire the fruit of life, Jesus Christ, we must possess the tree of life which is Mary. If we desire to have the Holy Spirit working within us, we must possess His faithful and inseparable spouse, Mary the divinely-favored one, whom as I have said elsewhere, He can make fruitful."[417]

Thus, with all due respect to the artist who designed the marble relief which hangs over the entrance of the Basilica of the National Shrine of the Immaculate Conception in Washington, D.C., as discussed in our introductory chapter, St. Louis Marie de Montfort helps us see that Mary offers us much more than merely holding our hand on the way to her Son as we receive the graces given by the Holy Spirit. While she is indeed a mere human being like us and in that sense really one of us, there is something of inestimable significance going on between her being and ours. Namely, the Blessed Virgin has been designated by God to function as our true and real Mother in the supernatural sphere. We might say that as the Father's adopted children we have each been entrusted by the entire Blessed Trinity into the spiritual equivalent of Mary's womb for our rebirth and continual transformation "from glory into glory."

In the mystery we call grace, it is thus only through, with, and even *in* our Blessed Mother, Mary, that our humanity is re-created and that we receive the inner life of divine Charity, called sanctifying grace, needed to transform us for entrance into eternal life with the Blessed Trinity. This life of grace is made possible for us only by the contributions of both the Incarnate Eternal Word of the Father, Jesus Christ, and the human woman and Mother, the Blessed Virgin Mary, by the Power of the Holy Spirit, as from one single principle in both the events of objective and subjective Redemption. St. Louis de Montfort clearly teaches that Mary is "our proximate end" and "our mysterious intermediary"[418] in receiving the full riches of Redemption, which is life with God.

Since all we have learned about the Blessed Virgin's role in both objective and subjective Redemption is true in the supernatural order of re-created being—even if those being redeemed are not consciously aware of this truth—St. Louis counsels that our explicit knowledge of, and loving surrender to, the Trinity's plan in regard to Mary is the "easiest way of reaching Him," i.e., the easiest way to union with Jesus Christ who "alone is our ultimate end."[419] This is why Montfort advises that we should literally "possess" Mary within us, as quoted above. We come to "possess" Mary by *consciously* giving "ourselves up to the spirit of Mary to be moved and directed as she wishes. We should place and leave ourselves in her virginal hands, like a tool in the hands of a craftsman or a lute in the hands of a good musician."[420] Practically speaking, we do this "by a mere thought, a slight movement of the will or just a few words as—'I renounce myself and give myself to you, my dear Mother.'" [421] When "the Holy Spirit, her spouse, finds Mary in a soul, He hastens there and enters fully into it. He gives Himself generously to that soul according to the place it has given to His spouse."[422]

In other words, if we desire to cooperate fully with what God has ordained in regard to Mary's role in Redemption, we must "let ourselves be perfectly contained and led by the humble Virgin without any reserve on our part."[423] Just as she cooperated with God's will for her life, so we should cooperate with His will for us. We accomplish this cooperation best by an intentional "surrender to her, body and soul, without reserve in order to belong entirely to Jesus."[424] The reason we choose to surrender ourselves to our Mother, Mary, is she "is a mold capable of forming people into the image of the God-man. Anyone who is cast into this divine mold is quickly shaped and molded into Jesus and Jesus into him. At little cost and in a short time he will become Christ-like since he is cast into the very same mold that fashioned a God-Man."[425] The mold of Mary "is the true likeness of Him."[426]

"Do Whatever He Tells You"

We are now at the heart of yet one last theological principle that provides the final support from sacred tradition for all that St. Louis Marie has helped us see about Mary's essential role in both objective and subjective Redemption. This principle is none other than the absolute necessity of the *imitatio Christi*, the imitation of the Second Adam who is the Head of the human race. It is here that our study of Montfort's life and thought come full circle as we pick up that significant thread that may well have found its beginnings in the early influence of Ignatian spirituality on this great Marian Saint mentioned in chapter 3.

The importance of the imitation of Christ for those being redeemed has its roots in the constant teaching of the Incarnate Word when He lived on this earth. "Go, sell what you have, and give to the poor, and you will have treasure in heaven; and come follow me" (Mark 10:21). While these words have been interpreted by the Christian community to mean that the life of discipleship will both accompany and be an expression of living faith in Jesus Christ as Lord and Savior, there has always been present throughout sacred tradition an abiding sense that these words are an invitation and a challenge to follow the example and life of Jesus, in a literal way, in order to enter into His paschal mystery.[427] "For if we have been united with Him in a death like His, we shall certainly be united with Him in a resurrection like His" (Rom. 6:5). In fact, St. Paul goes on to say that it is only if our old self is crucified with Christ that we will be freed from the bondage of sin. "For he who has died is freed from sin. But if we have died with Christ, we believe we shall also live with Him" (Rom. 6:6–8).

By the fifteenth century, this enduring sense that man needs to follow literally the life of Christ, especially by participating in His poverty and suffering in some way, in order to die to sin and be raised to the new life of grace expressed itself in the famous work entitled, the *Imitation of Christ*, attributed to Thomas à Kempis (1380–1471).[428] This work was widely circulated at the time it was written and is still considered a spiritual classic.

In his introduction to his translation of this classic, Joseph N. Tylenda, S.J., says that St. Ignatius of Loyola "read a chapter each day of his life" and "was in the habit of offering it as a gift to acquaintances."[429] Anyone who is familiar with *The Spiritual Exercises* of St. Ignatius can readily see the influence of Thomas à Kempis' opening admonition: "Let it be our main concern to meditate on the life of Jesus Christ. . . . If you want to fully understand Christ's words and to relish them, you must strive to conform your entire life to His."[430]

As discussed in chapter 3 above, a famous 20th century son of St. Ignatius, Karl Rahner, S.J., articulates well the theological imperative behind sacred tradition's enduring practice of the *imitatio Christi*, as encouraged by Thomas à Kempis, St. Ignatius of Loyola, and we can now add St. Louis Marie de Montfort:

> The Christ-conformation of existence is not
> merely the result of the abstract assumption of

human nature by the Logos, but comes about through the actual shape of existence. That is why we meditate on the life of Christ, why we say we will imitate our Lord in his poverty, why we say that our life is a participation in the death and in the cross of Christ.

All these things have a certain contingency in the life of Jesus; they did not need to be so, they are again concrete expressions of a free attitude of the Logos, who wanted to reveal himself just in this way. But it is the actual shape of the life of Jesus which then becomes the law of our life, whether we can draw this conclusion in a theoretical, abstract, moral philosophy or moral theology, or not. . . .

The life of Jesus as form of our life cannot be regarded merely as an alternative: either to reject it, to consider it as invalid for us, or to prove it to be appropriate in actuality by the standards of an abstract, fundamentally essentialist philosophy of the human person and what he ought to do. The Lord is the ultimate standard; there is none higher than he, since the ultimate standard of necessity is revealed to us just in this actual person.

For it is just here that the Logos became man and not simply any man, but this man, so that we cannot really accept a division in the life of Jesus between what is important for us and what can be left aside, however true it may be that the structure of this life bears within itself and thus also creates for us variations of significance and of necessity. All this remains a factor of this unique historical norm, and the imitation of Christ can be measured by no other standard than Jesus himself and his life.[431]

While Montfort did not have the gift of Rahner's clear theology on the *imitatio Christi* to substantiate his own thinking as we do today, St. Louis Marie is nonetheless clear that the pattern of the historical life of Jesus Christ is the standard and form for all those who desire to receive the full riches of Redemption. It is in this light and with this sense of urgency that St. Louis Marie holds up for our consideration a way to imitate consciously the surrender of the Eternal Word, and really of the entire Blessed Trinity, to the Blessed Virgin Mary. That way is intentionally "consecrating to her completely and for all eternity" our entire being, body and soul, both spiritual and material possessions, in order to follow the example of Jesus Christ.[432] Those who become subject and obedient to the Blessed Virgin as their Mother "are simply following the example set by our Lord Himself, who spent thirty of the thirty-three years He lived on earth glorifying God His Father in perfect and entire submission to His holy Mother:"[433]

> Our good Master stooped to enclose Himself *in* the womb of the Blessed Virgin, a captive but loving slave, and to make Himself subject to her for thirty years. As I said earlier, the human mind is bewildered when it reflects seriously upon this conduct of Incarnate Wisdom. He did not choose to give Himself in a direct manner to the human race though He could easily have done so. He chose to come through the Virgin Mary. . . .
>
> What immeasurable glory then do we give to God when, following the example of Jesus, we submit to Mary! With such a convincingly and well-known example before us, can we be so foolish as to believe that there is a better and shorter way of

giving God glory than by submitting ourselves to
Mary as Jesus did?[434]

By advocating consecration to Mary, Montfort is telling us
that the *intentional* submission of ourselves to Mary—who is ontologically (in the order of being) the Mother of our Redemption—
is the proven way we can become perfectly submissive to God.
When we consciously correspond to the *kenosis* of the Incarnate
Son by imitating His dependence upon Mary, we will discover the
sure way to be emptied of our disordered passions and our false
sense of self-reliance and control. In other words, for those who
want to take following and imitating our Lord and Savior Jesus
Christ seriously, submission to Mary is the way to do this perfectly.
We are foolish if we choose not to take the very path He took and
laid out for us. Practically speaking, this means intentionally
"beginning, carrying out and completing our actions through her,
in her, with her and for her in order to do them through Jesus, in
Jesus, with Jesus, and for Jesus, our last end."[435]

Montfort goes on to say that we need to undertake consciously this particular aspect of the imitation of Jesus Christ, the
Second Adam, because we are "extremely weak and change-
able. . . . (Our) human nature is deeply impaired. . . . (We) have
been fashioned from the same corrupted nature as the other children of Adam and Eve. . . . [436] Thus, how blessed we are if we
know and put into practice this "secret" he is revealing to us, "a
secret unknown to most Christians, even the most devout."[437] If
we want to be raised with Him into the life of divine Charity, the
way that Jesus Himself prepared for us is the surest way:

> You do not put choice wine into old casks that
> have contained sour wine. You would spoil the
> good wine and run the risk of losing it. . . .
>
> Do not commit the gold of your charity, the silver
> of your purity to a threadbare sack or a battered

old chest. . . . Otherwise you will be robbed by thieving devils who are on the look-out day and night waiting for a favorable opportunity to plunder. If you do so, all those pure gifts from God will be spoiled by the unwholesome presence of self-love, inordinate self-reliance, and self-will.

Pour into the bosom and heart of Mary all your precious possessions, all your graces and virtues. She is a spiritual vessel, a vessel of honor, a singular vessel of devotion. Ever since God personally hid Himself with all His perfections in this vessel, it has become completely spiritual, and the spiritual abode of all spiritual souls. . . .

Blessed is the man who has given everything to Mary, who at all times and in all things trusts in her, and loses himself in her. He belongs to Mary and Mary belongs to him. . . . (H)e can boldly say . . . with the beloved disciple, "I have taken her for my own" (John 19:27), or with our Lord Himself, "All that is mine is yours and all that is ours is mine."[438]

Through such a total surrender of ourselves to the Blessed Virgin, Montfort is advocating putting our confidence in what God has already accomplished in the Incarnation itself through, with, and in Mary—rather than in ourselves. And, lest anyone should think this exempts any of us from the hard work of dying to the false self that sanctification necessarily entails, St. Louis de Montfort reminds us that "only molten and liquefied substances may be poured into a mold. That means you must crush and melt down the old Adam in you if you wish to acquire the likeness of the new Adam in Mary."[439] If we are willing to undergo the process of daily examining our consciences, dying to sin, and crucifying our disordered desires and self-will, we will discover that it is by casting ourselves into her virginal bosom that we become filled with pure love, are purified from the least stain of sin, and are thus enabled to find Jesus in His fullness.[440] Having taken refuge in the very Virgin to whom the Father has entrusted the Son, we can more easily undergo our dark nights, learn to imitate Mary's virtues, and reproduce her ways. When we follow her advice and rely upon our Mother's direction, we, "like the stewards at the wedding in Cana" learn to "do whatever He tells you" (John 2:5)[441] and enter into the blessed life of the redeemed.

From all that we have already learned from Montfort about Mary's really and truly being our Mother in the supernatural order, it should be clear that he is not advocating a mere sentimental devotion to Mary. Rather, he is urging us to adopt an active relationship of dependence upon the Blessed Virgin as our Mother and Queen in our deepest interiority as our personal appropriation of what is really and truly transpiring in the order of grace. He is beseeching us to turn to her, and depend upon her, for direction and counsel, as our Savior did and still does. Bolstered by an intentional and constant relationship of loving dependence upon Mary, her sons and daughters learn to count upon this maternal mold and channel of grace to form them into her Son's image and likeness, especially amidst the suffering of persecution and the daily trial of carrying their cross.[442]

While we will still have "hard battles to fight and serious obstacles to overcome, . . . Mary, our Mother and Queen, stays close to her faithful servants. She is always at hand to brighten their darkness, clear away their doubts, strengthen them in their fears, sustain them in combats and trials."[443] "Her spirit will take the place of yours to rejoice in God, her Savior," if one faithfully consecrates oneself to so great a Mother.[444] For Mary, alone, is "not like other creatures who tend to lead us away from God than to Him, if we are over-attached to them. Mary's strongest inclination is to unite us to Jesus, her Son, and her Son's strongest wish is that we come to Him through His Blessed Mother."[445]

And, most importantly, the more we learn to depend consciously upon this Second Eve whom the Father, the Son, and the Holy Spirit have placed at enmity with Satan (Gen. 3:15), the more we discover that "Mary will safeguard us against the deception and cunning of the evil one."[446] Our own experience will validate the truth that "where Mary is present, the evil one is absent."[447]

St. Louis Marie de Montfort has named this way of intentionally turning to Mary as Mother and Queen, so she might form us into the image of her Son, as the "slavery of Jesus *in* Mary" or "slavery of Jesus dwelling and reigning *in* Mary." To become a slave of Jesus *in* Mary is to imitate perfectly the slavery of the Son of God Who humbled Himself to take the form of a slave, being born in the likeness of men, *in* her.

In light of all we've learned from this humble servant of the Blessed Virgin, we have no reason to let St Louis Marie's own use of the Bérulle French School's term 'slavery' bewilder us. In fact, it even seems fitting, strange as the language may still seem to our contemporary ears. For, without a doubt, "the principal mystery celebrated and honored" in Montfort's holy slavery of love is none other than "the mystery of the Incarnation where we find Jesus only *in* Mary, having become incarnate *in* her womb."[448] In the final analysis, it is *through, with, and in* Mary that Jesus Christ sets us free from the captivity of Satan as well as from our own slavery to sin and death resulting from original sin. It is only *in* Mary, who is His Mother and ours, that our Redeemer gives us the grace to be "born anew" as "slaves of God" by the Power of the Holy Spirit. The "return . . . is sanctification and its end, eternal life" (Rom. 6:22).

NOTES

[356] "True Devotion to Mary," *God Alone: The Collected Writings of St. Louis Marie de Montfort* (Bay Shore, NY: Montfort Publications, 1987) 364.

[357] *Catechism of the Catholic Church,* 2nd ed. (Washington: U.S. Catholic Conference Publications, 1997) 155.

[358] *Catechism of the Catholic Church* 165.

[359] *Catechism of the Catholic Church* 170–1.

[360] Karl Rahner, S.J., and Herbert Vorgrimler, *Dictionary of Theology,* 2nd ed. (New York: Crossroad, 1981) 432.

[361] Rahner, *Dictionary* 432; 434.

[362] Rahner, *Dictionary* 432.

[363] St. Thomas Aquinas, *Summa Theologica,* trans. Fathers of the English Dominican Province, vol. IV (Westminster, MD: Christian Classics, 1948) IIIa, q.26, art.1 2153.

[364] Reginald Garrigou-Lagrange, O.P. *The Mother of the Saviour and our Interior Life,* trans. Bernard J. Kelly, C.S.Sp. (Rockford, IL: Tan Books, 1993) 172.

[365] Garrigou-Lagrange, *The Mother of the Saviour* 172–3.

[366] "Lumen Gentium," *Documents of the Second Vatican Council,* ed. Austin Flannery, O.P. (Northport, NY: Costello, 1992) 418.

[367] "Lumen Gentium" 419.

[368] "Lumen Gentium" 418. Italics added for emphasis.

[369] "Lumen Gentium" 419.

[370] Richard P. McBrien, *Catholicism,* rev. ed. (San Francisco: Harper, 1994) 11.

[371] Michael O'Carroll, C.S.Sp., *Theotokos* (Collegeville: The Liturgical Press, 1982) 320–2.

[372] Garrigou-Lagrange, *The Mother of the Saviour* 177.

[373] Rahner, *Dictionary* 260–1.

[374] Rahner, *Dictionary* 261; 232.

[375] Rahner, *Dictionary* 460.

[376] Reginald Garrigou-Lagrange, O.P. *The Three Ways of the Spiritual Life,* trans. (Rockford, IL: Tan Books, 1977) 9–10.

[377] Rahner, *Dictionary* 460.

[378] Karl Rahner, S.J., "Reflections on the Problem of the Gradual Ascent to Christian Perfection," *Theological Investigations,* trans. Karl-H. and Boniface Kruger, vol. III (London: Darton, Longman and Todd, 1967) 21–2.

[379] Garrigou-Lagrange, *The Three Ways of the Spiritual Life* 11.

[380] *Catechism of the Catholic Church* 487.

[381] Josef Neuner, S.J., and Jacques Dupuis, S.J., ed., *The Christian Faith in the Doctrinal Documents of the Catholic Church* (New York: Alba House, 1998) 262 (DS 3370).

382 McBrien 12.

383 Neuner 152 (DS1330).

384 Neuner 152 (DS 1331).

385 Rahner, *Dictionary* 377.

386 Rahner, *Dictionary* 515.

387 This is underscored by Tertullian's claim in *Against Praxeas*, trans. Ernest Evans (London: SPCK, 1948) 172. Here Tertullian says that we must assert that function alone cannot differentiate the Persons of the Trinity in order to preserve the distinction of the Persons "without disturbing the permanence of the union." Thus, one important way to speak of the Their unity is precisely to say that the Father, the Son, and the Holy Spirit, though distinct, are of one substance and mind mutually engaged in doing one and the same thing—whether that be creating, redeeming, or sanctifying. Furthermore, this real distinction of Persons in the Trinity is necessary if we are not to divide Jesus Christ. "Those who contend that the Father and the Son are one and the same thing, now begin to divide them rather than to call them one. For if Jesus is one and Christ is another, the Son will be one and the Father another, because Jesus is the Son and Christ the Father. . . . (They will) make two of Jesus and Christ." The Incarnation can only exist if God is really both One and Three. Furthermore, it is essentially incorrect to refer to the Persons of the Blessed Trinity as "Creator, Redeemer, and Sanctifier" as this confuses function with the real distinction of Persons that is dependent upon origin within the Trinity rather than function.

388 St. Louis Marie de Montfort, "The Love of Eternal Wisdom," *God Alone: The Collected Writings of St. Louis Marie de Montfort* (Bay Shore, NY: Montfort Publications, 1987) 108.

389 Montfort, "True Devotion" 300.

390 Montfort, "True Devotion" 303.

391 Neuner 151 (DS1300–02). This language is taken from the Decree for the Greeks written by the General Council of Florence in 1439. It was written to explain "the procession of the Holy Spirit from Father and Son, allowing, however, also the dynamic formula , more in keeping with Eastern thinking, according to which the Spirit proceeds from the Father through the Son." This Council also defended as legitimate the insertion of the '*Filioque*' in the Creed.

392 Montfort, "True Devotion" 300.

393 Montfort, "True Devotion" 368–9.

394 St. Thomas Aquinas IIIa, q.48, art. 6 2281.

395 St. Athanasius. *On the Incarnation*, trans. and ed. A Religious of C.S.M.V. (Crestwood, NY: SVS Press, 1993) 33.

[396] St Athanasius 33.

[397] St. Thomas Aquinas IIIa, q.48, art. 6 2281.

[398] Montfort, "True Devotion" 293.

[399] Montfort, "True Devotion" 300.

[400] Montfort, "True Devotion" 300–1.

[401] Karl Rahner, S.J., *Foundations of Christian Faith*, trans. William V. Dych, (New York: Seabury, 1978) 316. Theologically, we might support this by saying that ". . . this Spirit who makes faith possible and who justifies is given in all times and places *intuitu meritorum Christi*, that is, in view of the merits of Jesus Christ." Coupled with this, we might add the insights of Garrigou-Lagrange, *The Mother of the Saviour* 183. "Under the Old Dispensation, graces were given—as it were on credit—in view of the future merits of Jesus, with which were associated those of Mary. Thus, Mary's merits *de congruo* extended by anticipation to the just of the Old Dispensation." In addition, it is important to remember that the "gates of heaven" were not even opened to the just of the Old Dispensation until the Lord descended "*ad infernum*" after His crucifixion and death, which Mary also shared in through her co-passion.

[402] Montfort, "True Devotion" 296.

[403] Montfort, "True Devotion" 301.

[404] Montfort, "True Devotion" 296.

[405] Montfort, "True Devotion" 296.

[406] Montfort, "True Devotion" 296.

[407] Montfort, "True Devotion" 297.

[408] Montfort, "True Devotion" 300.

[409] Montfort, "True Devotion" 297.

[410] Montfort, "True Devotion" 303.

[411] Montfort, "True Devotion" 303–4.

[412] Montfort, "True Devotion" 298.

[413] Montfort, "True Devotion" 298.

[414] Montfort, "True Devotion" 298.

[415] *"Lumen Gentium"* 418. The fathers of the Second Vatican Council used the term "mother in the order of grace" to describe the Blessed Virgin's relationship to us " in restoring supernatural life to souls."

[416] Montfort, "True Devotion" 341.

[417] Montfort, "True Devotion" 341.

[418] Montfort, "True Devotion" 374–5.

[419] Montfort, "True Devotion" 374.

[420] Montfort, "True Devotion" 372.

[421] Montfort, "True Devotion" 372.

422 Montfort, "True Devotion" 299.

423 Montfort, "True Devotion" 338.

424 Montfort, "True Devotion" 306.

425 Montfort, "True Devotion" 361.

426 Montfort, "True Devotion" 373.

427 Michael Downey, ed., *The New Dictionary of Catholic Spirituality* (Collegeville: Liturgical Press, 1993) 281–4. See the entry entitled, "Discipleship," for a brief history of how the concept of following Jesus in response to the Gospel imperative developed from the days of the post-Easter community until the present.

428 Thomas à Kempis, *The Imitation of Christ*, trans. Joseph N. Tylenda, S.J. (Wilmington, DE: Michael Glazier, 1984)14.

429 Thomas à Kempis 13.

430 Thomas à Kempis 29.

431 Karl Lehman and Albert Raffelt, ed., Harvey D. Egan, S.J., trans. ed., *The Content of the Faith: The Best of Karl Rahner's Theological Writings* (New York: Crossroad, 1993) 349.

432 Montfort, "Love of Eternal Wisdom"110–1. It is important for the reader to remember the earlier discussion we had in chapter 2 of this book about the meaning of the word "consecration" for Montfort. While Montfort is clear that God Alone, meaning the Father mediated to us through the Incarnate Son in union with the Holy Spirit, must be the ultimate End of all our consecrations, he is nevertheless advocating a consecration to Mary as the proximate means for reaching our ultimate End. While he also uses the term "surrender" in regard to our relationship with Mary, he is not hesitant to use the term "consecration" as the passage referenced above shows.

433 Montfort, "True Devotion" 351.

434 Montfort, "True Devotion" 332.

435 Montfort, "True Devotion" 324. St. Louis Marie recommends a precise plan of preparation and total consecration to Mary to help us do what he is recommending. See "True Devotion" 363 ff. See also *Preparation for Total Consecration According to St. Louis Marie de Montfort* (Bay Shore, NY: Montfort Publications, 1994) 83 for the wording of the entire formula of consecration to Mary. While this formula is quite lengthy, the most important segment of this prayer formula is as follows: "I, N_____, a faithless sinner, renew and ratify today in thy hands (O Immaculate Mary) the vows of my Baptism; I renounce forever Satan, his pomps and works; and I give myself entirely to Jesus Christ, the Incarnate Wisdom, to carry my cross after Him all the days of my life, and to be more faithful to Him than I have

ever been before. In the presence of all the heavenly court I choose thee this day for my Mother and mistress. I deliver and consecrate to thee, as thy slave, my body and soul, my goods, both interior and exterior, and even the value of all my good actions, past, present and future; leaving to thee the entire and full right of disposing of me, and all that belongs to me, without exception, according to thy good pleasure, for the greater glory of God in time and eternity." From this it is easy to see the Christocentric intent and end of Montfort's entire Mariological doctrine.

[436] Montfort, "True Devotion" 345–6.
[437] Montfort, "True Devotion" 346.
[438] Montfort, "True Devotion" 346.
[439] Montfort, "True Devotion" 361.
[440] Montfort, "True Devotion" 352.
[441] Montfort, "True Devotion" 351–2.
[442] Montfort, "True Devotion" 337.
[443] Montfort, "True Devotion" 336.
[444] Montfort, "True Devotion" 360.
[445] Montfort, "True Devotion" 313.
[446] Montfort, "True Devotion" 342.
[447] Montfort, "True Devotion" 342.
[448] Montfort, "True Devotion" 367–8.

CONCLUSION

Mary's Role in Redemption
is Mother

The Fruit of this Study of St. Louis Marie de Montfort

In the concluding paragraph of his Introduction to the encyclical on the Blessed Virgin Mary in the life of the Christian community, *Redemptoris Mater*, Pope John Paul II quotes from *"Lumen Gentium"* in offering an explanation for why we who are followers of our Lord and Savior, Jesus Christ, continually raise our eyes to the Virgin Mary, as we strive to increase in holiness along our pathway to eternal life with the Trinity. In the first place, the pope says we constantly turn to the Blessed Virgin because "'the Son whom she brought forth is He whom God placed as the first-born among many brethren (Rom. 8:29).'" In the second place, we turn toward her because "'in the birth and development' of these brothers and sisters 'she *cooperates with a maternal love.*'"[449]

From our foregoing study of the writings of St. Louis Marie de Montfort, it is my conclusion that the great gift this Marian Saint offers in understanding what the Catholic Faith holds about Mary's role in Redemption is not that the Blessed Virgin is merely affirmed as Mother of the Redeemer and thereby Mother of the Redemption. Rather, through his development of the specifically Marian line of thought inherent in the Bérulle French School's emphasis on the Incarnation, Montfort points us to the *substantial and ontological meaning of her motherhood.* And, because of this gift, we are enabled by the Holy Spirit to see more clearly the precise nature of the Virgin Mary's *maternal cooperation* in both the objective and the subjective Redemption.

By this, I mean that St. Louis Marie de Montfort has helped us see that the Virgin Mary's role in Redemption *is* precisely that of Mother, in the truest and complete sense of the word—with all that this entails in regard to physical and moral instrumental causality in the actual process of *birthing* God the Son as Incarnate, Redemption itself, and re-created human persons. Furthermore, to say that Mary really *is* Mother is essentially to make a statement about the *origin* of the Incarnate Redeemer and therefore Redemption itself, which are entirely and eternally inseparable. It is precisely in the substantial and ontological reality of *becoming and being* the Mother of God Incarnate that Mary *is* the Second Eve and *is* the 'helpmate' of the divine Redeemer in Redemption, a reality which she remains from the dual moment of her *fiat* and the Incarnation into the rest of time, as well as into all eternity.

Significant in this regard is the fact that Montfort has helped us clear up a misconception that frequently occurs when speaking of Mary as our spiritual mother as mentioned in the introductory chapter. In discovering the depth of meaning contained in Mary's actually *being* the Mother of the Incarnate Son and thereby Redemption itself, we can more readily appreciate the eternal mystery being pointed to in language that speaks of Mary's cooperation with the Savior "with a maternal love." It is inaccurate to reduce such a phrase to implying merely that Mary offers either her Son, or us, a nurturing presence or a maternal style of affection in the psychological sense. Similarly, it is erroneous to reduce her "maternal love" to meaning that Mary provides Jesus Christ, or us, with the labors of a homemaker in the sociological sense. While no slight of such important contributions by women to the actual rearing of children is intended, Montfort definitively shows us that to reduce or restrict the Blessed Virgin's maternal love and cooperation to either styles of affection or sociological roles undermines both the full meaning and the implications of the profound mystery of Redemption—revealed to us by the very fact of the Blessed Trinity's choosing a human woman, Mary, to be Mother of God the Son Incarnate.

Mary's *being* Mother of such a Son and cooperating in the Redemption "with a maternal love" means nothing less than her sharing in a human way, and therefore by definition necessarily subordinate, in the very *agape* love act of the Father and the Holy Spirit's begetting of the Eternal Son as Incarnate through her own self-offering—body, blood, soul, and humanity. Consequently, it is her freely offered, ever virginal, and human *kenosis* that both precedes and provides for nothing less than the Divine Son's eternal *Kenosis* as Incarnate for us. So much so, her relationship with the Trinity in the begetting of God the Son as Incarnate has drawn her into an essential, inseparable, and unique union with the Father, the Son, and the Holy Spirit that endures for all eternity.

Because of her substantial and inseparable union with all three Persons of the Blessed Trinity, brought about by the Trinity's own immanent mystery of the Incarnation and Hypostatic Union, she shares *a priori* in all that the Redeemer Himself accomplishes in Redemption—from the very moment of her freely allowing God the Son to be begotten by the Holy Spirit, as now Incarnate for all eternity, from the Blessed Virgin Mary's own flesh. This means that while she, as a creature, is by nature wholly subordinated to God the Father, the Son, and the Holy Spirit, she shares alongside Them in all that the Incarnate Word is and does, eternally—precisely because she has been lifted up from the very moment of the Incarnation into the Reality of the Godhead, in such an ineffable way, that she *is* perpetually Mother in the Trinity's mystery of God the Son Incarnate. She *is* thereby, *perpetually*, the instrumental cause of His very existence as Redeemer and Mediator, as well as *being* the instrumental cause of the Redeemed Life of Sanctifying Grace that flows from the Savior's Pierced Heart and is distributed to us in the sacraments.

And, since God the Son now remains Incarnate for all eternity, she *is* always an integral, entirely inseparable, and *substantial* partner in all that proceeds from the Father, the Son, and the Holy Spirit, on our behalf, in Redemption regardless of the extent to which we mere humans recognize and honor this mystery in God, during our sojourn on this earth. Like all the mysteries in God, we can only ponder this mystery at any depth with the Gift of the Holy Spirit, i.e., we mere humans must be given and willingly receive God's own Light both to ponder correctly and reverence rightly any of the mysteries of the Catholic and Apostolic Faith. Our natural reason alone is simply insufficient. It will always fail us in trying to grapple with, or rather be grasped by, any of God's own eternal mysteries.

And, as Montfort so insistently reminds us, the repercussions of our willing, conscious, and reverent reception of and correspondence to the Trinity's Marian mystery, while living on this earth, brings us wealth untold. After our death, the Blessed Trinity's profound Marian mystery will be seen as the Reality it is, by all. For the Blessed Virgin Mary is nothing less than the Blessed Trinity's Own Masterpiece, of both Creation and Redemption.

With all the above in mind, we must say that Montfort teaches us, masterfully, that the more we allow ourselves to ponder the many dimensions of the meaning of motherhood itself, beginning with its biological meaning,[450] the more we can see that Mary's *substantial and ontological maternal cooperation* in Redemption is exactly the way to substantiate that constantly recurring and developing theme in sacred tradition that many believe can be traced to the writings of St. Irenaeus. Namely, in Redemption, all flows from Mary, the Second Eve, alongside and in union with Jesus Christ, the Second Adam, as from one single source—while acknowledging that she is wholly subordinated to Him because she is a human person and He *is* God the Son Incarnate.

As a summary of all the marvelous theological insights we have gleaned from our study of St. Louis Marie de Montfort about the deeper meaning of Mary's role in Redemption, precisely as Mother, I offer the following major points:

1) As the literal Mother of God the Son Incarnate, Mary serves as the moral and physical instrumental cause through, with, and in whom the Second Person of the Blessed Trinity unites a humanity to His Divine Person and Nature, in the mystery of the Hypostatic Union, for all eternity. This means that the mystery of the Incarnation, which *is* essentially a mystery in God, has been established *only* through, with, and in the Blessed Virgin Mary for all eternity. This has been entirely accomplished by God but only with the instrumental cause of Mary's eternally resounding *fiat* to become His Mother, coupled with her substantial and required gift of her own body and person. The Blessed Virgin's humanity *is* nothing less than the substantial origin of God the Son's own Sacred Humanity by the Trinity's design and request, made actual only by means of her full consent and total, virginal self-oblation. It is Mary who mediates the Divine Son as Incarnate for us, in time and in eternity, by the Power of the Holy Spirit and Choice of the Blessed Trinity.

2) Precisely as Mother of the Incarnate Son, the entire Trinity has given the Blessed Virgin Mary a share in the Holy Spirit's eternal begetting of God the Son, as Incarnate, for all eternity. She has been lifted up by Them in such a mysterious way that she, though merely a human person, becomes a fully human participant in the Father's own divine fruitfulness and Authorship of the Trinity. Indeed, she reveals to us the human face of the Mothering aspect of the Trinity's own Fruitfulness, while not being a divine Person herself.

3) In choosing the Virgin Mary to be the Mother of God the Son Incarnate, the Trinity has *ipso facto* and simultaneously chosen Mary to cooperate alongside, while wholly subordinated to Them, in the entire work of Redemption. Her union with the Blessed Trinity by virtue of her having become eternally consubstantial with God the Son as His Mother, by the power of the Holy Spirit, is a wholly unique instance of bridal mystical union with the Holy Spirit. This means that while she forever remains a mere human person, she is everywhere doing one and the same thing with the Persons of the Blessed Trinity in regard to all that flows from Them in the Incarnation, including objective and subjective Redemption itself, by the Power of the Holy Spirit.

4) Her role in the Redemption *is* precisely that of Mother because the very Sacred Humanity that mediates and reveals God to us, serves as the saving meeting point of human nature and God, provides the Sacred Body and Blood that free us from sin and its effects, and is the Food of Eternal Life in the Holy Eucharist—is *entirely* derived from Mary's flesh in its bodily aspect—since she is the Virgin Mother of God the Son Incarnate, throughout eternity. She is also Mother of the Redemption because she *is* the required, substantial, maternal link through, with, and in whom the grace of Redemption is given to us by the Power of the Holy Spirit. Just as the Holy Spirit accomplished His work of incarnating the Son only through, with, and in her, so are we now "born anew" by the Holy Spirit only through, with, and in Mary, who *is* our Mother in the order

of grace. Likewise, we are mysteriously fed, liter-
ally, with the Substantial and Personal Body,
Blood, Soul, and Divinity of the Risen Lord *in* the
Holy Eucharist, under the outward appearances of
Bread and Wine, only through, with, and in
Mary—who in the eternal mystery of God the Son
Incarnate remains consubstantial with Him for all
eternity. This means that the Blessed Virgin is,
somehow, mysteriously involved in the daily mira-
cle of transubstantiation during the Mass, by the
Power of the Holy Spirit, and remains likewise
mysteriously "alongside" her Son in the Blessed
Sacrament, in all the tabernacles of the world.

As in the mystery of the Incarnation itself, she *is*
thus the physical and moral instrumental cause
through, with, and in whom we are redeemed,
transformed, and united with the Blessed Trinity
in this life and the next. This means that while
Jesus Christ is indeed the only Savior and Mediator between God and human persons, for all people, regardless of nation, race, culture, or creed,
both His very Mediation and the universal Salvation that He effects is always and everywhere *ex
Maria Virgine*. This is true because the very existence of the Mediator, God the Son Incarnate, *is*
only through, with, and in the Blessed Virgin
Mary, by the Power of the Holy Spirit. Thus, in all
truth we must say that the entire economy of salvation flows from the Blessed Trinity through,
with, and in the Blessed Virgin Mary because of
the Incarnation of God the Son only through,
with, and in her.

5) While the Blessed Virgin's role as Mother of the Redeemer and of the Redemption proceeds entirely from the Blessed Trinity as Source, God's graced action in Mary initially required nothing less than Mary's total self-offering and willing surrender to the Trinity, perpetually united with God the Son's Kenotic Self-offering on our behalf. This union of suffering and surrender began at the very moment of the Incarnation itself, continued through His Crucifixion and Death, and even to the moment of her own death and glorious bodily Assumption. While she was no doubt given the grace to make this personal and perpetual surrender, both at the moment of her *fiat* and every moment in this life thereafter, she, nevertheless, had to make a continual, willing, personal choice to cooperate freely with and correspond completely to all the grace offered her by God in this life.

In addition to the above discussion and summary, there are also some significant insights arising from the specifically virginal nature of Mary's Motherhood and relationship to the Blessed Trinity that have been aided greatly by our theological study of St. Louis de Montfort. Namely, just as Mary's maternal cooperation cannot be reduced to psychological characteristics or sociological roles typically associated with women, neither can Mary's virginal *fiat* be misunderstood as a psycho-sexual surrender of a female, the Second Eve, to a male, the Second Adam. Rather, Mary's *fiat* is the highest ranking gift of self to God ever made by a human person and is in no way meant to be a statement about gender roles between human men and women at all. Instead, the Blessed Virgin Mary is the *paradigm* for the perfect and total surrender of any and all human persons to God. Consequently, her subordination to Jesus Christ in the work of Redemption both inaugurates and typifies that total surrender of the human person to God required for grace to operate efficaciously and perfectively, in all humankind, regardless of gender. Mary's free, willing, and perpetually virginal self-offering and subordination to Jesus Christ, Whom we must remember *is* God the Son Incarnate, should be seen as the specifically human contribution that allowed the Father, the Son, and the Holy Spirit to act perfectly through, with, and in her as the instrumental cause chosen to be most closely associated with the Blessed Trinity in the entire work of Redemption. She shows us that in order for grace to work in us, both efficaciously and perfectively, we too must finally allow ourselves to surrender to Jesus Christ and co-operate with the Trinity's Plan for our lives—totally, willingly, freely, and even virginally, at least in our souls.

Moreover, the gift of God the Son to indwell the Blessed Virgin, to the point of becoming consubstantial with her flesh by the power of the Holy Spirit, is the ultimate Gift of God's very Self to humankind. God's unique indwelling of the Blessed Virgin in the Incarnation is both the beginning and the model for the indwelling of each and every human person by God in grace. Because she mediates God the Son to us and consequently the entire grace of Redemption, she is the Mother of the Divine Indwelling of each human person, through the Power of the Holy Spirit, as well as our sister in this gift.

Consequently, while it is correct to call the Blessed Virgin Mary the perfect disciple, as Luther and others have since the Reformation, this must always be accompanied with acknowledging that her perfect discipleship consists in nothing less than her consent to be, *substantially*, the Mother of both the Incarnate Son and of objective and subjective Redemption. While her selfless *fiat* is certainly the model for all subsequent disciples who seek to love, serve, and obey her divine Son, we must always remember that her perfect discipleship makes our discipleship possible in the first place. While her being a mere human person certainly makes her our fellow disciple, the Blessed Virgin's place in the hierarchical order of both redeemed humankind and the community of disciples will always be ontologically higher than—and indeed rank even before our very own—in the chain of instrumental causality that mediates the grace of the Mediator both to us as members of His Mystical Body and the world which we serve in His Name. It is her, not our, unprecedented self-gift to God that inaugurates the reversal of the sin of our first parents' disobedience and the possibility of all its effects in us. This truth is highlighted by Montfort's emphasis on the event of the Incarnation as an eternal mystery in God. It is this gift from Montfort that especially helps us realize that the Virgin Mary's *fiat* is not merely a moment in historical time that happens and is then quickly over. Instead, all that is inaugurated and signified by her initial *fiat* both continues throughout her earthly life and is being brought to fulfillment, in time and eternity, by virtue of the perpetual nature of her union with God the Son Incarnate.

Last, but not least, our study of Montfort continually reminds us of the importance of making these and any other bold claims about Mary's instrumental causality in the Mediation of the Son and Redemption, along with her consequentially superior place in the order of redeemed humankind and the Church, within the bounds of an orthodox Catholic understanding of original sin, concupiscence, the devil, mortal and venial sin, justification, sanctification, the sacraments, the Blessed Trinity, and Jesus Christ.[451] With Montfort, we must always allow the Catholic Faith itself to help us constantly reiterate that the Virgin Mary of Nazareth is not only the Mother of the divine Redeemer and Redemption, but also a daughter of Adam and Eve, as well as of Abraham and Sarah, and as such is totally dependent upon God with a humility that surpasses that of all God's creatures. In light of the 1854 solemn definition of the Doctrine of the Immaculate Conception, the Holy Spirit has helped the whole Catholic world expand on Montfort's assertions in this regard. We have now been given both the language and the certainty to say with confidence, as an Article of the Faith, that the perfectly redeemed one is not only our Mother but also our sister in Christ, totally dependent upon her Son, the divine Redeemer, for her own preservative Redemption.

Nevertheless, with Montfort we must constantly acknowledge that unless our sister had consented to become the Mother of the Incarnate Son and consequently the Mother of the Redemption, our rebirth in Christ would simply be an impossibility. In the mystery of Mary's virginal Motherhood of the Incarnate Son and spiritual Motherhood of us, created motherhood itself—in all its physical and spiritual dimensions—has been raised to the level of its ultimate meaning and dignity in God, a literal participation in the divine Authoring of Life Himself and the re-created life of the redeemed. Likewise, human motherhood has been revealed as a sacred reflection of the most intimate details of the inner Life of the Triune God, GodSelf. Truly, "blessed are you, among women," most Blessed Virgin Mary.

A Closing Portrait of the Blessed Virgin Mary

Since we began this conversation on the Blessed Virgin Mary by considering two seemingly contrasting Marian art forms at the National Shrine of the Basilica of the Immaculate Conception, I'd like to complete it by drawing our attention to an artistic image of Mary that shows forth both her humble humanity before the Blessed Trinity and her sublime dignity as Mother of God, as well as the Mother of all in the order of grace. That image is the miraculous portrait of Our Lady of Guadalupe captured on the tilma of Juan Diego, as proof of the authenticity of the apparitions of the Blessed Virgin to him at Tepeyac hill near Mexico City from December 9 to December 12, 1531. The significance of this particular image is that it can well be argued that among the countless art forms of the Blessed Virgin, this is the only one of supernatural origin and thus the only true self-portrait of the Mother of God in existence.[452]

In this famous image, the Blessed Virgin is seen as pregnant, standing on a cloud with a crescent moon under her feet, cloaked with a turquoise star-studded mantle, and completely surrounded by the brilliant light of golden rays—a portrait that is clearly reminiscent of Rev. 12:1–2. "And a great portent appeared in heaven, a woman clothed with the sun, with the moon under her feet, and on her head a crown of twelve stars; she was with child. . . ." When the image on the tilma was revealed to Bishop Zumárraga of Mexico City on December 12, 1531, in response to his request for proof of the apparitions to Juan Diego, the visionary recognized it immediately to be the portrait of the same woman who had appeared to him from December 9 to December 12.[453]

During her initial apparitions to Juan on December 9, the Blessed Virgin had spoken of herself by saying: "Know for certain, dearest of my sons, that I am the perfect and perpetual Virgin Mary, Mother of the True God, through whom everything lives, the Lord of all things, who is Master of Heaven and Earth. . . . I am your merciful Mother, the Mother of all who live united in this land, and of all mankind, of all those who love me, of those who cry to me, of those who have confidence in me. . . ."[454] And, similarly on December 12, she said to Juan: "Do not be troubled or weighed down with grief. Do not fear any illness or vexation, anxiety or pain. Am I not here who am your Mother? Are you not under my shadow and protection? Am I not your fountain of life? Are you not in the folds of my mantle? In the crossing of my arms? Is there anything else you need?"[455]

With these words, the Virgin Mary revealed herself in the apparitions at Tepeyac, immortalized on Juan Diego's tilma, in all the glory and the depth of meaning that is hers as both the Mother of God and our merciful Mother, the very fountain of Life.[456] And yet, perhaps the most stunning characteristic of the Blessed Virgin Mary's self-portrait in this image, known as Our Lady of Guadalupe, is the depth of her charity and the sincerity of her humility. Her head is gently tilted to the right and lowered in a posture of acknowledgement of Someone greater than herself. Her eyes are partially closed as if in deep prayer. Her hands are folded and pointing toward heaven. There is a profound silence and reverence about her person. She shows herself in this self-portrait to be none other than loving adoration personified, as she bears the divine Redeemer in her very womb along with the Redemption of all born from the Savior.[457]

This humble self-portrait of Mary, which reveals simultaneously the radiant glory of the most holy ever-Virgin Mother of God and Mother of us, declares that Mary herself is never confused about who she is and to Whom she owes everything. She knows that the Triune God, alone, is the real Source of all her brilliance. She knows that her divine Son, Jesus Christ, Whom she bears is not only the Savior of the whole world but her Savior as well. It is His Victory that her whole being so radiantly magnifies and perfectly manifests.

Yet, neither is she hesitant to show us by this pregnant self-portrait that the Father, the Son, and the Holy Spirit have lifted up her lowliness and uniquely united her to Their very Being in inviting her to be the very Mother of God the Son—Incarnate both in time and in eternity—and thereby the Mother of Redemption and even all humankind. If she is not confused, then let us not be. Amen.

NOTES

[449] John Paul II, *Redemptoris Mater*, Vatican trans. (Boston: Pauline Books, 1987) 10. Italics added for emphasis.

[450] In this regard, it's important to note that the mammalian ovum, contributed by the human female in the procreation of children, is a relatively recent scientific discovery that may not have yet been taken into account, sufficiently, in our appropriation of the mystery of Mary's role in both the Incarnation and Redemption, both theologically and otherwise. The ovum was not scientifically discovered until 1826 by Karl Ernst von

Baer. Prior to that time, it was commonly believed that the female mammal contributed merely "a simple formative liquid" within her womb that passively received, housed, and nurtured the male spermatozoa. (Charles Coulston Gillispie, ed. in chief, *Dictionary of Scientific Biography*, vol. 1 (NY: Scribner, 1970) 386.

Since the lower order of creation reflects, analogously, the higher supernatural order, as discussed throughout this book, it stands to reason that the more we learn about the exact nature of human motherhood, the more light the Holy Spirit will be able to shed on our limited human understanding of the Blessed Virgin Mary as Mother of the Redeemer, Redemption, the Church, and the redeemed, as well as on the mysteries of the Incarnation and the Blessed Trinity. Perhaps this is yet another reason why the Holy Spirit has waited "until now," as Montfort tells us, to bring us into a better understanding of Mary and her role in salvation.

[451] I wholeheartedly recommend that the reader interested in gaining a better understanding of these Truths consult the *Catechism of the Catholic Church* , as referenced in footnotes throughout this work.

[452] See Thomas Sennot, *Not Made by Hands* (San Francisco: Ignatius Press, 1998) for a good rebuttal of those who would say that the image of Our Lady of Guadalupe is a fraud.

[453] Francis Johnston, *The Wonder of Guadalupe* (Rockford, IL: Tan, 1981) 24–49.

[454] Johnston 26.

[455] Johnston 33.

[456]Johnston 56. The conversion of over 9,000,000 Aztecs has been attributed to the Blessed Virgin through her apparitions at Tepeyac and the miraculous self-portrait she left on Juan Diego's cloak.

[457] Johnson 13, 28. Oral tradition among persons gifted with a Mexican heritage makes these twin aspects of the Marian mystery seem all the more represented by this miraculous self-portrait of the Blessed Virgin Mary in light of the popular understanding of this image. Many say the rays surrounding the Virgin in this image depict, and therefore represent, the same rays the Aztecs used in the idol image of their pagan *sun* god, Huitzilopochtli. When a temple was built and inaugurated to this leading Aztec deity in 1487, it is recorded that at least 20,000 people were slaughtered on the temple's altars as commanded by the Aztec Emperor, Auitzotl. This human sacrifice was offered to appease this monstrous pagan sun god.

With this popular understanding in mind, the image of Our Lady of Guadalupe says that the Blessed Virgin is the woman who is both simultaneously filled with (pregnant with) and bringing the true *Son* to humankind. It is this Son, the Living and True God, Who conquers all false gods/goddesses and demonic spirits in order to end their enslaving hold on human persons. And the True Son and Living God chooses to come to us and conquer all that is opposed to God only through, with, and in Mary. Since the Blessed Virgin is credited with the conversion of so many Aztecs and saving many, no doubt, from the slaughter of human sacrifice, it is no wonder that Our Lady of Guadalupe is invoked in our contemporary world as the woman who will bring about an end to the horrendous and contemporary human sacrifice of legalized abortion.

Our Lady of Guadalupe *(December 12, 1531)*

Selected Bibliography

Alphonsus Liguori, St. *The Glories of Mary*. trans. Rockford, IL: Tan, 1977.

Bauer, Judith A., ed. *The Essential Mary Handbook*. Liguori, MO: Liguori Publications, 1999.

Bernard of Clairvaux, St. *Homilies in Praise of the Blessed Virgin Mary*. Trans. Marie-Bernard Saïd. Kalamazoo: Cistercian Publications, 1993.

Breen, Eileen, F.M.A., ed. *Mary: The Second Eve from the Writings of John Henry Newman*. Rockford, IL: Tan, 1982.

Buby, Bertrand, SM. *Mary of Galilee*. 3 vols. New York: Alba House, 1994–97.

Buono, Anthony M. *The Greatest Marian Prayers*. New York: Alba House, 1999.

Cyril of Alexandria, St. *On the Unity of Christ*. Trans. and Intro. John Anthony McGuckin. Crestwood, NY: St. Vladimir's Press, 1995.

de la Potterie, Ignace, S.J. *Mary in the Mystery of the Covenant*. Trans. Bertrand Buby, S.M. New York: Alba House, 1992.

Dictionary of Mary. New York: Catholic Book Publishing Company, 1997.

Doherty, Eddie. *Wisdom's Fool A Biography of St. Louis de Montfort*. Bay Shore, NY: Montfort Publications, 1998.

Gaffney, J. Patrick, S.M.M. *Mary's Spiritual Maternity According to St. Louis de Montfort*. Bay Shore, NY: Montfort Publications, 1976.

Gaffney, J. Patrick and Richard J. Payne., eds. *Jesus Living in Mary Handbook of the Spirituality of St. Louis Marie de Montfort*. Bay Shore, NY: Montfort Publications, 1994.

Gambero, Luigi, S.M. *Mary and the Fathers of the Church*. Trans. Thomas Buffer. San Francisco: Ignatius Press, 1999.

Garrigou-Lagrange, Reginald, O.P. *The Mother of the Saviour and Our Interior Life*. Trans. Bernard J. Kelly, C.S.Sp. St. Louis: Herder, 1949.

Gottemoller, Bartholemew, O.C.S.O. *Mary: God's Supreme Masterpiece*. Santa Barbara: Queenship Publishing, 1996.

Grignion de Montfort, St. Louis Marie. *God Alone The Collected Writings of St. Louis de Montfort*. Trans. team. Bay Shore, NY: Montfort Publications, 1976.

John Paul II. *Redemptoris Mater*. Vatican trans. Boston: Pauline Books, 1987.

———. *Theotókos: A Catechesis on Mary, Mother of God*. Boston: Pauline Books, 2000.

———. *Ut Unum Sint*. Vatican trans. Boston: Pauline Books, 1995.

Laurentin, René. *A Short Treatise on the Virgin Mary*. Trans. Charles Neumann, S.M. Washington, NJ: AMI Press, 1991.

———. *The Meaning of Consecration Today*. Trans. Kenneth D. Whitehead. San Francisco: Ignatius Press, 1991.

Macquarrie, John. *Mary for All Christians*. Grand Rapids: Eerdmas, 1991.

Manelli, Stefano, FFI. *All Generations Shall Call Me Blessed*. Trans. Peter Damien Fehlner. New Bedford, MA: Academy of the Immaculate, 1995.

Manteau-Bonamy, H.M., O.P. *Immaculate Conception and the Holy Spirit*. Trans. Richard Arnandez. Libertyville, IL: Franciscan Marytown Books, 1977.

O'Carroll, Michael, C.S.Sp.. *Theotokos: A Theological Encyclopedia of the Blessed Virgin Mary*. Collegeville: Liturgical Press, 1982.

Prévost, Jean-Pierre, S.M.M. *The Mother of Jesus*. Trans. Raymond ven der Buhs. Ottawa: Novalis, 1987.

Stravinskas, Peter M.J. *Mary and the Fundamentalist Challenge*. Huntington, IN: OSV Publishing, 1998.